Richard Wright Writing America at Home and from Abroad

Richard Wright

Writing America at Home and from Abroad

Edited by VIRGINIA WHATLEY SMITH

University Press of Mississippi / Jackson

www.upress.state.ms.us

The University Press of Mississippi is a member
of the Association of American University Presses.

Haiku: This Other World by Richard Wright (New York: Arcade Publishing, 1998): Copyright ©1998 Ellen Wright. Reprinted by permission of John Hawkins & Associates, Inc., and the Estate of Richard Wright and reprinted by permission of Arcade Publishing, an imprint of Skyhorse Publishing, Inc.

"Signifying and Self-Portraiture in Richard Wright's *A Father's Law*" previously appeared in *College Language Association Journal* L.II.I (September 2008): 55–73.

Manufactured in the United States of America

First printing 2016
∞

Library of Congress Cataloging-in-Publication Data

Names: Smith, Virginia Whatley, editor.
Title: Richard Wright writing America at home and from abroad / edited by Virginia Whatley Smith.
Description: Jackson : University Press of Mississippi, 2016. | Includes bibliographical references and index. | Description based on print version record and CIP data provided by publisher; resource not viewed.
Identifiers: LCCN 2016019879 (print) | LCCN 2016005802 (ebook) | ISBN 9781496807229 (ebook) | ISBN 9781496803801 (hardback)
Subjects: LCSH: Wright, Richard, 1908–1960—Criticism and interpretation. | BISAC: LITERARY CRITICISM / American / African American. | SOCIAL SCIENCE / Ethnic Studies / African American Studies.
Classification: LCC PS3545.R815 (print) | LCC PS3545.R815 Z8216 2016 (ebook) | DDC 813/.52—dc23
LC record available at https://lccn.loc.gov/2016019879

British Library Cataloging-in-Publication Data available

To my late parents
Norman and Willie Mae Whatley

Contents

Acknowledgments

Many thanks to people who encouraged me to complete this project besides my contributors: Mary Flowers Braswell, PhD; Susan Diane Mitchell, MA; Betsy Speight, MS; Warren Carson Jr., PhD, and my children: Sydney Smith, MBA; Alexis Smith Balkum, MBA; and Elworth Smith, BS.

Special thanks to those academic, government, and/or private and public agencies that have rendered services: The Wright Estate; John Hawkins and Associates, Inc.; Skyhorse Publishing, Inc.; the staff of the Beinecke Library, Yale University; the National Archives; and Wide World/photographer Fredi McCullough. Small grants from the University of Alabama at Birmingham also funded this project.

Richard Wright Writing America at Home and from Abroad

Introduction

—VIRGINIA WHATLEY SMITH—

Citizens and slaves of the White Republic: Race was produced through colonial law, but it was not yet connected to democracy.
—Joel Olson, *The Abolition of White Democracy* (39)

But it was slavery that particularly distinguished citizens from noncitizens and that has had the greatest impact on American citizenship.
—Joel Olson, *The Abolition of White Democracy* (41)

The votes of Jackson Democrats, combined with their fear and hatred of Black people, produced what the social Pierre van den Berghe calls a *Herrenvolk* democracy, a regime that is "democratic for the master race but tyrannical for subordinate groups."
—Joel Olson, *The Abolition of White Democracy* (42)

Citizenship was defined against slavery. Blackness and slavery were associated. Black and white were diametrically opposed. . . . Whiteness was not a biological status but a *political* color that distinguished the free from the unfree, the equal from the inferior, the citizen from the slave.
—Joel Olson, *The Abolition of White Democracy* (43)

In his study on white culture, the political scientist Joel Olson invariably addresses the collective experiences of Africans and their African American descendants who became subjected to the tyrannical laws and political machinations of British and then Anglo-American slave masters and politicians during the evolutions of the colonial and Federalist governments. Indeed, these transcontinental legislators perceived their visions of culture and society through racially biased lenses. They would grant unlimited to selective freedoms to whites, but contrarily would deny those same privileges to African Americans because they lacked the correct "*political* color," meaning skin color, according to Olson's research. Blacks ranked lowest on the scale of the reviled *Herrenvolk* "subordinate groups" of anticitizens. Anglo-Americans despised the

600,000 European immigrants who became settlers during the reign of seventh president Andrew Jackson in the 1830s. Jackson founded the Democratic Party, which putatively claimed that the government should be administered for and by the people. But the citizens and their chosen governmental electorates deliberately designed arcane laws defining human rights that excluded European migrants and African Americans. The public believed that "black[s] and white[s] were diametrically opposed" (43), and that each racial group had evolved as humans at different time periods (Nott and Gliddon 388). Blacks were even decreed to be on the bottom rung of the Great Chain of Being but just above the animal kingdom, and definitely the polar opposite to the "master race" (Olson 39–43).

Olson's contemporary study is quite relevant as far as examining the career of Richard Wright. Wright became a short-term member of the Communist Party from 1933 to 1936, but he remained a diehard Marxist all his life. American politics, regardless of the party, always occupied the mind-set of America's foremost African American writer from 1936 to 1960, the years that comprised his writing career. The introduction to this collection reflects Wright's self-assessments in the 1950s about his "Americanness," his American citizenship, and his views on American policies as a whole (Fabre, *World* 188). The "freedom" to be a "man," a "citizen," and a "whole person" always remained uppermost in Wright's mind—whether at home in America or living abroad. His literary analyses with their sociological and political implications actually preceded Olson's 2004 study by some eighty years when Wright launched his literary career as a poet with the publications of "I Have Seen Black Hands" in 1934 and "Between the World and Me" in 1935 (Wright and Fabre, *Richard Wright Reader* [*RWR*] 243, 246). Both pieces exposed the harsh realities and daily sufferings experienced by African Americans because of the political regulations, labor conditions, and violent activities that Southern whites enforced in order to keep blacks subdued. Wright would stress these issues again and again in his massive canon of poetry, fictions, autobiographical writings, travel books, and speeches.

Although Wright died at age fifty-two in 1960, it is never too late for scholars, creative writers, or the general public once again to engage in interrogating the prescient nature of Wright's mind and to reassess his life and body of writings, especially those directly concerned with American culture and its racial dynamics. This present collection, *Richard Wright Writing America at Home and from Abroad,* is significant because its design brings to light several new ways of looking at the author's life and works. First, the subject matter is focused on American culture—its theme resonates throughout Wright's body of writings. Second, Wright became a masterful writer of crime fictions. Indeed, no critical studies have considered the full significance of his canon of crime fictions that

Wright developed and that still exist in both published and unpublished forms. The cover photograph of Wright posed at his typewriter on March 27, 1945, signifies how he, an American, turned his creative ideas into works of art that informed the public about what it feels like to be a Negro in America. The essays in this collection stress that point. Additionally, this collection captures that latter phase of the self-liberated artist and man, Richard Wright. His poetry and prose works became more interdependent in the last two years of his life, 1958 to 1960, even though American culture remained in his thoughts. However, he turned inward and embarked upon a spiritual journey by delving into and creating a Wrightean form of haiku poetry by synthesizing Eastern Zen Buddhism with African philosophy that, together, finally set him spiritually free from the torments of his American childhood, youth, adolescence, and adulthood.

American Politics and Disfranchisement Policies

Although they had or have fought in America's domestic and foreign wars, African Americans have not become fully fledged citizens, even today after having reached the ideal state of equal opportunity by having an African American president in office. During Richard Wright's life span (1908–60), such a reality seemed implausible. As a self-appointed cultural spokesperson, Wright captured in his writings such as *12 Million Black Voices: A Folk History of the Negro in the United States* ([*12MBV*] 1941) a photographic text, the arbitrariness of American laws that whites designed to keep Negro Americans economically oppressed. Blacks rejected the unjust social and political policies by outcry, mimicry, and subversive tactics (30). The multiple narratives of enslaved, freed, or fugitive slaves led to the formal establishment of a first-person confessional genre, which attracted Richard Wright because of the slave legacies on both sides of his paternal and maternal heritages.

Wright was not Northern born nor a member of an elite, educated class like W. E. B. Du Bois, who was carving out his career as an intellectual and cultural spokesperson at the turn of the twentieth century before Wright was born in 1908. For nineteen years, Richard Wright lived the turbulent life of an Andrew Jackson anticitizen from age four onward while living in Natchez Mississippi, his birthplace; Jackson, Mississippi; Elaine, Arkansas; and Memphis, Tennessee, before fleeing to Chicago, Illinois, in 1927. He experienced firsthand or by way of his family and relatives the absence of democracy: unfair wages, poverty and hunger, limited education, and often violence in or toward his family. He graphically portrays the grisly reality of his Southern upbringing in his autobiography *Black Boy* (1945), which magnifies how maladjusted he had become by the time the nineteen-year-old Wright finally reached and then settled in Illinois for a period of ten years (1927–1937). Chicago, in Richard Wright's case, came to symbolize beginnings—a pivotal site marking the start of his career as a professional writer—just as Paris, France, came to signify endings—a foreign but ambivalent location of success, freedom, and then disappointments as a result of Wright's years of unsuccessful publications, loss of financial stability, and failing health.

For readers, *Richard Wright Writing America at Home and from Abroad* brings together a unique body of knowledge that follows the trajectory of Wright's combative relations with and analyses of the country of his nativity through the discourses of his crime fictions and relational mini-narratives of escapism and/or death as also portrayed in his poetry. They converse even if they are different genres. Wright never let America's racial impediments hinder his ambitions. Instead, he learned to use words like *linguistic armor.* In 1938, he visualized and then theorized a sociological pathway to freedom in order to inform culturally subjugated and racially amnesiac blacks of a way to rethink the ontological factors causing their fractured psyches as outcast African Americans. His "gnostic" theory embedded in his 1938 essay "Blueprint for Negro Writing" teaches them how "to know" and to recognize that a pathway to freedom exists.[1] He writes:

> Negro folklore contains . . . the collective sense of Negro life in America. Let those who shy at the nationalist implications of Negro life look at this body of folklore, living and powerful, which rose out of a unified sense of a common life and a common fate. Here are those vital beginnings of a recognition of value in life as it is *lived*, a recognition that marks the emergence of a new culture in the shell of the old. (1994 "Blueprint" 100)

Wright applauds the "folklore" arising from the "*lived*" experiences of Negro people—their parents and foreparents. The customs serve as epistemological truths, cautionary tales, and guides for their survivals. He does not demean his people by referring to them as the *Herrenvolk* as would a Jackson Democrat. Instead, Wright extols the "folks," meaning those from the lower class of African Americans in which he was born (*White Man, Listen* [*WML!*] 758). From their lips, declares Wright, the oral messages passed from parent to child in forms of the "blues, spirituals, . . . folktales," and "work songs" have all formed the repositories of knowledge "through which the racial wisdom" of black culture has been formed (98–99). Regardless of the racial or class makeup of his audiences, Wright never altered his candid remarks about America's racial prejudices during the World War II–Jim Crow era of the 1940s or the Cold War period of the 1950s.

America in Black and White

Noteworthy is that Wright, during exile, never relinquished his American citizenship, but used his citizenship rights to critique America. In pictures and in words, *Richard Wright Writing America at Home and from Abroad* provides a visual and verbal conversation about Richard Wright, the man, and his responses to his native country. It begins with the cover photograph of the thirty-seven-year-old author of *Black Boy* (1945) posed at his typewriter in New York in 1944, which depicts his rapid rise to international acclaim at this significant time of his writing career. Additionally, this book follows the trajectory of Richard Wright's domestic and foreign productions of his crime fictions about America. The cast of black and white characters whom Wright has created derive from the "folk" class of the masses. While some may ascend to higher classes or educational levels, they still have grassroots ties that keep them grounded about the realism of America's unjust and biased democratic system. They do not chatter about the reigning Democratic or Republican parties, but take a mediate or neutral position that either group headed by white politicians is generally partisan and racially opposed to them, the perceived anticitizens. The same mediate stance applies to Wright. As a devout Marxist, he recognized that American politicians, regardless of party affiliation, had continued to betray the Negro as well as himself as a member of that outside, racial group. Living in exile broadened his theoretical perspectives about race, class, and American capitalism. As he applied newer psychological and philosophical theories to his crime fictions, he also revealed or implied his own sophisticated, global perspectives. Common to all of Wright's crime fictions as well as his newest haiku poetry are themes of escapism and/or death confronting his black and/or white protagonists in America or his persona of the poet from 1958 to 1960.

Without fully revealing Wright's typical plot narratives in his crime fictions and related poetry, we can now turn to the critical analyses of Wright's works by the essayists in this collection. In part 1, "Writing America at Home, 1930–1947," Ginevra Geraci delves into the meaning of the "Life and Death of a Black Man(n) in Richard Wright's 'Down by the Riverside.'" She applies the theories of Fredric Jameson, Georges Lukács, and Terry Eagleton to illustrate how Anglo-America's combined or singular naturalistic and realistic sociopolitical systems hinder Brother Mann's efforts to acquire medical services for his pregnant wife as natural forces seemingly like a biblical deluge also hamper his progress.

Next, Virginia Whatley Smith views *Native Son* as a prison narrative in "Down South/Up North: Bigger Thomas's Carceral Societies in *Native Son*." The Southern plantation prison system adopted by British and American colonial politicians also functioned as a surveillancing system to keep slaves in the

South from starting uprisings. The ensuing lynching rituals mimed the frenzied crowds at European public executions. Michel Foucault's descriptions of the sociopolitical conditions in Europe that influenced the birth of the Benthamite panopticon prison in 1830 for long-term incarceration, and that Americans adapted, accounts for Bigger Thomas's restrictive and claustrophobic, Jim Crow habitations in both the South and North as being racially designed carceral worlds. In another work, Wright's analyses of black youth reveal that Anglo-America's rules of law have deleterious effects upon some African Americans.

Robert Butler in "Richard Wright's *Rite of Passage* and a Reconsideration of His Portrayal of Women" rejects the claims of 1970s and 1980s feminists who charged Wright with being a misogynist. The suppression of Wright's unpublished manuscripts has led to misrepresentations of Wright's works, which is the case of this 1940s novella that only was published in 1994. Butler illustrates how the positive nurturing of the nonbiological black mother in the novel reflects an undetected pattern of Wright's positive portrayals of black women in his other unpublished and published works after *Rite of Passage*. It is not nurture that fails the youthful black protagonist; instead, it is the inhumane social service system that undermines the mother's love for her foster child.

Part 2, titled "Writing America from Abroad, 1947–1960," contains two essays that concern Wright's classic existentialist novel *The Outsider*, published in 1953. Floyd W. Hayes III probes a conundrum in his essay "Richard Wright and the Dilemma of the Ethical Criminal: Can One Live beyond Good and Evil?" Using the ideas and theories of Nietzsche and Fanon, he provides an assessment of how the American conditions of slavery, postslavery, and current urban targeting of blacks have fostered what Fanon cites to be "a crisis of black existence in an 'antiblack world.'" Hayes argues that America's continued dehumanization of African Americans is among the reasons that Wright has created a novel of ideas with a superintellectual, existential-nihilist protagonist. Cross Damon's heretical thinking and amoral ethics make him a greater danger to American society than the average black criminal.

From another perspective, Joseph Keith, in "Keeping Secrets: The Cold War and the Politics of Un-Belonging in Richard Wright's *The Outsider*," explicates the concept of *secrecy* that Wright establishes in the first part of *The Outsider*. This theme reveals how the repressive effects of the new, post–World War II Cold War between the United States and the Soviet Union especially decimates black Americans. Cross Damon, a stateless person, develops an amoral creed that fosters the uprisings and discordance of blacks throughout the United States and accelerates more anticolonial revolts already sweeping across Africa and Asia in the 1950s.

In "Lying, Deception, Truth-Telling, and Self-Negation: Ironies and Failures of Nation-Building in Wright's African Parody *Savage Holiday*," Virginia

Whatley Smith argues that Wright's nonfictional travel book *Black Power* published in 1954 in reversal becomes white power in America. Wright in *Savage Holiday,* a novel, rescripts the methods that Kwame Nkrumah, the aspiring president of the Gold Coast, must employ to first dismantle the governing tribal and gender traditional customs of the people in order to rebuild from bottom to top a political nation-state run by one president. By writing Nkrumah's actions in Africa as the political and personal experiences of Erskine Fowler in America, Wright traces Fowler's rise to middle-class status in an American nationwide insurance company only to become "de-tribalized" and decentered after an in-house coup. He then implements a vengeful, Freudian-driven, nation-building moral uplift campaign based upon lies and self-deception.

Toru Kiuchi recognizes the Freudian implications in Wright's 1954 novel, but also suggests that the work is a psychoanalytical study more about the author in "Psychoanalysis as Self-Reflection in Richard Wright's *Savage Holiday*." He notes Wright's experience at documentary writing starting in the 1930s as arising from his penchant for converting real-life American crime stories into fictions, such as his employment of the Clinton Brewer case as the basis for *Savage Holiday*. Such extratextual resources have served as kernel ideas for Wright's crime fictions, but Kiuchi argues that *Savage Holiday* more accurately resonates not only of Freudian allusions pertaining to the main white male character, but also reflects Wright's personal struggles in America with his own mother and grandmother.

Moving onward, Wright's novel *The Long Dream*, published in 1958, and its accompanying short story "Five Episodes of Island of Hallucinations" were meant to be part of a trilogy of novels that Wright never completed. As John Lowe notes in "Wright on Patmos: The European Refiguration of Mississippi in *The Long Dream*," the ending of the novel shows Fishbelly in flight from America and bound for Paris, France. The "Islands" short story fragment reflects Fishbelly's reactions to displacement in Paris's multicultural, foreign environment. Yet, as Lowe illustrates, the fully developed published novel is a "protean work" consisting of "separations, flights, departures, and new visions." The work concerns shattered illusions about Fishbelly's childhood and maturation in Mississippi. He follows a deadly path of crime in the footsteps of his father, which sends Fishbelly into a series of international flights and then a final return to an alternate place in America.

Again on the father-son note, Robert Butler in "Signifying and Self-Portraiture in Richard Wright's *A Father's Law*" also views *Native Son* as an intratextual parody in order to magnify some themes recurring in Wright's unfinished novel finally published in 2008. With both the lives of Bigger Thomas the young adult and Ruddy Turner the mature father figure being tied to Chicago, Butler illustrates how Bigger's criminal activities as a lower-class hood take on a different patina when the black family moves up a class level and becomes economically sound and educationally ascended. Yet, as Butler indicates, the happy family life that reflects the American dream of equal wealth and education for blacks in America soon transforms into a nightmare of blindness and self-deception. Wright's own autobiographical experiences in America resonate throughout the novel.

The personal statements or allusions that the essayists have noted as recurring in Wright's fictional works repeat in his poetic creations as well. The words and images also allude to Wright's personal upbringing in the agrarian American South and/or his persona's interactions with nature. For this reason, I have chosen *not* to place the essays about Wright's haiku in a separate section so that they will be construed as extensions of his creative fictions, particularly during the period 1958 to 1960.

In "Richard Wright and the American South," Sachi Nakachi argues that, while Wright expressed an interest in Japan in 1955 and considered it also to be a "colored nation" after attending the Bandung conference held for Africans and Asians in 1955, he was not "absorbed in Zen philosophy." Nakachi finds more thematic elements about the American South located in Wright's photographic text *12 Million Black Voices* (1941) that more accurately parallel the seasonal descriptions that one finds in the four volumes of poems by R. H. Blythe. He helped Wright to refine his knowledge of the form and content expected in haiku. But Wright's haiku differ from the Japanese form that disallows any "grotesque imagery in the natural world" to seep into the poetic moment. His aversion to religion also accounts for Wright's departure from the strict, spiritual directives of haiku writing.

Contrarily, John Zheng in "Richard Wright's Poetic Spirit through the Influence of Zen" says that Wright's versions of haiku often appear as "complete prose statements" and phrases, unlike the two- or three-line, seventeen-syllable, traditional haiku structure. This is more of a compliment than a criticism, since Wright had been writing novels and short stories in this 1958 to 1960 time period. But Wright does become a masterful haiku writer because of his interest in the poet's ability to transcend life's imperishability by altering into a spiritual state of fulfillment. Zen Buddhism in Japan translates to *meditation.* Wright demonstrates such meditative, haiku moments in his poems such as *sabi*—the poet's achievement of a state of "loneliness" to purge himself of his personal emotions. Reading R. H. Blythe's poems helped Wright's persona to become receptive to Zen Buddhism and to realize his "real being with nature."

Different from Nakachi and Zheng, Yoshinobu Hakutani in "The Triangular Vision of Richard Wright: The African American Poet's Achievement of Solace by Means of Eastern Poetics and African Philosophy" suggests that Wright's admixtures of Zen Buddhism with the African philosophy of life enabled the poet to achieve the ultimate state of *mu* or no-self before his death. Hakutani, too, acknowledges the haiku writings of R. H. Blythe as being Wright's introduction to the Eastern form. But Wright was also attracted to the spiritual nature of Zen philosophy espoused by the early haiku masters, and the form's spiritual aesthetics that make no distinctions between the life and death of an individual. By noting how the Eastern and Southern global cultures share similar spiritual beliefs, Hakutani demonstrates how the African American poet of Wright's haiku finally achieves spiritual solace by attaining the ultimate state of *mu*.

To conclude, *Richard Wright Writing America at Home and from Abroad* demonstrates Richard Wright's definitions of his "Americanness" as expressed by means of his front cover photograph and the preponderance of words that he expressed that delineate events in his professional career and private life. The volume brings new insight to his reading public by Wright's not only theorizing a knowable pathway to freedom in "Blueprint for Negro Writing" (1938), but also his having *lived* the experience of British American legal measures that branded black Americans as "*Herrenvolk*" anticitizens. By means of his unique crime fictions and Wrightean-styled Afro-Asian haiku poetry, the essayists reflect how Wright critiques America by means of intratextual parody, extratextual resources, and new theories on race, gender, and sexuality emerging in the 1950s. Overall, Wright's audiences will grasp his personal struggle leading to the spiritual solace of this cultural theorist, global humanist, and African American intellectual who could never be contained or constrained by his native America.

Note

1. *Negro* has been a term used by whites in public discourse as an alternative reference to people of African descent and their African American descendants. Whites also used the "N-word" as a slur on *Negro*, which black people began to repeat as well. The less popular word *colored* came into usage after the 1830s. During the 1960s, *Afro-American* and *black American* became popular references, which blacks themselves displaced in the 1980s and 1990s with the term *African American*.

Part I

Writing America at Home, 1930–1947

Life and Death of a Black Man(n) in Richard Wright's "Down by the Riverside"

—GINEVRA GERACI—

Two basic forces shape language and imagery in "Down by the Riverside," the second of Richard Wright's five short stories that comprise *Uncle Tom's Children* (1938). The first concerns the naturalistic representation of the general conditions and inescapable circumstances of life and death for blacks living in the American South. The other specifically concerns the African American hero Brother Mann. He tries to rescue his family during a period of martial law because of the massive flooding of the Mississippi River; however, he is forced into conscription and then shot by white soldiers for killing a white man. During the series of mishaps complicating Brother Mann's rescue operations, the reader senses the modernist presence of his voice and thoughts as well as the interiority of his being and selfhood. Wright captures the hero's subjectivity by employing the modernist techniques of vernacular interior monologues as well as using a symbolic mythic framework that reflects the biblical deluge.

Wright places the hero's predictable failure within a system of hard facts that will defeat him according to race, milieu, and epoch. Brother Mann perceives the white-dominated American social structure as a solid, impenetrable wall and feels compelled to obey orders and give himself up to white authority.[1] He lives in the Deep South where racial conditions have changed very little since slavery. To illustrate, Wright insinuates the contradictory social conditions that frustrate Mann's attempts to act as a man. He also uses opposite pairings throughout the text to balance the fluid transition between the external, third-person narrator's voice and Mann's personal, desperate, and alienated voice.

Critics have repeatedly highlighted Wright's ability to fuse different elements and techniques into his writings, including those that focus on American culture. With regard to "Down by the Riverside," Michel Fabre mentions the author's ability to "blend and fuse elements and techniques borrowed from Joyce, Hemingway, Gertrude Stein, Conrad, and even James"—all being white European and American writers. Fabre also stresses that, in his depictions of natural disasters, individual loneliness, and existential numbness complicating the lives of his African American characters, Wright chooses to utilize philosophical theories as an alternative mode to writing protest fiction (Fabre, *World* 68). In his introduction to the HarperPerennial edition of *Uncle Tom's Children*, Richard Yarborough also considers the different disciplines and influences occurring in Wright's collection, and especially notes the literary influences ranging from American naturalism to modernism to African American folklore (xiii–xxii). Similarly, Yoshinobu Hakutani places Wright in the African American modernist tradition by stressing its affinity with Anglo-American modernism in terms of their shared interest in traditions, myths, and legends (Hakutani, *Cross-Cultural* 8).

Yet, in assessing Wright's American-based short story, it is also possible *not* to consider naturalism as an expression of social commitment and modernism as a concern with form and craft, and, therefore, as naturally contrasting principles. In "Culture and Finance Capital" from *The Cultural Turn*, Fredric Jameson proposes a dialectical theory of "realism as modernism, or a realism which is so fundamentally a part of modernity that it demands description in some of the ways we have traditionally reserved for modernism itself—the break, the *Novum*, the emergence of new perceptions" (148).[2] On the other hand, in reviewing Marxist theories of literature, Terry Eagleton defines naturalism as a distortion of realism. Choosing Lukács's interpretation of realism as a starting point, Eagleton considers the passage from realism to naturalism as a process of deterioration; in fact, "the great realist writers arise from a history which is visibly in the making. . . . For the successors of the realists . . . history is already an inert object, an externally given fact no longer imaginable as men's dynamic product. Realism, deprived of the historical conditions which gave it birth, splinters and declines into 'naturalism' on the one hand and 'formalism' on the other" (28).

By combining these two notions of naturalism and modernism, they *can be* considered as deeply related perspectives on the world, and even as a means to gain a tentative renewed alliance between man and history in the writer's conscience after the reification of historical perception as mentioned by Eagleton. Thus, naturalism and modernism *are not* opposing forces: the former provides the theoretical background against which the social and economic analysis implied in Wright's short story can be assessed; the latter supplies a range of technical tools that make the character's subjectivity come to life while stressing the artistry of the writer's effort. Wright himself had acknowledged naturalism's inability to delve into the characters' psychology as one major flaw. In *Uncle Tom's Children*, Wright seems willing to balance that inability through "the complexities of the narrative line, the twists and turns of the plot [that] are essential for an understanding of the characters' feelings and the nuances of their emotions" (Margolies, "Wright's Craft" 76).

"Down by the Riverside" is set in American culture, the Deep South, and the racial and cultural conditions existing in the 1920s and 1930s. It provides an example of such interplay between naturalism and modernism that is further processed through solid imagery on the one hand, and fluid tropes on the other. External reality, which is consistent with the naturalistic and protest fiction angles that take into account the hard life of vanquished African Americans, is depicted as a solid, impenetrable wall erected by violent nature, hard unfriendly whites, and iron-like American racist authority.[3] This solidity, metaphorically representing the deterministic nature of social and historical conditions, has a balancing principle in the liquidity of both sounds and images. The modernist elements thus include water imagery, thematic representations of individual isolation, and stylistic techniques that capture the qualitative levels of the African American hero's voice.

Wright portrays, and Mann perceives, white people and white authority as a solid barrier that symbolizes "the inflexibility of the Southern status quo" (Howard 60). His perception of whites is no different from that of Bigger Thomas in *Native Son.* This solid inalterability of the social system is also expressed in the "unrelieved bleakness symbolized by the endless waters of the flood or the silt-draped landscape left after it" (Howard 48).[4] Nature, too, is unrelenting and resistant to Mann's endeavors.

Throughout the narrative, the African American character's psyche remains detached and even subordinated to external reality because, as Eagleton writes about naturalism, "the dialectical relations between men and their world give way to an environment of dead, contingent objects disconnected from characters" (28). An example of such estrangement is the frequent juxtaposition of Mann's thoughts with white people's orders. Social reality in general in the form of white authority coincides with the specific moment that dominates the external reality in Mann's consciousness. After being sidetracked from acquiring a boat to take his pregnant wife Lulu to a hospital, Mann's thoughts are still on his personal mission at hand: "Lawd, Lulu down there somewhere, Mann thought. Dead! She gonna be left there in the flood . . ." (Wright, "Down" 103). The suspension dots at the end make it evident that Mann is not fully allowed to indulge in his train of thought because a soldier's voice interrupts it to urge him to get back to work.[5]

Wright depicts American whites as being similar to rock-hard surfaces reflecting, according to circumstances, fear, hatred, or disgust. When Mann approaches the white man Heartfield and asks him for help with his sick wife, even nature seems hard-edged as the surrounding darkness is disrupted by solid light: "A pencil of light shot out in the darkness, a spot of yellow caught the boat. He blinked, blinded" (79). To Mann, an enraged Heartfield appears heartless: "He watched a white man with a hard, red face come out onto a narrow second-story porch and stand framed in a light-flooded doorway" (80). Darkness is intercut by lightness or whiteness. White authority is also metonymically represented by white soldiers, whose faces seem to Mann to be "like square blocks of red and he could see the dull glint of steel on the tips of their rifles" (83). Here the impenetrable wall of racial prejudice is portrayed as being made of square blocks and steel rifles. Later in the concluding scene, Mann will perceive the pressure of pursuing whites as being equivalent to physical weight: "Mann knew they were behind him. He felt them all over his body, and especially like something hard and cold weighing on top of his head, weighing so heavily that it seemed to blot out everything but one hard, tight thought: They got me now" (113).

Wright's imagery in this short story recalls similar tropes in *Native Son* (1940) with its setting being in the American North, and specifically urban Chicago, Illinois, and its segregated South Side. The African American hero Bigger Thomas, another product of the South but now having grown up in the North, registers his disappointment with his oppressive environmental and economic conditions. Bigger feels as if the snow covering the city is weighing down on him and is symbolically like another white mass crushing him: "White people were not really people; they were a sort of great natural force, like a stormy sky looming overhead" (Wright, 1987 *Native Son* [*NS*] 129). Mann's external environment in the South shares the same menacing quality, as it is clear in this scene shortly preceding his arrest: "The landscape lay before his eyes with a surprising and faithful solidity. It was like a picture that might break. He walked on in blind faith, he reached level ground and went on past white people who stared sullenly. He wanted to look around, but could not turn his head. His body seemed encased in a tight vise, in a narrow black coffin that moved with him as he moved" ("Down" 114). Mann feels that his own mortality is imminent.

Ironically, Mann contributes to his own ending from the very beginning of his desperate mission to transport his pregnant wife to a hospital. First, he signs a note to be repaid for a boat that he steals and that will later be used against him as evidence of his theft. Second, he is indicted by means of another note carrying Heartfield's address that compels him to rescue the family of the man he has just killed in self-defense.[6] These notes predate symbolically the derisive one inscribed by Dr. Bledsoe that Ellison's Invisible Man carries in his briefcase to white patrons in the North and that reads: "Keep this nigger boy running."[7]

The text also refers to the problem of inaction by the larger community—the black sector that Wright does not fail to represent in its shortcomings. Mann feels more at ease when he is with "his people"; yet, no help comes from them during his travails and tribulations. In fact, when he is arrested and members of the black community are present, he notes that "the black faces he passed were blurred one into the other" (117). He despairingly wonders: "Why dont they hep me?" (117). They, too, are subjugated victims of white oppression and powerless to save themselves against white authority. Mann turns out to be a typical, powerless black man, a condition Wright continually presents as a contradiction to the claims of equality written in the Declaration of Independence and freedom guaranteed to blacks according to the Emancipation Proclamation. In the South, however, Mann is not a "man"; he is still a "boy" to whites, no matter at what age because he is black.

In essence, Mann is an aspect of Wright's other typical, black male heroes who become thwarted by white society from achieving their ambitions. His story gains additional parabolic force by Mann's efforts to save his pregnant black wife who will never be delivered of her child (Brigano 18). This African American adult male is also a painfully isolated hero, a desperate and lonely modernist character wobbling in an American sea of white and some black faces staring indifferently at him. The passage concerning Mann's puzzlement over his black community's inaction has been interpreted as a hint of Wright's pessimism regarding black culture's failure to live up to the nationalistic ideals it often extols (Kent 46).

The proof of a modernist intention is evinced by Wright's incorporation of its stylistic techniques. Extending his analysis to *Uncle Tom's Children* as a whole, Richard Yarborough equates Wright's use of the "stream of consciousness," especially in "Long Black Song," to Gertrude Stein's "Melanctha," included in *Three Lives.*[8] The modernist frame of reference in "Down by the Riverside" is further suggested by Wright's use of the flood metaphor as a variant of the biblical deluge. He repeats this water imagery in his other short story, "The Man Who Saw the Flood," also included in *Eight Men.* As modernist literary echoes, they resonate the water imagery enveloping the symbolic elements in T. S. Eliot's *The Waste Land* (1922). In addition, Mann's desperate effort to fight the current additionally recalls the equally hopeless confrontation with nature that the Bundren family in Mississippi experience in William Faulkner's *As I Lay Dying* (1930). During one scene, Cash and the family's wagon are swept away while crossing a river similarly as forceful and powerful as the one impeding Mann's efforts.

Edward Margolies also notes that there is "a certain epic quality to the piece—man steadily pursuing his course against a malevolent nature only to be cut down later by the ingratitude of his fellow men: "The scenario is suggestive of Mark Twain or Faulkner. And Mann's long-suffering perseverance and stubborn will to survive endow him with a rare mythic Biblical quality" (Margolies, "Wright's Craft" 80). Michel Fabre has also included Faulkner into Wright's sources of inspiration (Fabre 1973 *Unfinished Quest* [*UQ*] 17, 112–36). Yet, the experimental nature of a text like that of *As I Lay Dying*, which powerfully relies on fragmentation and disorder as a gnosiological method and as a metanarrative meditation on the nature of the authorial process, may appear unparalleled in comparison to Wright's reworking of a modernist perspective (Rubeo, "Fragments" 209–12).

However, Wright's short story and Faulkner's novel do have a few elements in common. As already mentioned, while evoking a hopeless confrontation between man and nature, Wright endeavors to follow the character's mobile, flowing train of thought as it is being pitted against a stone-like background that seems to mock him. Consistently, the reader has to deal with a "confused rush and whirl of events and is swept along, like Mann, as if in the flood itself. Wright's main means of engaging the reader in this way is his rapid and frequent shifts in point of view from third person to first person and back" (Kinnamon, *Emergence* 89). Nature consistently undercuts human efforts.

Faulkner's novel, too, displays a complex combination of naturalistic and modernist elements. In fact, the naturalistic setting of Mississippi in which man struggles with indifferent nature, and the material and spiritual ruin of the Bundrens have their modernist counterpart in ways similarly represented in Wright's short story. There is the challenging fragmentation of characters' thoughts, scenes, or events in the text over several sections. The different points of view and narrative voices for each section in Faulkner's longer work tentatively outline or provide an overall picture of persons living under chaotic conditions. Faulkner questions the very nature of literary creation by opposing two essential linguistic modes against each other. For example, there is the strictly referential, even dreary language used by Anse as opposed to the creative but incoherent "imagist" language used by Darl and Vardaman. They "speak with a freedom that allows them to get directly to the essence of things, and thus expose, quite unintentionally, the hypocritical redundancy, the labyrinthical course of what is commonly accepted as 'normal speech'" (Rubeo, "Fragments" 208). Their fragmentary and/or incoherent expressions are modernistic.

Wright, too, embeds the motifs of fragmentary and/or incoherent references in his modernist short story "Down by the Riverside." The work suggests an analogous contrast: the matter-of-fact language of authority of white men, such as the case of Mann being given orders by the soldiers, as well as the more extensively naturalistic language clashes with the strongly emotional or at times broken language of the main character. Wright portrays Mann as someone who is much more verbal when talking to himself than he can ever be when talking to others, especially white people. The story is a multifaceted combination of discursive levels unceasingly shifting from pure third-person narration to first-person vernacular interior monologue to direct speech. The liquid transition between these levels adds force to the figures of fluidity, to the water imagery that Tracy Webb has extensively discussed as a predominant feature not just in "Down by the Riverside," but also throughout *Uncle Tom's Children* (5–16).

From the very first pages, the third-person narrator's voice and the character's interior monologue alternate constantly to bring the reader back and forth between the world outside and the world inside. This alternating combination becomes at times intricate, as in the following quotation that shows an alternation of direct speech, interior monologue, third-person internally focalized narration, and nonfocalized third-person narration, all in the space of a few lines:

> "Ah sent Bob wid the mule t try t git a boat," he said . . . he swallowed with effort. . . . No boat. No money. No doctah. Nothing t eat. N Bob ain back here yit. Lulu could not last much longer this way. If Bob came with a boat he would pile Lulu in and row over to that Red Cross Hospital, no matter *what*. The white folks would . . . have to take her in. They would not let a woman die just because she was black. . . . He grew rigid, looking out of the window, straining to listen. ("Down" 65–66)

The sentence "Lulu could not last much longer this way," in particular, seems an example of imperfect free indirect discourse. While it is a statement that can only belong to Mann in terms of subjective knowledge and especially because of the proximal deictic *this*, it is in standard English, not in black English as it should be in order to faithfully reproduce the character's thoughts and speech patterns. In these terms, then, the passage should be read as narrative report provided by an internally focalized narrator. The use of the italics, too—"no matter *what*"—indicate an emphasis that should belong to the character, although the register does not.

Wright also pays extreme attention to other formal issues, such as the pure sounds of the flooding waters. Says the narrator: "To all sides of Mann the flood rustled, gurgled, droned, glistening blackly like an ocean of bubbling oil" (74). In this case, a series of alliterations of *l*, a liquid consonant, reinforces the fluid imagery in the text. From the very beginning the water enters the scene as a leading actor. It inundates Mann's world: "Each step he took made the old house creak as thought the earth beneath the foundations were soggy. He wondered how long the logs which supported the house could stand against the water . . ." (62). The description has a complexity symbolized by its alternating nuances: "In the morning the water was a deep brown. In the afternoon it was a clayey yellow. And at night it was black, like a restless tide of liquid tar" (62). The water all around the house comes to stand as a primordial, all-encompassing element indifferent to human events. Says the narrator: "And water was everywhere. Yellow water. Swirling water. Droning water. Four long days and nights it had been there, flowing past" (64). As Mann comments, "water was everywhere"; however, as in Coleridge's *The Rime of the Ancient Mariner*, there is "nor any drop to drink." Without another choice, "he took a gourd from the wall and dipped some muddy water out of a bucket. It tasted thick and bitter and he could not swallow it" (64).

Wright makes his descriptions of the flood and Mann's struggles more complicated than naturalistic solidity and modernist liquidity. In the context of Jameson's reassessment of the close relationship between realism and modernism as a commitment to the *novum*, both of which insist upon "the necessarily subversive and critical, destructive, character of their realisms," the two perspectives melt into each other (147). Consequently, Wright characterizes the water as almost solid, like a wall opposing Mann: "The current became stiff and the darkness thickened. For awhile he had the feeling that the boat was not moving" ("Down" 75). As Mann proceeds to row in complete darkness against a thick, heavy current, while, at the same time, also staving off a growing numbness in his tired body, the air and the water become more and more unyielding like "an invisible wall" (77). Mann's world is hostile; nature is as life-threatening as humans in Mann's southern climate.

The rock-hardness of Mann's defeat is partially attenuated by his desperate attempt to escape. In a truly naturalistic perspective, the postslavery historical circumstances, hereditary laws, and economic poverty meant to hinder blacks work inexorably to subdue man, and in this case, a black man living in a white-dominated world. The fact that Mann eventually tries to escape conscription in a desperate final act to save Lulu is perceived by whites as an act of incipient rebellion—a "boy" socialized by the white South tries to act like a "man." The one tangible evidence of his success is that Mann is able to choose when to die. George E. Kent stresses Mann's will to survive, which he expresses "by determining the moment when he will die . . .although he is killed by the soldier, they have been forced to accept the time that he offers" (45). This is an "existential triumph" also acknowledged by Richard Yarborough (xxiv). In analyzing the ideological functions of death in Wright's fiction, Abdul JanMohamed argues that choosing the terms of one's death is a claim of irreducible selfhood against American oppression. It must be understood in the context of postslavery Jim Crow laws first and marginalization and/or segregation secondarily. In fact, rebellion is the way in which the oppressed subject—generally African Americans—challenges the threat of physical annihilation that whites use to control him or her (*Death-Bound* 19).

The way the collection is organized as a whole tells the reader that *Uncle Tom's Children* may start in life as being mere victims such as Big Boy's friends, but they end up like ungovernable subjects and act accordingly. Therefore, the first tableau of "Big Boy Leaves Home" portrays a lynching ritual that Big Boy witnesses. In the last one titled "Bright and Morning Star," Aunt Sue, a stubborn, decisive, black mother figure, comes gradually to life as a proactive character when whites kill her son. She finally understands the nature of her son's Communist leanings, and gradually, the devout Christian woman realizes that she, too, is ready to kill in order to achieve freedom. At the paratextual level, the table of contents to *Uncle Tom's Children* sums up the thematic trajectory of Wright's message for the collection: what begins with "Big Boy Leav[ing] Home" ends up with a "Bright and Morning Star" materializing after a dark night.

In this sense, there is a progression of resistance throughout *Uncle Tom's Children*, and the topic will be further developed in *Native Son* in the form of a conflict between a marginalized man and a white-dominated, oppressive American society. The harsh determinism of race and environment is revealed in terms of the emergence of African American subjectivity and resistance. Such a combination accounts for the changing nature of liquid and solid objects in "Down by the Riverside." Accordingly, the solid quality of the naturalist angle is diluted into something more fluid as the tragedy works itself to resolution. The hardness of the sky that Mann sees itself converges with the "wobbly sea of brown water stretching away to a trembling sky" (122). Both seem limitless as sky and water converge on the horizon. Colors become liquid, and light becomes fluid: "the sun was shining, pouring showers of yellow into his eyes" ("Down" 122).

The text provides another variation of the solid and fluid properties, as in the following example occurring when Mann and Brinkley finally rescue Mrs. Heartfield and her children: "A voice whispered over and over in his ears, Ah gotta git outta here . . ." (111). In this case, the third-person narration smoothly slides into vernacular interior monologue with no punctuation marks except for a comma; yet, the latter is introduced by the verb *whispered*—as it would be in the case with direct speech or at least reported speech. However, while the voice is said to whisper in Mann's ears, thus suggesting its otherness, it speaks in the words Mann himself would use. Undergoing a process of distancing and objectivization, Mann becomes estranged from his own voice, hearing himself speak and watching himself act: ". . . as though he were outside of himself watching himself, Mann felt himself stand up. He saw his hands reaching for the window ledge . . ." (109). Mann's tendency to observe himself from the outside provides another link to Faulkner, since such detachment from himself recalls Addie and Darl Bundren's aloofness and estrangement from their own thoughts and actions (Rubeo "Fragments" 202).

While the text relies on a modernist sensibility as to symbols and narrative technique, it also displays a naturalist awareness of material conditions that is also made possible by the specific attitude of African American modernist writers such as Langston Hughes, Wright, Ellison, and, later, James Baldwin, who, as Yoshinobu Hakutani explains, "were intent on conveying their universal visions, their world views informed of other cultures" (*Cross-Cultural* 8–9). And it is all the more interesting how metaphors of fluidity abound when discussing the relatedness of modernism, tradition, and the role of the artist. In "Blueprint for Negro Writing," Wright reworks African American modernism in terms of themes and points of view that can create value by relying on a "consciousness that draws on the fluid, historically influential lore of the great people" (qtd. in Hakutani, *Cross-Cultural* 3).

Yet, the most evident tribute that Wright pays in developing the symbolism of the river is to Langston Hughes's "The Negro Speaks of Rivers." However, he does something more than just reiterate a literary motif. In Hughes's poetic imagination, the Mississippi River is more immediately associated with slavery. It also recalls an African past, and establishes a temporal connection through which memory, like the river itself, flows powerful and majestic. Not only is the Mississippi River a metaphor for the inner relatedness of past and present, it is also a natural embodiment of black people as a community, as a repository of tradition (23). In Hughes's case, such tradition is also enriched by biblical references, which further expand the metaphor of the river to include the identification of the Mississippi River with the Jordan River (Piccinato 81–86).

This brings us back to the biblical overtones in "Down by the Riverside." First of all, the title is taken from a spiritual Mann and his family sing before they leave their decrepit, sagging house and literally travel down by the riverside on a stolen boat. As already mentioned, Mann thus becomes a prototypical man, a Christian Everyman. In perfect harmony with Wright's use of the Bible as a mythic framework, Mann's wandering on the enraged river is, at the same time, a metaphor for the plight of black people and a symbolic representation of an individual's fight against nature and society. Here, Wright is rewriting the African American poetic tradition. His hero must cross the river by performing an act similar to the acts of fugitive slaves who had to cross the Ohio River in order to be free at last. The crossing paradigm only makes Mann's death on the river bank all the more meaningful. No more placid flowing for him, no more grandiose evocation of a past when black people were kings, no more River Jordan to cross to get to the Promised Land.

The river, additionally, is a powerful trope not just in African American culture, but also in what eventually emerged as a pattern in the writings dominated by white Americans. And as such, it lives on in Twain's portraits of "Life on the Mississippi" as well as in Herman Melville's *The Confidence Man*. As for travelers—be they just two as Huck and Jim or a motley and diverse human microcosm traveling on board of the *Fidèle*—they become a narrative tool to represent social practices. Especially regarding Melville's novel, the travelers problematize the fluid identities and shifting tenets that being an American encompasses. While in Melville's novel the mutable beauty of the river mirrors the protean nature of American life as a new and constantly renewed world where the con man prevails and the impostor finds his personal heaven, in Wright's short story the blackness of the water stands for the direness of circumstances in Mann's life as the fury of the loosened river discharges the harshness of racism. Wright does not stop here in terms of reformulating canons. In the highly symbolic and richly evocative texture he weaves, every key object suggests a network of meanings that make the text intelligible against "the American grain."

Wright's text shares specific features—the blackness of the water and its solidity—with an American classic. In Poe's *The Narrative of Arthur Gordon Pym,* the *Grampus* is surrounded on every side by the furious sea "which tore it away lifting the after portion of the brig entirely from the water, against which trumpeted in her descent with such a concussion as would be occasioned by going ashore" (1075). The water seems to close upon the defenseless ship and Pym and his companions are "stunned by the immense weight of water which tumbled upon us" (Poe, "Narrative" 1076). Later, upon his arrival in Tsalal onboard the *Jane Guy,* Pym is struck by the color and the apparent thickness of a brook crossing his path and is astounded in noticing that the water does not seem transparent, although it is, but appears as a solid object:

> Upon collecting a basinful and allowing it to settle thoroughly, we perceived the whole mass of liquid was made of a number of distinct veins, each of a distinct hue; that these veins did not commingle. . . . Upon passing the blade of a knife athwart the veins, the water closed over it immediately. . . . If, however, the blade was passed down accurately between two veins, a perfect separation was effected, which the power of cohesion did not immediately rectify. (Poe, "Narrative" 1141)[9]

Along with Coleridge's ephemeral presence in "Down by the Riverside," the echo of *The Narrative of Arthur Gordon Pym* within Wright's text on the one hand, and the resonance of *The Rime of the Ancient Mariner* in Poe's on the other (Rubeo, *Agghiacciant*i 29–32) tighten the intertextual network and make "Down by the Riverside" a multifaceted literary prism.

In molding diverse literary reminiscences, Wright's text fully reveals a truly modernist approach as he collects diverse materials and reassembles them into a new form that critiques American culture. In addition to the multilayered symbolism of the river, other specific objects perform this function: the boat, the gun, and the axe. Such strategy based on the use of "second-hand objects" tallies with the modernist perspective in which Wright's text demands to be read and interpreted and where, as among the ruins of "the waste land," tradition is sometimes altered, distorted, maximized, or downsized. It should not be overlooked that Wright and Eliot moved in very different directions. Eliot, an American and a well-educated white man, is known for his political conservatism and positive horror over modern chaos; namely, urban masses and immigration. His conservatism and resistance to cultural changes in the flux of modernistic trends has little to do with Wright's personal background as an African American with a ninth-grade education but self-taught writer with an artistic commitment. Concerning the place that subaltern or lower classes have within modernist aesthetics, Eric Shoket reads literary modernism at large and Eliot's work in particular "as a reconceptualization of the working-class forms that tries to control the economic and social anxiety of modernization" and, therefore, is "not an aesthetics of liberation, but an aesthetics of management that was symptomatic of incipient configurations within the industrial labor process" (14). He notes that "Taylorist" production methods are adopted along with managerial systems to better organize them (18).[10]

When Wright's modernism deals with poor, beleaguered African American subaltern subjects lost in the Mississippian waste land as well as in the new urban wilderness of the North, it does articulate a problematic aesthetic of liberation posited against a realistic appraisal of material condition. As already stressed, economic oppression accounts for the specificity of black modernism. However, Wright conveys his own version of degradation and dehumanization. While in *Walden* Henry Thoreau borrows an ax (32) and goes into the woods to live "live deliberately . . . deep and suck out all the marrow of life" (74) to stress his rejection of bourgeois values such as property, Mann uses his axe more prosaically to force open the window of Mrs. Heartfield's house in order to rescue her and her children. Momentarily, he is even tempted to use it against them to save his own life. His hesitancy will be costly; it finally causes him to be recognized as Heartfield's murderer. The gun does not assist him in achieving a heroic grandeur like that in the wild West, either, but it is, at the same time, an instrument of self-defense as well as a cause of his final ruin. Paradoxically, the only way a black man can hope to point a gun at a white man in self-defense and not be convicted for murder is to let himself be killed.

Lastly, the rowboat with which Mann tries to steer a difficult course against the liquid-solid fury of the Mississippi River will not be a lifesaver for his wife, who dies before getting to a hospital, nor for him. It is stolen property and, significantly, white in color. The little white boat fights against the black water, and the chromatic contrast could not be more symbolically charged. Its whiteness makes it more easily recognizable and certainly more visible in the darkness of the surging river and heavy rain. Keneth Kinnamon highlights the symbolic meaning of the contrasts between the light and dark colors, between the brown and yellow of the water and the whiteness of the foam, the boat, and Heartfield's shirt (*Emergence* 89–90). Finally, the boat is not a vessel carrying the character through an epistemological process as the metaphor of difficult navigation might suggest. It is not Huck and Jim's raft; in fact, it resembles more Arthur Gordon Pym's various makeshift crafts. Mann's difficulties in recognizing places and objects call to mind Pym's failure as a subject capable of reading and interpreting nature (Rubeo, *Agghiaccianti* 28–29): "He began to look for the cotton-seed mill that stood to the left of the railroad. He peered, longing to see black stack-pipes. They were along here somewhere. . . . Quickly he retraced in his mind the route over which he thought he had come. . . . He rowed from the stack-pipes, rowed with the houses in his mind, yearning for something to come out of the darkness to match an inner vision" ("Down" 75). Wright blends all these elements and shapes to characterize the paradigmatic African American and black Christian going through his own personal pilgrim's progress, which, at the same time, opens onto a collective horizon. The plot unfolds as the river overflows, and exposes the impenetrability of an American, white-dominated social system that makes black people especially vulnerable in times of natural catastrophes. It is the same trajectory developing in the "Man Who Saw the Flood" as well as in recent time when Hurricane Katrina took a heavy toll on black Louisiana residents.

There is another way in which Mann's boat explores the metaphor of the ship as a representation of the world; namely, the way in which it questions the nature of interpersonal relationships within the black community. Mann is a lonely character, a modernist, desperate hero. He does not confide in Brinkley, the young black man who helps him rescue the Heartfields. Therefore, one might argue, how can he expect "his people" to help him at the end when he cannot trust his fellow men even when they are, literally, on the same boat? Hence, his defeat at the end of his solitary war can also be faulted as his own inability to ask for help (Kinnamon, *Emergence* 87, 92).

The relationship between the individual and his or her community is a constant concern in Wright's work, which is especially evident in *Uncle Tom's Children*, even when the characters seem lonely and isolated. Wright tries to unravel the contradictions of such a relationship, especially when it proves to be a failure. Thus, the black community is relegated to the background like the members of a chorus in a Greek tragedy or, at other times, they are totally absent. While in "Big Boy Leaves Home," the minimal presence of the black community performs a function that could be defined, in narratologic terms, as that of the helper since Big Boy is assisted by a black neighbor in escaping a lynching, it is a silent spectator in "Down By the Riverside." In "Long Black Song," Sarah goes adrift and becomes lost in loneliness that leads to adultery. In response, her husband Silas opts for the most dramatically solitary choice of all by setting fire to his own house and choosing to die in it. The transition from individual to plural is tentatively achieved in "Fire and Cloud" in which Reverend Taylor takes his place at the center of the final group picture. This singular to group action occurs also in "Bright and Morning Star" when Aunt Sue joins the other blacks in the community and organizes a group of Communist activists to fight local economic oppression.

At a macrotextual level, another element adding continuity to Wright's themes and poetics is violence, especially individual violence. It interweaves with the fabric of a moral dilemma in which fierceness is either a response to chaos or a desperate act of rebellion. Big Boy kills in panic as well as Bigger in *Native Son*. Their intertextual relationship is first and foremost evident in the similarity of their names, the latter being an accretion of the former, and both suggesting a story of increasing violence. Wright's meditation on solitary acts of violence, and on murder in particular, develops further in the novels written during his self-imposed exile in France. The theme of deliberate assassination takes on a Dostoevskian nuance as the similarities between *The Outsider* and *Crime and Punishment* illustrate—especially regarding the relationship between murderers and inquirers in the respective couples comprised of Cross Damon–Ely Houston and Raskòl'nikov-Porfirij Petrovič.

As to the specific cases of violence in *Uncle Tom's Children*, there are many. Brother Mann kills in self-defense; Silas murders as a result of anger and kills himself in defiance of an authority he no longer is willing to acknowledge after a lifetime of exasperation; Sue kills to protect the welfare of other members of the Communist Party. In reading "Down by the Riverside" in light of Burke's *Permanence and Change,* Eugene Miller stresses the emergence, in Wright's work, of transitional figures in which the old and the new are contending forces. Violence indicates the explosion of this tension and the materialization of something new, according to which Mann "asserts himself both in killing Mr. Heartfield and his decision to bring about his own death" ("Down" 193). Such a character performs a crucial function in taking upon himself "the voltage of conflicting orientations" in American society (193). In this context of American culture and the Deep South, the newer synthesized form could be an embodiment of the *novum* which Wright has chosen to express himself in modernist-naturalistic terms.

In conclusion, "Down by the Riverside" is carefully constructed as a critique on American culture. The text pivots around two literary principles: naturalism, which molds the representation of Mann's predictable failure, and modernism, which takes on the familiar look of a certain Faulknerian narrative style. Wright's wide range of literary influences, stretching from Joyce to Dostoevsky, has already been studied. It has been noticed that his work possesses a certain paradoxical quality, especially regarding the impossibility to separate the naturalistic, protest fiction tenets from the existentialist slant that does not exclusively belong to his French period.[11] The two areas unceasingly intersect to expose American culture. Thus, "Down by the Riverside" constitutes an effort to harmonize psychological interrogation and social commitment in an unorthodox mode of protest fiction. Such an approach responds to the complexity of Wright's position as an African American writer whose battle with American culture had to be fought by taking into account specific economic, social, and historical issues depriving blacks of equal citizenship. All of these issues could only be waged on a cultural level by his facility with words. Richard Wright, as a "black boy," achieves the mission that he had declared at the end of *Black Boy* (1945). He says: "I would hurl words into this darkness and wait for an echo, and if an echo sounded, no matter how faintly, I would send other words to tell, to march, to fight, to create a sense of the hunger for life that gnaws in us all, to keep alive in our hearts a sense of the inexpressibly human" (1987 *Black Boy* [*BB*] 384). He successfully proves his point in illuminating Mann's struggles against the insidious forces of unfriendly nature and hostile human beings causing his tragic but manly defeat.

Notes

1. Writing about *Uncle Tom's Children*, Edward Margolies points out that the characters perceive whites as "blurs," "bogs," "mountains," "fire," "ices," and "marble." Margolies, "Wright's Craft: The Short Stories," 75.

2. Kevin Bell considers Jameson's account of modernism as an act of "all-but-wholesale Dismissal . . . on the grounds of its supposed flight from reality into formalistic ephemerality." Kevin Bell, *Ashes Taken for Fire: Aesthetic Modernism and the Critique of Identity* (Urbana: University of Illinois Press, 2007), 5.

3. Concerning Wright's attitude as a child, Abdul R. JanMohamed explains: "Between the young child's vague understanding of the culture of social death and the mature writer who begins to investigate that world in *Uncle Tom's Children* lays the vast and pernicious world of social death, the most brutal and dispiriting aspects of which he had yet to experience and which were to become the subject matter of his fiction." JanMohamed, "Negating the Negation," 113.

4. See Fabre, *Unfinished Quest*, 110.

5. Howard points out Mann's defeatist, fatalist belief instilled by Southern society and that, although he can fight the force of nature, he is vanquished by the force of white racist society (60). Margaret Walker Alexander says the basic story line of *Uncle Tom's Children* concerns "the tragic fate of a black man in the hostile white world of a violent South land." Margaret Walker Alexander, "Richard Wright," *Richard Wright: A Collection of Critical Essays*, ed. Richard Macksey and Frank E. Moorer (Englewood Cliffs, NJ: Prentice Hall, 1984), 34. Similarly, Maria K. Mootry points out that "his characters are typologies which personify the hero in opposition to the environment." See Mootry, "Bitches, Whores, and Woman Haters," Macksey and Moorer, 122.

6. Edward Margolies stresses the excessively contrived coincidences in the story ("Wright's Craft," 79) as does Michel Fabre (1973 *UQ* 158). Concerning the "implausibility of the plot," see also Kinnamon, *Emergence*, 88.

7. The origin of this element can be traced back to a trick white people would play on slaves asked to deliver letters having the sole aim to keep them running from plantation to plantation. See Leon Forrest, "Luminosity from the Lower Frequencies," in Kimberly W. Benston,

ed., *Speaking for You: The Vision of Ralph Ellison* (Washington, DC: Howard University Press, 1987), 316.

8. Margaret Walker Alexander reports "Wright used James Joyce as an example when he was writing *Lawd Today!*, being struck by a book that kept all the action limited to one day, but he considered *Lawd Today!*, which I retyped for him, as one of his worst works." See Margaret Walker Alexander, "Richard Wright," Macksey and Moorer, 25.

9. Ugo Rubeo considers the lack of limpidity of Tsalal water in the context of Emerson's concept of nature as a transparent and perfectly intelligible system; therefore, the opacity of the water implies the opacity of the world. Rubeo, *Agghiaccianti simmetrie*, 85.

10. Shoket's evaluation diverges from Kevin Bell's above-mentioned appraisal of modernism as an instrument that opens "other registers of signification by which those realities less visible or less audible to official history and representational writing" (5). Bell's study focuses, among others, on Faulkner, Ellison, and Himes, while Shoket discusses Eliot's early poetry. Yoshinobu Hakutani points out that "one of the striking differences between Anglo-American and African American modernists has much to do with their attitudes toward their crafts. Hughes . . . advocated an aesthetic of simplicity and, like Whitman, voices of democracy. All, in all, African American modernists shunned an elitist attitude which Western modernists at times betrayed." Hakutani, *Cross-Cultural Visions in African American Modernism*, 8.

11. Patricia D. Watkins considers the paradox at the heart of *The Man Who Lived Underground* as "an effort to reconcile apparently irreconcilable approaches such as a naturalistic, and therefore deterministic, fable . . . and an existential, and therefore anti-deterministic, fable." Watkins, "The Paradoxical Structure," Rampersad, 148.

Down South/Up North: Bigger Thomas's Carceral Societies in *Native Son*

—VIRGINIA WHATLEY SMITH—

> My father was a white man. He was admitted to be such by all I ever heard speak of my parentage. The opinion was also whispered that my master was my father; but of the correctness of this opinion, I know nothing; the means of knowing was withheld from me. My mother and I were separated when I was but an infant—before I knew her as my mother.
>
> **—Frederick Douglass,** *Narrative* (12–13)

In *Narrative of the Life of Frederick Douglass, an American Slave, Written by Himself,* published in 1845, Douglass's remark concerning plantation gossip about his paternal heritage indicates just one of the multiple ontological conundrums that occurs throughout his life and that repeats over time as one of numerous enigmas confronting Bigger Thomas, the African American protagonist in Richard Wright's 1940 novel *Native Son*. The reason that Douglass raises the biological issue of paternity has nothing to do with his memory loss. Unlike the birthright of white children of knowing their ages and/or biological heritages, Douglass very early had recognized that half of his identity and ontological well-being remained hidden in the suppressed information about his paternity: the name of his real father, the race of his biological father, and the absence or presence of this mysterious father figure. He, as a powerless slave child, had no legal rights to learn the "truth" about his paternal heritage. It remained buried under a labyrinth of oral speculations, secretive written records, and legal lies that had been manufactured, mobilized, and manipulated by the past and present European American slaveholders and their powerful legal networks. These lawful constraints gradually caused Douglass to become a "restless spirit" or the type of inquisitive or rebellious slave whom masters dreaded. To squelch revolts, white male and female slave owners routinely used barbaric forms of discipline and punishment to keep unruly slaves bound to the strictures of the slave laws and confined within the physical borders of the plantations. Such plantations were deliberately partitioned into sectors like prisons in order to house captives, willing slave spies, masters and their families, and overseers (Douglass, *Narrative* 12).

Nearly one hundred years later, the same antebellum epistemological, ontological, biological, and sociological problems of African American identity, birthright privileges, paternal lineage, and racial placement from Douglass's era have recurred to conflict the mind-set of the fictional character Bigger Thomas, despite obvious temporal, spatial, and demographic changes in the southern and northern regions of the United States by the 1940s. That is because signatures of race transcend time and place. Indeed, Michel Foucault's publication about the birth of the prison in *Discipline and Punish* (1979) provides clarity about the contradictory cultural messages causing turmoil for Bigger Thomas because penal systems have repeated and transformed over time as well. Foucault's work is a significant historical study on penology that elucidates how the European-modeled, American plantation prison systems altered minimally over three centuries, and eventually adapted the panopticon penitentiary structural design completed in 1843 as an alternate means of surveillancing prisoners while keeping them in long-term confinements. Both of these penal institutions were still operating in America in the 1930s and 1940s. Thus, when readers start to explore carceral representations in American literature, they most likely will recover the works of African American writer Richard Wright and his depictions of carceral societies both South and North in his canon of crime fictions. He published eight works by the time of his death in 1960: *Uncle Tom's Children* (1938); "Almos' a Man" (1940); *Native Son* (1940); *The Man Who Lived Underground* (1941); *Black Boy* (1945); *The Outsider* (1953); *Savage Holiday* (1954), and *The Long Dream* (1958). Five of Wright's crime fictions were published posthumously—*Eight Men* (1961), *Lawd Today!* (1963), "Five Episodes/Island of Hallucinations" (1963), *Rite of Passage* (1994), and *A Father's Law* (2008). Of these, Wright's signature crime novel is still considered to be *Native Son*, which immediately cast the struggling author into national and international prominence as the foremost black writer in America. Moreover, with Wright's publication of his 1941 photographic text, *12 Million Black Voices: A Folk History of the Negro in the United States*, he proclaimed himself to be the post–Du Boisian spokesperson for black/Negro Americans. All of these works portray American society both South and North as a kind of prison.

Wright's graphic depiction of the making of an African American male into a double-edged murderer in *Native Son* was meant to "shock" society, particularly white society, in order to awaken their social consciousnesses to America's economic and racial disparities, unequal civil rights laws, and biased justice and penal systems. All of these have fostered the unhealthy sociological and environmental conditions that cultivated the "restless spirit," rebel, and criminal Bigger Thomas. Wright makes this clear in his essay "How Bigger Was Born"

(433).[1] Indeed, Wright does not spare imaging the disunification of a black family that still bears all the antebellum signs of the Virginia Slave Law of 1662 that changed the African patriarchal household into an African/African American matriarchal household, and the corresponding Virginia slave law of 1669 that worked in tandem both literally and/or figuratively to "kill off" the black male's presence in and/or power over his family. This latter legal ruling enabled with impunity the white master or his agent to murder any slave who dared to raise a hand in rebellion against him or her ("Virginia Slave Laws" 14). Wright envisions how these aforementioned American slave laws set up the plantation prison system as the forerunner to the Foucaultian carceral world inhabited by the Thomas family now residing in the North in the late 1930s and early 1940s.

Foucault's discussion on how the Benthamite panopticon prison model became adopted in Europe in 1843 and later adapted in America illuminates how this architectural advancement actually augmented America's Virginia slave laws of 1662 and 1669 and the 1896 *Plessy v. Ferguson* decree mandating Jim Crow segregation of blacks from whites. Hence, Foucault's analyses on how and why power figures in the European feudal systems first utilized the penal practices of swift, outdoor punishment for criminals and then later supplanted it in the nineteenth century with a newer form of long-term, indoor incarceration help to clarify why Richard Wright adapts these historical European American policies of class values, penal codes, and mechanisms. All of these containment devices foster the rebellious and criminal actions of the fatherless "boy-man" Bigger Thomas by ironically setting him on an amoral pathway to freedom that inevitably ends with his being sentenced to die in the electric chair.

Down South: Carceral Roots of Slavery in Bigger Thomas's Ancestry

One does not have to read all of Frederick Douglass's 1845 *Narrative* to grasp how the antebellum plantation prison system transformed into the static, neo-slave peonage system that had ensnared the Thomas family prior to their flight to the North. In his 1938 essay "Blueprint for Negro Writing," Wright indicates that the way for African Americans to gauge "truth" that contradicts the European, scientific approach is by the humanistic method—that is, by recovering, studying, adopting, and/or adapting the oral expressions, sociological practices, and cultural experiences of lower-classed African Americans (Wright, 1994 "Blueprint" 98). It is at the lower depths of African/African American society that one finds the purer cultural expressions of black people because they have been the least corrupted by bourgeoisie European American class policies, educational propaganda, and biased written histories. The cultural knowledge on how blacks can survive in America is dispersed between and among the "words of wisdom" found in their slave narratives, folk tales, novels, dramatic works, poetry, and the blues, spirituals, and work songs that have been passed down from "mouth to mouth" to generation after generation for more than three centuries (99). Bigger Thomas is exemplary of someone from the lower depths of African American society. However, he is an introspective black male who engages reticently in direct discourse with his family, gang members, girlfriend, or the law. As a twenty-year-old, educationally limited adolescent African American male with low self-esteem, he has been forcefully promoted to male head of household and chief breadwinner by his mother. But her admonishments and pressures for Bigger to "man up" and to replace his deceased father as household head only frustrate Bigger. He secretly resents his family's poverty and sufferings, and contradictorily feels ashamed and angry that he lacks the educational skills to alleviate their impoverishment by providing a better economic lifestyle for them—preferably as an aviator (Wright, 1998 *NS* 17).

Thus, readers frequently learn about Bigger's family history, his absent father, and his emotional and intellectual anxieties by means of his introspections or by way of the oral-based, question-and-answer sessions with members of the Dalton family; Jan Erlone, a Communist; legal representatives; and others whose interactions with Bigger often simulate courtroom trial scenes. For Bigger the uncommunicative protagonist, such interrogations are psychologically taxing and emotionally humiliating. However, these examinations often reveal hidden aspects about Bigger's earlier life in the South, which would otherwise be unknown to readers since the novel's central setting is in the North and takes place in the 1940s, the present time period of Bigger's impending adulthood.

For example, the trope of the absent father figure continues to be as much of a problem for Bigger as it was for Douglass. Take the scene of Bigger being forced to drive Mary Dalton, the rich white heiress, and her Communist boyfriend, Jan Erlone, to a Black Belt café on the South Side of Chicago, Illinois, where the Thomases live. The educationally privileged white children wish to engage in field experience and learn firsthand how black people live. Bigger becomes their case study. Jan Erlone starts to gather data by probing into Bigger's personal life:

> "Where were you born, Bigger?"
> "In the South"
> "Whereabouts?"
> "Mississippi."
> "You live with your people?"
> "My mother, brother, and sister."
> "Where's your father?"
> "Dead."

> "How long ago was that?"
> "He got killed in a riot when I was a kid—in the South."
> There was silence. The rum was helping Bigger.
> "And what was done about it?" Jan asked.
> "Nothing, far as I know." (74)

Clearly, Bigger's terse responses to Jan's questions reveal that the Thomas family had been subjected to barbaric treatment in the South. The absent husband–father figure had been "killed in" Mississippi and thus "1669d" or "killed off" in yet another act of white vigilante violence. Bigger offers no explanation for the action because the main point is the totality of its meaning: a black man had been violently murdered. The momentary silence should be a grisly and sobering wake-up call for Jan Erlone and Mary Dalton. At Ernie's Chicken Shack in the segregated part of town, they are confronting the grim reality of "Negro" life far from the safety of Mary's upper-class home or prestigious university in Hyde Park, the white section of Chicago, and possibly Jan's experiences as an aspiring Communist fieldworker who is attempting to become the savior of economically deprived black people. In fact, Jan's inquiry about Mr. Thomas's death only bolsters his determination to arouse Bigger's dormant "political consciousness" about America's heinous atrocities against black men. His next question to Bigger about the famous 1930s case in Alabama of nine black youths known as the Scottsboro Boys being charged with the rape of two white prostitutes also disappoints Jan. Bigger nonchalantly replies that he had "heard" of the case; he does not express shock, indignation, or rage over the violent death of his father or the South's continued violence against blacks and specifically black males (74).

Why is Bigger so benumbed over his father's violent death from having been "killed off" in a riot in Mississippi as well as the impending legal lynchings of the Scottsboro Boys in the adjoining state of Alabama? The reason is that Bigger shows all the signs of having a black Atlantic personality, the term that Paul Gilroy has devised to describe the "fractured psyches" of the slaves who had been kidnapped from their homes in Africa, locked down in the bottom of ships transporting them across the Atlantic Ocean, and then deposited onto a foreign land to work indeterminably (Gilroy 11, 15). The kidnappings and resettlements were excruciatingly traumatic for the slaves and caused many of them to commit suicide, suffer nervous breakdowns, or fall into dark states of depression. Their physical abuses at the hands of the white seamen, slave speculators, and new masters and mistresses only exacerbated their distresses in mind, body, and spirit. They were forced to forget their African heritages and to accept new identities, new languages, and new work ethics that were reinforced by savage forms of discipline and punishment. Centuries later, Bigger Thomas and his family express similar traits of black Atlantics with fractured psyches. Just the novel's title of *Native Son* reveals Bigger's ironic situation as a black male who is continually treated like an anticitizen in his own native country. All of his family members know that whites consider them to be disposable property because of the recent murder of their husband-father. The Thomases, to paraphrase Wright, have "lived" the personal experiences of brutality and economic bondage that European Americans have continued to force upon black people since 1619 when Africans first arrived on American shores (Wright, 1994 "Blueprint" 99).

Bigger and his family are still oral-based people like their unknown African ancestors. Their methods of authenticating "truth" still continues to follow the pattern of oral-based transmissions utilized by illiterate African/African American slaves prior to, during, and after Douglass's time. When the slaves would relay tales about repeated forms of abuse, the oral narratives would syncretize into a collective story about the methods that whites had designed to discipline and punish them. Their oral practices of forging a collective narrative illustrate how they continued to reinforce the African, Nommo form of orally transmitting a story from person to person in order to document and to "authenticate" its veracity (Alkebulan 28). The slaves' chains of gossip about Douglass's white master being his father is an example. It contradicts the method by which Jan Erlone and Mary Dalton would use to ascertain the verisimilitude of a claim. Jan Erlone, a practitioner of Marxist dialecticism, and Mary Dalton, a college student, probably would be more inclined to accept written discourse as a more logical means to gauge a "truth" from a fiction about "Negroes." They also would probably be knowledgeable about the plethora of written, European American legal decrees that were perpetuated by seventeenth-century philosophers, statesmen, and natural scientists such as David Hume of England (49), Immanuel Kant of Germany (53), Georges Leopold Cuvier (54), and Thomas Jefferson of the United States (45), whose texts have continued to flourish in European American cultures. These writers castigated "Mongolians" and especially "Negroes" as being inferior races to "Caucasians." As both Jan and Mary know, whites have produced all of these legal documents in order to keep blacks in restrictive states of bondage and servitude. The written pamphlets published by the Communists that Erlone attempts to foist upon Bigger exemplify the Western form of recording and authenticating history.

As Wright demonstrates, the written texts of the above-named white statesmen, inclusive of Marxist writers, would mean nothing to Bigger Thomas. He may not be able to articulate the chronological history of slavery in America in a recitation, as would be the cases of his educated, white companions, but Bigger, like other African Americans, has "lived" history and experienced firsthand the violence of southern whites. His acute intuitive skills and common sense have enabled Bigger to recognize hierarchies of white power. In the street scene in front of his slum tenement, Bigger expresses to his gang member Gus that "they own the world." He is speaking from his own empirical knowledge as a dispossessed black man that the white military officers, bankers, and statesmen whom they have been emulating in a game of playacting "white" all have control over his life (Wright, 1998 *NS* 22). Even sitting at the table with Jan and Mary, Bigger remains deferential to their power. Embedded in his cautious statements to them or outspoken comments to Gus are the signifiers of white power that control Bigger's life and that of black people as a whole: the Virginia Slave Law of 1662 that destroyed the African patriarchal family, and the companion Virginia Slave Law of 1669 that, with impunity, allowed any white master, mistress, or agent to "kill off" any rebellious slave ("Virginia Slave Laws" 14). Bigger and his family have experienced the consequences of both legislative acts that have kept the black American family operating in a household with a disempowered father figure or none at all.

Foucault's discussions help to clarify Bigger's position as a fatherless boy-man as he sits at the table with Jan and Mary. I call him a "boy-man" because Wright's black males—whether they are at the stages of child, adolescent, adult, or elderly—are never allowed to function independently as self-actualized "men," but invariably end up in actual situations of social bondage or being assassinated. For instance, Foucault precedes his commentary on the birth of the prison by discussing how Europeans in earlier times handled criminals swiftly by housing them for short-term confinements in jails and stockades. The rapid indictment process would involve three or four participants: the criminal, the judge, the executioner, and the public spectators. However, "spectacle" is the noun that best describes the swift, public performance (Foucault 32). And Wright, in his unpublished novel "Tarbaby's Dawn" and other published novels and short stories that he began to write around 1934, has commenced to illustrate in literary form how American whites not only adapted European penal practices, but also engaged in public spectacles in Mississippi during the 1930s even prior to Bigger's father's tragic demise. The boy-men victims would rarely make it to or through the formal stage of being housed in an actual jail or stockade.

Up North: Plantation Rituals and Penitentiary Symbols in Bigger Thomas's Carceral Society in Southside Chicago

Bigger's incarceration in a Northern jail is merely pro forma for a brief but swift, predetermined fate. For, despite the flights of Wright's boy-men protagonists to the North with or without their families, they find no consolation once landing in urban areas. The reach of Southern whites interjects itself into Northern domains to validate that race transcends time and space, and that their racist penal laws restricting the physical movements of African Americans never applied to them. Once Bigger Thomas is jailed in Chicago for the murder of Mary Dalton, Edward Robertson, "editor of the *Jackson* [Mississippi] *Daily Star,*" posts a column in a local Chicago newspaper about Bigger's boyhood days in the South. He writes:

> Thomas comes of a poor darky family of a shiftless and immoral variety. He was raised here and is known to local residents as an irreformable sneak thief and liar. We were unable to send him to the chain gang because of his age. (1998 *NS* 280)

> I think it but proper to inform you that in many quarters it is believed that Thomas, despite his dead-black complexion, may have a minor portion of white blood in his veins, a mixture which generally makes for a criminal and intractable nature. (281)

While the editor alludes to seventeenth- to nineteenth-century genetic theories that mixed-race blood lineage causes aberrancy, this prohibition of interracial sex was built into the Virginia Slave Law of 1662. It did not, on the other hand, deter white men such as Douglass's father from contravening the law and having forced assignations with slave women that produced mulatto children whom they refused to acknowledge. However, mixed-blood lineage appears not to be Bigger's case, for Robertson only speculates on the matter, and then proceeds to contradict himself by describing Bigger as bearing a "dead-black complexion" (281). He, like other European American whites, has clung to archaic genetic, climate, and physiological suppositions that were recapitulated in 1845 by the race theory of "polygenesis" professed by Alabama scientists Josiah Nott and George R. Gliddon who claimed that blacks and whites evolved at different time periods (388–89). They also produced side-by-side sketches depicting blacks as descendants of apes in an attempt to revitalize the "ape" theory earlier promoted by Georges Leopold Cuvier of France. Also, the team sought to prove that polygenesis is the reason for the different skin pigmentations of whites from blacks. Editor Robertson definitely affirms himself to be a member of the polygenetic group, which is most evident in his editorial spiel that claims Bigger's putative one drop of white blood and/or his black melanine complexion are the reasons for his aberrant, criminal behavior (Wright, 1998 *NS* 281).

Signifyin' is an African/African American form of oral expression in which, according to Henry Louis Gates Jr., one calls out another's name by indirection (Gates, *Signifying Monkey* 110). This does not apply to Editor Robertson; he blatantly utters Bigger Thomas's name in his remarks. But Wright adopts the African American mode of indirection to "signify upon" the dated race theories espoused by the Robertson types. He deliberately resists scripting lengthy, physical details about his black characters because, to white society, they monolithically project a single mental image when their racial designation of "Negro" is written or pronounced. Says Wright in *12 Million Black Voices*:

> The WORD "NEGRO," the term by which, orally or in print, we black folk in the United States are usually designated, is not really a name at all nor a description, but a psychological island whose objective form is the most unanimous fiat in all American history . . . which artificially and arbitrarily defines, regulates, and limits . . . the vital contours of our lives, and the lives of our children, and our children's children." (1941 *12MBV* 30)

Such are the psychological reactions and mental projections that whites experience when they utter or write the word *Negro* or refer to a person by the slurs of *darky* or *nigger*, as does Editor Robertson (Wright, 1998 *NS* 281). American whites murdered Mr. Thomas based upon their imaginations, arbitrary fiats, and vigilante codes that have enabled them to act upon their whims. Editor Robertson also reveals how whites have still enforced another arbitrary fiat—the 1896 *Plessy v. Ferguson* decree of Jim Crow segregation in order to deter "Negro" males from coming into contact with white women. He states: "Crimes such as the Bigger Thomas murders could be lessened by segregating all Negroes in parks, playgrounds, cafes, theatres, and street cars. Residential segregation is imperative" (281). Although he is extolling how the South has contained blacks, most likely Editor Robertson knows or should know from newspapers that similar Jim Crow segregationist policies exist in the North. The escaped Thomas family, just by being "Negroes," found themselves being housed in a more modern state of confinement. Bigger tells his friend Gus that the steel, stone, and wood high-rise buildings make him feel as if he were "living in jail!" (20). That is because his urban settlement is no more than a concrete variation of the agrarian southern plantation prison. Again, the Thomases are limited in movements by northern Jim Crow laws that mandate them to reside separately from whites. Moreover, because of their economic plight, they have been forced to live in a subaltern sector of the overpriced slums in South Side Chicago. Overall, Bigger and his fatherless family have been both economically and socially punished because of their physical "Negroid" features.

Foucault notes that the punishment of social offenders changed in Europe by the mid-eighteenth century from public trial and spectacles of beheadings, disembowelments, and hangings to the enclosed prison, and then by the mid-nineteenth century, to the penitentiary system of "surveillance and observation" modeled upon the penitentiary panopticon designed by Jeremy Bentham in 1843. No longer was the prison a mere place of brief detention. Instead, the prison became the site par excellence for "disciplinary subjection" of criminals to forms of behavior modification designed specifically to produce or to induce their moral reforms (Foucault 231–32). This penal surveillance system, which also became adapted in the United States, failed in its intent of moral transformation. The carceral system instead produced from its environmental conditions the "second self" of the criminal—that is, the "delinquent" or "recidivist" self (238, 265).

Why? Foucault suggests that networks that engage in discipline, observation, and surveillance—that is, hospitals, schools, reformatories, military systems, and factories—are themselves carceral modifications of the panopticon system designed for the penitentiary. His definition should include plantation prisons and urban ghettoes, according to Wright's perceptions. At its highest level of simulating the ever-present gazing eye, the government, with its "silent, vigilant, mysterious" and even "unperceived vigilance" of its citizenry, has ultimately transformed the state into a "carceral society" (280). The penitentiary facility itself consists of partitioned cells for the prisoners, with sectors blocked off for the management staff. Foucault includes a drawing of a European panopticon tower rising in the middle of gated prison cells. Both of Bigger's Southern and Northern domiciles have simulated that "surveillancing" towering eye structure. His family's urban, one-room kitchenette on the South Side is no different from the agrarian slave quarters–cum–farm labor housing for Tarbaby's family who continually have remained under the watchful eye of the white plantation owner's surveillancing gaze. A difference between the regions is that Bigger's vertical, high-rise building is just one of many in his densely populated slum sector.

Indeed, a towerlike panopticon surveillancing system does operate in Bigger's ghetto. The scene that illustrates this literal carceral network occurs in the street setting after Bigger leaves his rat-infested apartment in the early pages of the novel. He first loiters on the street by watching workmen erect a poster that bears the picture of state's attorney David A. Buckley who is running for reelection. Says the narrator:

> He looked at the poster: the white face was fleshy but stern; one hand was uplifted and its index finger pointed straight out into the street at each passer-by. The poster showed one of those faces that looked straight at you when you looked at it and all the while you were walking and turning your head to look at it it kept looking unblinkingly back at you until you got so far from it you had to take your eyes away, and then it stopped, like a movie blackout. Above the top of the poster were tall red letters: YOU CAN'T WIN! (Wright, 1998 *NS* 13)

The poster of Buckley with its caption and his pointing finger is a "punitive" sign cited by Foucault and one that reflects the "rule of perfect certainty," which warns Bigger that should he break the law, he will receive an equal degree of punishment to fit the crime (Foucault 94–95). The incontrovertibility of the state government's threat is later confirmed after Bigger accidentally murders the white heiress Mary Dalton and is captured. Buckley informs him, "You're *caught*," and "we got the evidence" of her burned remains (Wright, 1998 *NS* 338). The expectation that Bigger's punishment will be equivalent to his crime is also revealed during Buckley's conversation with Boris Max, Bigger's Communist lawyer, when Buckley states that the "grave wrong" done to the "poor old parents" of the murder victim will result in their wanting "to see that this boy *burns*!" (293). Already, the state's legal system has predetermined Bigger's "fate."

The poster of Buckley has a secondary meaning. His white face and unblinking gaze symbolizes the "faceless gaze" or omnipresent, transparent, vertical eye of surveillance in Bentham's panopticon penitentiary (Foucault 200). The square of Bigger's ghetto is its modern-day simulation. Bigger says that living in the Black Belt slums is like "living in jail" (Wright, 1998 *NS* 20). Walls or metaphors of barriers to restrict Bigger's movements across race, class, or gender lines appear in the forms of his small apartment, a bedroom curtain, Cottage Grove Avenue (which separates his black ghetto from the upper-class Hyde Park estate of the rich Daltons), the Dalton's front gate, and Mary Dalton's bedroom. It is more difficult for Bigger to breathe easily in a densely populated urban area that causes claustrophobia versus on an open, agrarian plantation that is not usually glutted with people. Additionally, Bigger's ghetto prison is blatantly controlled by a mechanism of white authority figures: uniformed policemen, government officials, and citizenry whose purposes are to "prohibit [Bigger's] entering certain areas" (Foucault 18). Hierarchically, the towering eye of the prison state is signified by Buckley's personage, both figuratively in the poster and literally when, at the jail, a visiting Buckley towers over a seated Bigger. Additionally, Buckley's signification as the ever-present, vigilant eye of the government is borne out by Buckley himself when he tells Max, "My job is to enforce the law of this state" (Wright, 1998 *NS* 295).

Certainly, Editor Robertson, too, is a signification of state power in Mississippi. His newspaper is as lethally and legally judgmental as Buckley's position as state's attorney in Illinois. Robertson, like Buckley, is the human panopticon whose gaze tracks Negroes proclaimed to be the Bigger Thomas types of criminals. The editor encourages Northerners to forget formalities of the penal process and resort to the old-fashioned, swift system of Southern justice, which would be lynch mobs who could direct excessive punishment upon Bigger's body like they had done to his father. Says Robertson: "Had that nigger Thomas lived in Mississippi and committed such a crime, no power under Heaven could have saved him from death at the hands of indignant citizens" (281). Robertson is acutely aware of the human nature of whites in general since the Northern ones turn out en masse to track down Bigger when he goes into flight after killing Mary Dalton. The swarming crowds scream Robertsonian-type epithets of "Kill 'im!"; "Lynch 'im!" and "Kill the black ape!" once Bigger is caught and jailed (270).

Admittedly, there is no prehistory of Bigger having thrived in a nurturing, loving familial environment in the South even while his father was alive, because the Jim Crow, segregated living conditions were racially "intractable by nature," to paraphrase Editor Robertson (280–81). Because of the constant turbulences of threats of violence, death, and/or imprisonment, the Thomases lived in a destabilizing state of persistent fear from the Robertson types. Bigger and his family were all benumbed by the murder of Mr. Thomas, and probably fled North immediately like that of Wright's own family when his Uncle Hoskins is murdered by whites. The macabre deed invariably forces Aunt Maggie Hoskins and Richard's mother, brother, and himself to take immediate action and flee in the night without belongings across state lines to West Helena, Arkansas (Wright, 1993 *Black Boy/American Hunger* [*BB/AH*] 54). Bigger and his family simply followed an archetypal pattern of flight that had impelled frightened slaves and free persons before and after Frederick Douglass's time to escape to other regions, states, or countries because of impending threats of death.

A question arises as to how much time elapsed before or after Mr. Thomas's death that the boy-man Bigger began his evolvements into a "delinquent" and then a repeat offender or "recidivist," to use Foucault's terms? (Foucault 238, 265). Editor Robertson presents undocumented evidence that portrays Bigger as having become an "irreformable sneak thief and liar" while living in the South; he only escaped the "chain gang" because of his "age" (Wright, *NS* 280–81). Since no scenes exist of Bigger performing such deeds during or after Mr. Thomas's death, readers must turn to the Northern sequences for corroboration of orally expressed or written evidence tracking Bigger's recidivist tendencies. To understand society's advanced ideas about how to reform criminals, Foucault's remarks are necessary here. He perceptively analyzes the social treatment of offenders in Europe from the mid-eighteenth century to modern times. Although Foucault focuses on the object—the body and its subjection to punitive measures—he implies a human subject, a social offender, to whom society has responded. White society's methods to deter criminality have been in forms of public torture, dismemberment, and execution before constructing enclosed penal facilities in the nineteenth century (such as the jails holding Douglass and later Bigger Thomas). But, with mid-eighteenth-century reforms and then nineteenth-century scientific studies being implemented, the "technology of the body" became displaced as the central focus of scientists and educators in favor of the newer interests about the "technology of the soul" (Foucault 30). In both technological studies, society's efforts to discipline, punish, and reform malefactors led to their being formally codified as criminals so that they could serve as moral deterrents to others. Editor Robertson, without proof or scientific credentials, has chosen to codify Bigger Thomas as a criminal and to clamor for swift justice so that Bigger's execution will be a deterrent to other Negroes.

On the other hand, all of these advanced studies became mere hyperbole once "race" entered into the assessment processes. And because of such exaggerated double standards, Wright has chosen to expose white society's acts of racial hypocrisy that have operated overtly or covertly when these hosts of laws, fiats, and systems had or would become applicable to the fatherless, boy-man Bigger Thomas. Two scenes illustrate these fables. After Bigger examines Buckley's poster, he expresses contempt toward the attorney's threat of incarceration. Bigger knows about the "police-prisoner-delinquent" trilogy described by Foucault. The latter remarks that the prison environment only fosters corruption, fear, and disloyalty among prisoners and between prisoners and law officials (Foucault 18). Bigger's cynicism about the falseness of the law stems from his previous stint in reform school after his arrival in Chicago. The evidence of his criminal history is exposed during the "trial scene" or question-and-answer dialogue between Mr. Dalton and Bigger when the latter reports for his interview about the chauffer's position. In his hand, and submitted upon Mr. Dalton's request, is the emblem of Bigger's past: his "case note/relief record" that all the Daltons know exists. And the positions of power and powerless are intense during Bigger's interrogation. Mr. Dalton is the overbearing, panopticon eye even though he is seated. Meanwhile, Bigger stands with his hat in hand and assumes the body posture of averted gaze, slumped shoulders, and bent knees to express deference. Mr. Dalton knows his power; he attempts to ease into the subject of Bigger's reform school history by confessing that he, too, "once had been a boy." Bigger explains in limited vocabulary that he had been caught "stealing," but implies that he had been convicted because of his guilt by association with other juvenile thieves on the South Side (Wright, 1998 *NS* 50–51).

Most interesting is that both Mr. Dalton and Bigger deliberately "lie by omission," which illustrates that the truth is arbitrary and its veracity is dependent upon the racial domain and power of the speaker and/or listener. Mr. Dalton exaggerates the truth about having grown up a "boy" like Bigger. He, in fact, grew up wealthy and privileged, and later invested his wife's fortune, which enabled him to become a real-estate mogul. He is simply an upgraded version of Jim Hawkins, the white land baron in Tarbaby's world. And although Bigger knows the truth, Mr. Dalton never admits that he is the owner of the South Side Realty Company where Bigger and his family pay an excessive rental fee for slum housing. Mr. Dalton, in fact, has fostered a breeding ground for liars and petty thieves by sending Ping-Pong tables to the South Side Boy's Club; his donations to "colored" schools have somehow never trickled down to members of the lower-level masses like Bigger, Buddy, and Vera—the latter attending sewing classes at the local YWCA instead of high school or college. The family's stay in the North has not been economically or educationally progressive, which Mr. Dalton knows. In a later interview with Jan, Bigger admits that he and his family had been living in Chicago "about five years" and that he had completed the eighth grade after two years in the public schools (74). Calculations of Bigger's inexact figures suggest that Bigger is a representation of "Tarbaby," Wright's prototype adolescent criminal, who at age seventeen had only passed to the fifth grade at the conclusion of the novel. Since Bigger is presently aged twenty, his two years of regular school and then his additional time in reform school—probably a two-year sentence mimetic of Tarbaby's term for killing Jim Hawkins's mule—explain how Bigger has spent the past five years being constricted in different carceral networks. His past, agrarian life in the violent South, his present, urban life in the punitive North, and his continuously restricted and monitored movements at home, in public school, and/or in reform school all illuminate why the boy-man, non-adult Bigger has become criminally astute. He is Foucault's recidivist who has refined his street-smart, intuitive skills of plotting crimes and/or assessing dangerous situations. Bigger, too, lies by omission and does not dare reveal to Mr. Dalton that he and his predatory gang had been plotting to rob Blum's delicatessen that very morning. On the other hand, Mr. Dalton appeases his own guilt for overcharging the Thomases on their rent by including an extra five dollars a week for Bigger's personal expenses while the remaining twenty dollars of his salary must go to his family.

Bigger has evolved into a hard-edged, predatory, social offender or recidivist at age twenty from having grown into manhood under repressive economic conditions that have only exacerbated his reform school survival skills. No surrogate black father figures have volunteered to replace Bigger's absent father in order to offer the adolescent positive guidance. His subaltern class level among the poor, black masses has not only kept him devoid of contact with bourgeoisie blacks, but also left Bigger unsupervised to "father" a gang and sire crafty deeds in order to circumvent the strangulating power of white men like Mr. Dalton. Even he is a predator because of his siphoning the lifeblood from poor African Americans by charging them excessive rents and contributing to the delinquency of impoverished black males by offering them Ping-Pong tables to occupy their idle times instead of jobs. His slum-level, cramped housing breeds family incest, community spies, and juvenile delinquents. Indeed, Wright's use of literary naturalism to paint Bigger's world as being predatory accounts for Bigger's evolution into a monster. The preexisting conditions of infinite poverty in Bigger's industrialized worlds in the South and North have never economically nurtured his mind, body, or spirit. Instead, these "lacks" or voids have made Bigger's recidivism inevitable.

Another new modern discipline predicting Bigger's ascension into crime is the advent of criminology as a science. Emergent in the nineteenth century, criminology brought together psychiatrists, psychologists, educators, and judges to understand criminals as well as the nature of their crimes (Foucault 18). The relief agency controlling Bigger's family and tracking his actions is an example; the prison psychologist assessing Bigger's condition as being pathological is another. Criminology, according to Foucault, represents the vertical and collective eye cast downward through which Bigger is scrutinized by society. On the one hand, the various forms of seeing and unseeing in the novel—sightedness, blindness, the averted, silent, or direct gazes—all signify upon the penal surveillance mechanisms circumscribing Bigger's life and activities. On the other hand, Wright privileges the inverted gaze; that is, the view from the masses that is from below to above. By crafting the novel's limited perspective from Bigger's angle of vision, readers perceive how Bigger views his environment both through his inner eye, the mind's eye, and through his outer eye, the physical eye. This inner-outer eye dichotomy allows Bigger's dual perspectives to indict society and its scientific methods as failures. His welfare record and his cumulative criminal biography are proofs of this failure (Wright, 1998 *NS* 53). He had become a social offender in the North by about age seventeen after completing two years of public school. Thereafter, Bigger was sent to reform school for approximately two to three years. Now at age twenty, his carceral experiences have neither "[neutralized] his state of mind" nor "[altered] his criminal tendencies" (Foucault 18).

Bigger's growth into manhood under the supervision of his mother has also exacerbated his criminal behavior because of his disregard for black female authority. The Virginia Slave Laws of 1662 and 1669 subverted African masculinist traditions of authority, and the transcendent effects of these decrees of instilling contempt for black female authority in the minds of the junior and/or senior African/African American males in the family have still remained resilient in the 1940s. Even with her constant nagging, Mrs. Thomas has been unable to control Bigger in her unwelcome role as the matriarchal head of household. Like Tarbaby, Bigger normally undermines his mother's commands by acting upon his own whims. Hence, Bigger's loitering on the street corner or at the pool parlor and his pillaging of the South Side with his gang are all symptomatic of the "illness of idleness" that social scientists have identified as a factor that promotes crime. But employment or unemployment, according to Wright, depends upon race, class, and gender. Mrs. Thomas still works as a washerwoman as she had done in the South, and Vera is doomed to follow in her footsteps of performing unskilled or semiskilled manual labor. Bigger, the boy-man of the house, has an eighth-grade education that limits his employment choices. For lack of funds, he had dropped out before pursuing the ninth grade and above, contrary to other financially supported high school or college-bound African American youths. His derailed ambitions to finish high school and then college or aviation school had left Bigger unqualified to become a pilot whose position would have elevated his family both in class and economics (353). Foucault says that forced labor as a punishment and as a curative (and also as a means to enlist slave labor) diminishes in an industrial society and is replaced by mechanisms of "corrective detention" (Foucault 25). Bigger feels that he had been bound by "corrective detention" to live in a ghetto because of his color and class long before he began to commit illegal acts against his own black people (Wright, 1998 *NS* 296). These racist-classist penalties are evident when Bigger insists to Mr. Dalton that he had been wrongfully detained for stealing tires and sent to reform school (56). Detainment is repeated when Bigger's gang members are picked up as suspects in Mary's murder because of their color, class, and association with Bigger (298). Bigger's environment continues to be one unchanging repetition of nurturing the criminality of African American males. Buddy does not attend school and aspires to be like Bigger, his hero. Bigger's detention in reform school and then release back into the same depressed conditions have not corrected or modified his behavior. Reform school has only exacerbated his rage and criminal tendencies, which are reflected by his actions and expressed through his stream of consciousness. He is "forced" into labor by the welfare office (via his mother) and then by Mr. Dalton. Their ideas are that work as a chauffeur, a lower-level job than that of an aviator, will transform his "soul" and lead him to moral reform (283).

However, at the opening of the novel, Bigger the fatherless boy-man is already in a dangerous state of mind because of carceral-type preconditionings. The reform-school experience, petty thefts, and assault on Gus are only a prelude to the capital crime awaiting Bigger's destiny. His plot to rob Blum's, although self-thwarted, is an interim step. The team of scientists, psychologists, educators, judges, the juvenile courts, the welfare office, Mr. and Mrs. Dalton, Mary Dalton, and Jan Erlone all act in concert as a carceral network to, in the words of Reverend Hammond, convert Bigger's "soul" to their two opposing ideologies of Christianity and Communism (283). Bigger's prior "activities and efforts or achievements" (if one uses Raymond Williams's definition of "work" in its basic sense [335–36]) do not come under the category of work as paid employment until Bigger accepts the job as Mr. Dalton's chauffeur. The street scene in book 1 unleashes a maelstrom of reasons that Bigger resents the limiting aspects of his carceral world. His suppressed anger is symbolized by the burning in his stomach and by the raging furnace into which he stuffs Mary Dalton's body.

Bigger's transformation from petty thief to murderer follows a recurring pattern of plot and incident in Wright's criminal fictions, which also reflect

Foucault's descriptions of the physical and/or sociological aspects of the carceral network. There are seven stages:

1. The scene opens with the hero enclosed in a visible or invisible restricted, four-cornered barrier like a prison cell (a baseball diamond, field, house, or region) and facing a strange adversary, strange ally, or familiar opponent (a person or thing). *Native Son* opens with Bigger and his family trapped in their ghetto apartment and facing a familiar opponent: Mr. Dalton's rat.
2. The hero has a psychological or physical battle with the adversary or ally (a person or thing). Bigger's environment is a breeding ground for predators, both human and animal. He is attacked by the rat, but Bigger kills it.
3. The hero interacts with his black or white community (authority figures or others demanding accountability). Bigger feels trapped in his carceral world. He berates his family, beats up Gus, but then, out of fear, acts deferential in situations with whites: the Daltons and later Jan Erlone.
4. The hero has an accident or makes an error in judgment that alters the course of his life (a lawbreaking act requiring punishment). Bigger the recidivist errs by carrying the drunken Mary Dalton to her room only to find that his chivalrous act has positioned him for charges of rape by Mrs. Dalton. As a reflex action, he accidentally smothers Mary to death with a pillow while trying to remain undetected by Mrs. Dalton.
5. The hero feels fear because of his error (adopting a fight-or-flight strategy to escape punishment). In Mary's bedroom, Bigger recognizes that he is a dead man if caught. Reform school has not "neutralized" his criminal mind-set, but sharpened his skills at outwitting the penal system. He sets a plan in motion to frame Jan Erlone with the latter's own Communist literature.
6. The hero takes flight to outwit his opponents (a physical and/or psychological tactic to evade capture and/or outwit the law). Bigger first takes a psychological flight to demonstrate his humanity that has escaped all social service and penal authorities. After the discovery of Mary's bones in the furnace, he takes physical flight within his familiar ghetto-prison. White police and lynch mobs turn the chase into a "spectacle" simulating the European system of outdoor punishment.
7. The hero confronts his fate—usually death and often by gunfire (the power of the white carceral authorities). Bigger's trial and sentencing are emblematic of how carceral systems work to validate Buckley's and white society's predetermined judgments. Simulating the Virginia Slave

> Laws of 1662 and 1669, both Bessie Mears, Bigger's real victim, and Bigger Thomas end up being treated like disposable property for crimes they did not commit (Bessie did not betray Bigger, and Bigger never raped Mary Dalton).

Native Son opens with carceral imaging of Bigger being imprisoned in a figurative Benthamite-type square, his apartment, and concludes with Bigger literally being locked into another square, an actual Benthamite jail cell. The repetition of Bigger's prison environment is "regressive," as defined by James Snead, since the ending of the novel cuts back to Bigger's beginning status of enforced confinement in the ghetto. Nonetheless, the linearity of the novel's three-part structure shows that Bigger's psychological growth is "progressive" (Snead 50, 67). Bigger moves from dreaming to waking and from a nonbeing to an existential hero empowered by his own self-creation (Fabre, 1973 *UQ* 171). Close attention to these stages of plot development reveal the contradictions arising from Wright's paired oppositions by race, class, gender, and so on: two races; two families; two spatial areas; two economic levels; two female victims.

Bringing out these dualities leads to other social oppositions. Bigger's game of "playing white" with Gus (Wright, 1998 *NS* 17) is paired opposite to Mary Dalton's "playing Negro" with Jan Erlone (which shows how whites, whether rich or Communist, misread the text of the Negro). As the exploited laborer responding to the capitalist yoke, Bigger enacts the Communist's fantasies of Jan and Mary when, after killing Mary, he steals the money from her purse and then attempts to extort ransom for her in retaliation against her capitalist father, who had charged Bigger's family excessive rents for a slum dwelling. Nevertheless, neither of the Daltons ever sees Bigger as a human being (just as slaves were perceived as estate property). For the Daltons, Bigger is another object of their scientific experiments in Negro philanthropy. Had the Daltons not been class-bound and color-blind, they would have noticed that their prize experiment, the black chauffeur Green, had side-by-side pictures of famous black prizefighters and famous white, blonde Hollywood actresses displayed in his room. The Daltons do not read correctly their experimental data, for Green, more blatantly than Bigger, coveted the forbidden white doll-woman in the way that his idol Jack Johnson had done.

If the Daltons misread Bigger's text, the law does so, too. Bigger the boy-man becomes a self-defined "man" by using his readings of *Real Detective Magazine*—one of the crime magazines about heroes and antiheroes arising from the birth of crime literature mentioned by Foucault—to outwit his investigators. At the inquest for Mary Dalton, one *Tribune* reporter describes Bigger in the stereotypical language invented by French scientist Georges Leopold Cuvier, who claimed Negroes to be descendants of "apes" (54). His racist theory was enhanced by Josiah Nott and George R. Gliddon of Alabama who belonged to the 1830s "School of Ethnology" and published their book *Types of Mankind* in 1854. They assured readers that they would not have far to travel to discover the animal features of "ordinary field-Negroes [found on farms] in the United States." Their nearly century-old, dated theory has remained active in the mindset of the public in *Native Son* during the 1940s (Nott and Gliddon 388). The *Tribune* reporter's descriptions of activities at Bigger's inquest simulate those racist, ape theories:

> "He looks exactly like an ape!" exclaimed a terrified young white girl who watched the black slayer . . . after he had fainted.
>
> Though the Negro killer's body does not seem compactly built, he gives the impression of possessing abnormal physical strength. He is about five feet, nine inches tall and his skin is exceedingly black. His lower jaw protrudes obnoxiously, reminding one of a jungle beast.
>
> His arms are long, hanging in a dangling fashion to his knees. . . . (Wright, 1998 *NS* 179)

During his creative schemes as a fugitive to mislead Detective Britten and the police, Bigger had resorted to playacting a shuffling, minstrel figure to reinforce society's assumptions that Negroes are illiterate and lazy as commonly stereotyped. His purpose had been to deflect suspicions away from himself. The police even miss the giveaway Black English Vernacular in the phrase "the letter say" inscripted in Bigger's ransom note, which should have alerted them to the race of the note's author (177). At the inquest, however, Bigger's playacting only confirms white society's assumptions about Negroes as being bestial.

The elements of public spectacle that Editor Robertson had pronounced as still being an active process in the South recur in the scenes of Bigger's capture and trial in the North, and again contrast with the criminal justice system's movement from outdoors to indoors. The white mobs clamoring for Bigger to be lynched or immediately executed show how little social progress and social justice have advanced for blacks in the 1930s and '40s. They prejudge Bigger as a rapist-murderer, hurl epithets at him, chant death songs, and refer to him as a beast, thereby recalling the brute level of eighteenth-century society that turned the punishment and execution of criminals, especially black criminals in America, into a sport. The theatricality in the three stages of indictment—inquest, trial, and sentencing—is Wright's method of emphasizing that American society's denigrations of Bigger have produced Bigger's second persona, the delinquent. The interrogations that begin with Bigger's encounter with the Daltons and that conclude with Max's questioning of Bigger illustrate that white society has continued to avert its gaze even when it knows the truth of its own guilt.

Wright's images of whiteness, from the characters to the cat to the snow, symbolize the dehumanizing, naturalistic forces that have imprisoned Bigger and have effaced his blackness and thus his humanity. But in accidentally colliding with that white power, with those white laws and mechanized systems, Bigger the boy-man actually becomes a self-actualized, existential "man" by means of his own self-definitions. He finds at a basic level that his killing in the darkness of the night is his amoral awakening into the autonomy of his manhood and selfhood. He breaks out of prison mentally, making blackness empowering as he schemes to outwit his opponents. The irony is that Max, his Communist lawyer who has acted as his voice in a twenty-two-page propaganda speech at Bigger's trial, is too frightened to confront Bigger's humanity in the final scene of the novel—an extension of Bigger's "last confession" of the condemned man. Bigger's assertion of his existential credo to Max, "But what I killed for, I *am!*" (429) is, as Foucault would say, "an outburst of protest in the name of human individuality" (Foucault 289). And even if Max comprehends the black English connotations of self-definition implicit in Bigger's unusual statement in standard English, which is doubtful, he never conveys Bigger's confession to the courts or society, thereby suppressing it and thus ensuring that Bigger never rises as a human being or a social hero—as was the practice in the eighteenth century of suppressing the glorification of the criminal as hero.

Obviously Frederick Douglass was the exception to the rule as the real-life fugitive and antihero who became "glorified" because of the abolitionist movement and publication of his autobiography. But Bigger Thomas, the fatherless, boy-man, fictional character, lacked group support and only garnered infamy in the eyes of the public. Nonetheless, Wright's protagonist succeeded in becoming a father figure as a simulacrum of Tarbaby as well as a composite of the multiple black males who have become caught in the web of America's criminal justice system and its unjust treatment of Negro Americans in both the South and North. White society's invention of "technology" to mark the black body began with the arrival of African slaves on America's shores in 1619, and the passage of legal edicts—the Virginia Slave Laws of 1662 and 1669—to contain them in plantation prison systems before society's adaptation of the Benthamite panopticon penitentiaries more skillfully applied in the 1930s and 1940s of Bigger Thomas's lifetime. His was not a case of ten to fifteen years of appeals, but that of rapid execution like that of the old-fashioned public spectacle. Wright precedes Foucault, but Foucault expresses in *Discipline and Punish* what Wright elaborates upon in his criminal fictions, especially *Native Son*. Wright's depiction of a carceral society of surveillance, observation, and imprisonment both South and North in 1940 served as a warning to American society that the penal system was producing recidivists like Bigger Thomas who would attempt to win their equal rights at any cost. The novel is still a prescient work. By reading the "South" in *Native Son* by means of the Virginia Slave Laws of 1662 and 1669 and the 1896 *Plessy v. Ferguson* ruling, and the "North" in *Native Son* through the lens of Foucault's *Discipline and Punish*, American society can deepen its understanding of Wright's critique of America.

Note

An earlier version of this article appeared as "*Native Son* as Depiction of a Carceral Society." *Approaches to Teaching Wright's 'Native Son.'* Ed. James A. Miller. New York: MLA, 1997. 95–101.

1. Unless otherwise specified, all references to *Native Son* by Richard Wright in this essay will pertain to the Restored Text Established by the Library of America, New York: Perennial Classics, 1998.

Richard Wright's *Rite of Passage* and a Reconsideration of His Portrayal of Women

—ROBERT BUTLER—

Although Richard Wright died in 1960 when his critical reputation was perhaps at its nadir, within a few short years he achieved status as a major American writer and a seminal figure in the development of African American literature. As Margaret Walker noted in 1971: "I think it is safe to say that at least in fiction of the Twentieth Century in Black America we can mark or date everything before and after Richard Wright. Like Russians who say they all have come out of Gogol's 'Overcoat,' most of our writers have come out of Wright's cloak" (*Impressions* 66). A year later, Keneth Kinnamon characterized Wright as "one of the most important figures of twentieth century American fiction" (*Emergence* 118). By 1991 with the appearance of the Library of America editions of Wright's major works, Wright's canonical status had been firmly established.

But throughout Wright's career a troubling doubt has been sounded about a perceived weakness in his art and vision. It started with Zora Neale Hurston's 1938 review of *Uncle Tom's Children* that claimed that the book was centered in male "wish fulfillment" to lash out with hatred and violence against an oppressive white system: "There is lavish killing here, perhaps enough to satisfy all male black readers" ("Stories" 3). Hurston found Wright's preoccupation with violence to be a severe limitation in his vision of African American experience, resulting in his neglecting "the broader and more fundamental phases of Negro life" that would have enabled him to incorporate much-needed "understanding and sympathy" in his work ("Stories" 3).

Many feminist critics from the 1970s onward have supported and amplified Hurston's serious criticism of Wright's work, deploring its excessively narrow male perspective, which has reduced his portrayal of feminine experience to harshly stereotypical terms. Sylvia Keady complained in 1976 that Wright's characterization of women must be termed "prejudiced and stereotyped" because the women in his fiction "do not exist as equal partners and full human beings but function as convenience for the resolution or development of masculine dilemmas" (101) . She adds that "most of Wright's women . . . are frequently described as being childlike, whimpering and stupid" (100). Calvin Hernton in 1984 used *Native Son* as an illustration of his thesis that "the complexity of black female experience has been fundamentally ignored" in modern black literature, citing Wright's portrayal of Bigger's mother and sisters as "nagging bitches" and his description of Bessie as "a pathetic nothing" (139). Barbara Johnson, likewise, objected to a "careless misogyny" (120) in *Native Son*, arguing that Wright excuses his violence toward women by implying that white society forces Bigger into such actions. And Joseph Skerrett, while generally sympathetic to Wright, nevertheless concluded that much of the violence in *Native Son* was rooted in the author's repressed resentment and hostility toward women (125). Maria K. Mootry perhaps put the case against Wright most strongly in "Bitches, Whores, and Woman Haters: Archetypes and Typologies in the Art of Richard Wright." Surveying all of Wright's major fiction but centering on *Native Son*, Mootry faulted Wright for articulating a crude macho ethic that is "brutal and unfair to women" (127).[1]

Important feminist critiques of Wright's work continue to the present day. Tara Green has recently observed that black women play very limited roles in Wright's fiction and white women assume more importance because "his black characters find the nurturing they need in white women" ("Virgin Mary" 44). But Green also finds that Wright's white women are little more than flat stereotypes—Virgin Mary, Eve, and Mary Magdalene figures drawn from male-imagined biblical narratives. Qiana J. Whitted argues that Wright's abiding hostility toward his grandmother and her severe Seventh-Day Adventist religion resulted in his rejecting "a female way of looking at the world" (2009 "Using My Grandmother's Life" 133). Whitted claims that Wright came to see religion as "emasculating" (133) and she ties his rejection of religion to his "troubling fictional characterizations of black women" (132).

Cheryl Higashida, however, has called for a reassessment of Wright's portrayal of women. In what she describes as her "own feminist rereading of *Uncle Tom's Children*" (2009 "Aunt Sue's Children" 75), she offers "an important corrective to limitations in certain strands of feminist analysis" (93) that have resulted in oversimplified readings of Wright's novels and stories. She detects a kind of "blindness" in many previous interpretations that "do not do justice to his work" (93) and has "led to grossly oversimplified views of his gender(ed) politics" (75). Her close reading of "Bright and Morning Star" corrects what she believes are serious misreadings of the text that reduce an important character, Aunt Sue, to a "Mammy stereotype." For Higashida, Wright's story begins with a "masculine aesthetic" but develops into a much more "nuanced perspective" (75) that envisions Sue as a heroic figure whose rebellious actions epitomize the "revolutionary struggle" (93) to which Wright was strongly committed in 1940 as a member of the Communist Party. Far from epitomizing the female impotence that feminist scholars typically see in Wright's women, Sue ultimately affirms "a new radicalism" (78) that matches or even exceeds the political actions and sacrifices made by Wright's strongest male characters.

My purpose in this essay is to follow Higashida's lead by reexamining certain texts in which Wright clearly does provide very positive, even heroic, images of feminine experience. By carefully examining this important aspect of Wright's work, which has never received the careful critical attention it merits, a more balanced and nuanced understanding of Wright's overall vision may be attained, one that honors the full complexity and richness of his work.

Perhaps the clearest and most dramatic example of Wright's sometimes affirmative portrayal of feminine experience is *Rite of Passage*, a novella that was begun in the spring of 1945 when he completed *Black Boy*, extensively revised late in his life, and published posthumously in 1994.[2] This book, which has received scant critical attention, focuses on three worlds: (1) an impersonal bureaucratic system that treats the central character, Johnny Gibbs, as a thing to be manipulated rather than a person to be respected; (2) an aggressively male existence on the streets of New York that reduces him to an animal; and (3) a woman-centered life of school and home that nurtures Johnny and offers him a human life of love and possibility. At the beginning of the story Johnny is presented as a healthy adolescent boy whose life is focused around school, where he is an A student, and his family, which supplies him with love and understanding. (Unlike most of Wright's protagonists such as Bigger Thomas who suffer from shaky, one-parent families, Johnny benefits from a full family consisting of a mother, father, brother and sister who care deeply for him and meet his material, psychological, and emotional needs.) But he is suddenly plunged into orphanhood when he is told that he is a foster child whose biological parents are dead and the New York City Welfare Department's "policy" (*Rite of Passage* [*RP*] 25) has been invoked that requires him to be placed in another foster home at age fifteen. Johnny's entire life then is restructured around the "rule" (14) of a faceless bureaucracy composed of anonymous functionaries who never personally encounter Johnny or see him as a human being.

Johnny's reaction to this sudden loss of family is to be "struck stone still" (15) with shock and he starts developing the "cold fury" (15) that debilitates Wright's alienated male characters. He quickly descends into the world of Bigger Thomas and, like Bigger, he leaves home and enters the world of the streets where he gets the illusion of a new "family" in the form of a gang of young black men living on the margins of American life.

From the very beginning of the novel, the male-dominated world of the streets is consciously contrasted with the female-centered worlds of school and home. In the book's opening paragraphs, Johnny is pictured as a student in a schoolroom illuminated by "a flood of sun" while listening to the "silvery voice" of his "white woman teacher" (1), Miss Alma Reid. Although he has the understandable desire of a young boy to await impatiently the end of the school day so that he can play with his friends in the street and then go home to a nourishing supper of beef stew, Johnny likes school and takes pride in being an A student. His teacher is a helpful, nurturing figure whose first name is the Latin word for *nourishing* or *love* and her last name highlights the skill of "reading" that she teaches, a skill that Wright equates in *Black Boy* with self-transformation and mastery of experience. Johnny eagerly seeks the approval of his teacher, which makes him "glow with pleasure" (3). As a student, he is convinced that "the world was rosy and he was happy" (3).

But when he leaves the school and enters the street, he experiences a radically different world. He spots a boy "flashing a knife" and is told by his friend Billy that his brother Jack is on leave from the army and has brought a "gun" (3) home with him. For the remainder of the novel, the streets are portrayed as a menacing underworld of violence, crime, and self-destructive macho values. Although at first Johnny and Billy go "in opposite directions" (5) as one returns home and the other seeks adventure in the streets, Johnny will soon join his friend in the streets when he discovers that his home has been destroyed by an impersonal bureaucratic system. Bolting out of his family's apartment after he discovers that all the coordinates of his life have been destroyed and he has been reduced to the status of a lonely orphan, Johnny is "glad to disappear" into the subway, losing himself in a city that he hopes will provide him with a "new life" and a "new self" (27, 187).

The illusory new life that Johnny seeks on the streets, however, bears an ominous resemblance to the toxic "new life" (105) that Bigger Thomas experiences after killing Mary Dalton, for it promises a macho power but delivers death. Rejecting the school that is described in terms of "sun" (1) and his home that is presented with images of physical and emotional warmth, Johnny descends into an urban netherworld characterized by coldness and darkness that closely resembles Bigger's Chicago South Side ghetto. Such an "unstable" and "unreal" (3) setting is a powerful reflector of his intense fear and deep alienation. Replete with "yellow streetlamps glowing in the hazy dark" (36), "cold wind" (30), and tall buildings whose windows look like a "thousand vacant eyes" (40), the city becomes a stark reversal of the school and home that have nurtured him. It is a Poesque landscape of nightmare that threatens to destroy Johnny.

Recoiling from such a "naked reality" (29) that closely resembles the existential situations faced by Wright's adult protagonists such as Fred Daniels and Cross Damon, Johnny becomes part of a youthful gang when his friend Billy sees him wandering aimlessly on Forty-Second Street and invites him to become part of "The Moochers." This exclusively male gang composed of boys from broken homes and school dropouts is seen by Wright as a grim inversion of family and community, offering its members a sense of belonging and kinship but producing meaningless violence and death. The group's predatory, irrational behavior, which Billy wrongly claims will convert Johnny into a "man" (51), can only turn him into an animal or a corpse. Significantly, most of the members are described as "ghosts" (99), "rats" (111), "beasts" (79), or "robots" (107). And Johnny's gang-assigned name is "Jackal" (85), signifying his loss of humanity and becoming part of a Darwinian jungle that will lead to his downfall.

The gang, which takes a special delight in mugging "a university teacher" (103) and chides Johnny when his educated diction makes him "sound like a schoolteacher" (113), is a complete reversal of the school that has previously triggered Johnny's moral and intellectual growth and helped to make him a happy and secure young man. It reduces him to the level of an animal, forecloses his prospects of a fruitful life, and threatens him with imprisonment or death.

Wright's distaste for this grotesquely masculine world based on violence, competition, and death is vividly revealed in his description of two important scenes of graphic violence late in the novel: Johnny's savage fight with the gang's leader, Baldy, and the gang's mugging of a white man in Central Park. (These two scenes are so strongly written that they may have been the main reason that Wright had difficulty publishing the book in the mid-1940s.) It is important to remember that Wright stresses that only a part of Johnny's divided self participates in these two episodes. While his outer nature is forced by circumstances to engage in violence, his inner nature draws back from the action and longs for more humane options. His fight with Baldy is "forced upon him" (72) and, although part of him becomes a fierce beast that goes "wild" (79) during the fight, another part of him is repulsed by the scene. In the same way, Johnny does not really want to participate in the Central Park mugging but goes along with the gang because he is fearful of their response to his objecting to their actions. As he walks to the park with them, he secretly wished "to flee to the shelter of one of those dark, looming houses and knock on the door and be admitted into the warmth of a home where people lived with smiles and trust and faith" (102). Like most of Wright's protagonists and heroes, he has two conflicting selves, a humane self seeking love and community and an artificially imposed social self forced into acts of suicidal violence.

It is important to realize that Wright consistently associates Johnny's best self with feminine values and influence while he links his worst self with masculine values and influence. Irresponsible flight, for example, is connected with Johnny's biological father, who quickly abandons his mother after she becomes pregnant, thus forcing her to place Johnny in a foster home. And compulsive violence is always associated with male figures like Billy's brother, who endangers his family by bringing home his army gun, or Baldy, who erupts in terrible violence whenever his ego is threatened. Johnny's humane self, however, is activated whenever he thinks of the women who have touched his life in positive ways. Soon after he runs away because the "City" (18) authorities have decided to place him in another foster home, he has the strong desire to talk with someone and immediately thinks of his teacher, Mrs. Reid. When he imagines his biological mother, whom he discovers has gone insane and become institutionalized, his moral nature is activated and he feels "enormously guilty" (51). Although this guilt is irrational, it does help to counterbalance the destructive rage boiling in him when he finds out about his father's abandonment and society's arbitrarily moving him to another foster home.

In the novel's final scenes, Johnny's humane self is vividly dramatized by his desire for female presence and influence. As he trudges the "empty silent streets" (102) with the gang as they make their way to Central Park to randomly beat up and rob white people, Johnny's inner self "yearned to sink to his knees to some kind of old black woman and sob: Help me . . . I can't go through with this!" (102). After he has participated in the mugging, he hears the voice of a "Negro woman" (103) screaming her disapproval of the gang's behavior by shouting in denunciation, "You Boys! You Boys!" (107). Although it is highly unlikely that this woman is objectively real since only Johnny hears her repeated calls and nobody actually sees her, she is crucially important in the story because she is the voice within Johnny, a moral voice like the voices of Mrs. Reid and his foster mother that direct him away from crime and violence and encourage him to respond to the world in productive, humane terms.

The active presence of this "feminine" voice within Johnny, therefore, endows *Rite of Passage* with a very measured and qualified hope. As the gang "huddled together, panting" (107) like pack animals trapped in a cycle of inward compulsion and outward conditioning, Johnny is "alone" (117) in a positive sense because the street values that control the gang have not yet swallowed up his entire personality. He surely has not become Baldy, who is finally described as a psychopath, and he has not yet fully become Jackal, a jungle animal. He is repulsed by the gang's nihilistic behavior and, more importantly, wants to share his humane, "feminine" self with them:

> Again Johnny wondered if he ought to tell them about the woman; he turned his head and looked over the park, but no one was in sight. Had he imagined that he had seen and heard the woman? No, he had seen her, had heard her. He found himself identifying with the woman, pictured her running and looking for them, and he wanted her to find them. (108)

Identifying more strongly with the woman and what she represents than the gang and what it represents, Johnny is only superficially taken in by a destructively male ethic and still has a chance of remaining human in an increasingly brutal world. Moreover, he has a strong desire to tell the gang about the woman and hopes that she may "find" them; that is, redeem them by rejuvenating the feminine side of their personalities.

One might say that Johnny finally becomes more than a bit like Wright himself, who dedicated his masterwork to his mother because she activated within him an artist's voice as she took him on her knee when he was a child and taught him "to revere the fanciful and the imaginative" (1993 *NS* ii). By nurturing a humane and creative voice within Wright that enabled him to tell his "story" and share it with others, Wright's mother provided him with resources that enabled him to find imaginative alternatives to the social environment that crushes so many of his characters.

Although Johnny Gibb's humanity is not apparent to anyone on the scene in Central Park when he participates in a gang mugging, the reader is well aware that he is a tragically divided person rather than a vicious animal because the reader realizes that Johnny's mind is "still full of the running and invisible woman he had seen and heard" (*RP* 109). Because he sees this woman and her humane voice arises from the deepest levels of his own consciousness, he has not yet been consumed by the gang values that could turn him into a robot, beast, or ghost.

Wright began composing *Rite of Passage* just five years after the publication of *Native Son* and perhaps was signifying on his earlier novel as a way of broadening his vision with a more hopeful perspective on African American life. There is certainly much internal evidence in *Rite of Passage* that indicates that he intended his readers to make connections with *Native Son*. Both books open with their central characters being awakened by harshly cacophonous sounds, with Johnny brought out of his daydreams with the *BRAAAAAAAANG!* of a bell announcing the end of the school day and Bigger being jolted into consciousness with the *Brrrrrrrriiiiiiiiiiiiiiiiiinng!* of his alarm clock. Like Bigger, he seeks a "new life" (5) in crime because he finds himself trapped in a coldly impersonal society that denies him the things he needs to build and sustain a human identity. Feeling "a deep sense of estrangement" from the dominant culture that regards him as a "nothing" and a "nobody" (52), Johnny rebels and, like Bigger, retreats into an underground world symbolized in *Rite of Passage* by the "dirty room" in the basement of the school that his gang calls "the hole" (61). Like Bigger also, Johnny throughout the novel is described as physically and emotionally hungry, trapped in a world that starves both his outer and inner selves.

Henry Louis Gates in *Figures in Black* has argued that "signifying" is a mode of discourse at the heart of African American literary, folk, and musical traditions that creatively engages previous discourse, thus creating a kind of conversation between current and earlier texts. As such, it can take two forms: (1)

honorific signifying that broadens and deepens a contemporary text by echoing motifs from an earlier work in a positive way, and (2) ironic signifying in which the meaning of an earlier text is reversed or undercut by a contemporary text, thus creating what Gates terms a distinctive "black difference" (xxviii).

Wright consciously used both kinds of signifying in *Rite of Passage*. In connecting his story about a psychologically healthy fifteen-year-old black youth who is on the verge of descending into a self-destructive life of crime and violence to the story of a twenty-year-old, educationally limited adolescent African American male who has been destroyed by such a life, Wright is reminding us that Johnny Gibbs could easily turn into Bigger Thomas. In this way, the shadow of *Native Son* hangs ominously over *Rite of Passage*, making it a more serious and troubling narrative than a simple tale about a "juvenile delinquent" engaged in adolescent testing of limits. But the vision at the center of *Rite of Passage* also contrasts with the much bleaker outlook provided by *Native Son*. While Bigger must finally confront his own death alone and will get no second chances of turning his life around, Johnny may avoid such a fate because his healthy family and school lives have prevented him from incurring the psychological damage suffered by Bigger and also because he still hears the humanizing feminine voices that call him to a better life. (In this sense, Johnny resembles the narrator of *Black Boy/American Hunger* whose life is transformed in part by his education.) While Bigger admits that "I reckon I never was in love with nobody" (1993 *NS* 352), Johnny has been raised by a loving family until the age of fifteen and at the end of the novel can respond to the love, wisdom, and kinship offered by the women who have raised him and taught him. Even though the black woman who finally calls him away from the toxic male values of the gang is invisible, she is not inaudible, and has not disappeared. Because he is still capable of "identifying" with this woman and "wanted her to find him" (*RP* 108), there is still hope for him. He is not locked into the two "rhythms" of Bigger's life, the "indifference and violence" (29) that trap and ultimately destroy him.

Tara Green asserted that "we must offer new perspectives in critiquing the women of Wright's fiction" and also stressed that "there are a number of questions that have been unasked and unanswered regarding the women of Wright's fiction" ("Women" 416). One important question that needs to be explored more fully by contemporary critics is this: Has the full story been told of Wright's treatment of women in his fiction and autobiographical writings? Is it fair to label Wright as a misogynist who was unable to represent women in any but crudely stereotypical ways?

A careful reading of *Rite of Passage* clearly reveals that Wright was well aware of the redemptive values of feminine experience and was equally aware that certain macho values such as the valorization of violence and unrestrained egoism were profoundly self-destructive forces in African American and American cultures. But *Rite of Passage* is by no means an isolated and anomalous example in the Wright canon. A careful investigation of works written throughout Wright's life also provide very positive, sometimes heroic, images of feminine experience. As Cheryl Higashida has convincingly argued, an important story written at the outset of Wright's career, "Bright and Morning Star," contains a female character who transcends the stereotype of the "Mammy" and achieves heroic status that is surely the equal of anything attained by his male rebels. When Sue rises up against white oppressors in an act of personal and political violence, she becomes what Higashida calls a "self-conscious agent of historical change" (92).

Wright's *12 Million Black Voices*, published in 1941, a year after the appearance of *Native Son*, also provides an extremely positive vision of black female experience and may be seen as a kind of balance or corrective to the extremely negative vision of women in that novel.[3] Whereas Wright employed a strict first-person point of view in *Native Son* that limited his vision to Bigger Thomas's brutally stereotyped images of women, in *12 Million Black Voices*, he broadened his perspective with a first-person plural point of view. The "we" of Wright's brilliant documentary account of African American life enables him to project the world of both black men and women with what Hazel Rowley terms "unusual tenderness" (237). Wright offers a warm endorsement of black family life and religion, both of which he sees as anchored in and nurtured by women. Wright credits black women from the time of slavery onward as being the repository of "our folk wisdom" (*12MBV* 36) and praises black mothers for providing their children with "an irreducible human feeling that stands above the claims of law or property" (61).

The photographic text of *12 Million Black Voices* powerfully reinforces this extremely affirmative vision of black womanhood. All but one of the seventeen photographs focusing on women portray them in dignified ways and none envision them as threats of any kind to black male identity.[4] Several picture women as struggling against racist systems in both the North and the South but doing so with personal courage and self-respect. A number of other remarkable photographs center on women in church services as they engage soulfully in prayer or rapturously sing gospel music. But these images do not evoke in any way clichéd suggestions of women using religion as a narcotic providing them with compensatory release from the real world. Rather, these images portray strong women tapping into spiritual resources that will enable them to deal more fruitfully with the problems that beset them in their daily existences. The final photograph of women in the book contains truly heroic meanings as it envisions a group of women engaged in a political demonstration in front of the White House. As they protest the federal government's failure to pass antilynching legislation, their erect carriage and determined facial expressions foreshadow the heroic photography produced years later in the civil rights movement.

Black Boy/American Hunger also contains many positive images of women, although most critics have paid but little attention to this. It is common for contemporary readers of Wright's autobiography to interpret it as a story of male self-assertion against an oppressive world where black women are part of the problem because they force Wright to passively accept white injustice rather than devise ways of opposing it. Qiana J. Whitted, for instance, argues that Wright's grandmother was an "archetypal oppressor" (124) because she imposes on him a harshly puritanical religion that deprives him of freedom and directs his energies to achieve an otherworldly "salvation" rather than seeking social justice in the real world. It is possible that other readers might claim that Wright is traumatized by what he describes in *Black Boy* as his mother's "meaningless suffering" (1993 *BB/AH* 118), which makes her a passive victim who is unable to help him, and also by the "strange woman" (38) in Memphis who lures his father away from his family.

But this surely does not tell the whole story about the ways in which women are portrayed in Wright's autobiography. It is important to realize that several women teach Wright how to read and he stresses how the achievement of full literacy was his first step to achieving "new ways of looking and seeing" (294) that he needed in order to liberate himself from a society that regarded him as nonhuman. Although his grandmother's religion in certain ways trapped him, in other ways it liberated him. The daily readings of the Bible that she required of him steeped him in religious narratives and symbols that he would make abundant use of in his poetry and fiction. And the lengthy sermons he heard in his grandmother's Seventh-Day Adventist church would sometimes put him to sleep but could also fire his imagination.[5]

Two other women play important roles in *Black Boy/American Hunger*. His aunt Maggie, whom he describes as his favorite aunt and "another mother" (77) was both a role model and a friend to Wright. He saw her as one of the few adults whom he could trust and confide in as well as a person who would come to his aid in family quarrels. When his father abandoned the family and his mother became seriously ill, it was Maggie who brought Wright, his brother, and his mother to live with her and her husband, Silas Hoskins, in Elaine, Arkansas. Maggie and Silas treated Wright as a kind of adopted son and his period of living with them is one of the few bright spots in his early childhood. The other woman in Wright's autobiography who would later play a role in his writing was an unnamed black woman whose husband was killed by a white mob and who worked out an ingenious and effective mode of revenge. She wrapped a loaded shotgun in a sheet and humbly implored the men who killed her husband to allow her to prepare his body for burial. After securing permission to do so, she prayed over the body, lulled the armed whites into trusting her, and then quickly unwrapped the gun and shot four of them to death. The young Wright clearly saw the woman as a heroic rebel and later used her as the model for Sue in "Bright and Morning Star." After telling the story of this anonymous woman in his autobiography, he added, "I resolved that I would emulate the black woman if I were ever faced by a white mob" (1993 *BB/AH* 86).

While he was working on *Black Boy/American Hunger,* Wright recalled another black woman whom he could use as a role model of a heroic black rebel and, surprisingly enough, it turned out to be his grandmother. In an unpublished essay, "Memories of My Grandmother," which Wright probably wrote in either 1944 or 1945 and perhaps revised later in life,[6] he describes Margaret Bolden Wilson in terms usually reserved for his male rebels such as Bigger Thomas and Cross Damon as a woman who rebelled fiercely against a society that attempted to "deny her humanity" ("Memories" 8). This certainly calls into question the view that has become standard in Wright criticism that his maternal grandmother had a completely negative influence on Wright and was one of the main sources in his difficulties of relating to women or representing them in his fiction. Margaret Walker, for example, saw her as a "religious fanatic" (1988 Amistad ed. *Daemonic Genius* [*DG*] 33) who tyrannized Wright and implanted in him puritanical hang-ups about sex that resulted in his lifelong hostility toward women, especially black women. Walker argued that "there is not one whole black woman in Wright's fiction whom he feels deserves respect" (179).

But Wright's depiction of grandmother Wilson in "Memories of My Grandmother" creates a radically different impression of her as a deeply respected role model who could inspire him to "transform the world" through heroic acts of will and self-assertion. Wright's view of his grandmother as a rebel also challenges the idea that Wright regarded black women as threats to male independence and freedom. Trudier Harris, for instance, has argued that African American women in Wright's fiction, particularly *Native Son*, tend "to be supporters of the status quo" and thus are portrayed as "being in league with the oppressors of black men." Such women "stifle" the "dreams of black men" because they lack the courage to oppose racist oppression and encourage black men to stay safely within the limits created for them by white society (qtd. in Kinnamon, *Emergence* 63). But by the time Wright composed his autobiography, he regarded his grandmother as one who declared "war" on the status quo of the segregated South, which viewed black people at best as second-class citizens and at worst as soulless animals. Wright came to understand that Margaret Wilson, more than any other person he knew while growing up, possessed a potent system of beliefs that assured her that she was a spiritual being who could achieve salvation despite being caught in a material world that was both a hell and a prison.

Instead of categorically rejecting his grandmother's religion, as many critics have claimed over the years, Wright secularized it. While rejecting the outward practices and dogmatic doctrines of Seventh-Day Adventism, Wright embraced his grandmother's belief that it was possible to undergo what she understood as a "conversion" from an imprisoning old life to a liberating new life. It is not by accident that he titled the second part of his autobiography "The Horror and the Glory," asserting that in Chicago he could transcend the Gothic nightmare of the segregated South and achieve a kind of transcendence through art and politics.

Black Boy/American Hunger tells the story of how Wright as a child and young man rebelled aggressively against his grandmother and what she represented. But as an adult who wrote "Memories of My Grandmother," he could step back from his youthful perspectives and understand how he had misunderstood and underestimated her. Ironically, he ultimately realized how much he resembled her and how her influence helped to shape the stronger parts of his own character. He sees both himself and his grandmother as rebels who are at war with their inherited social systems. And he is clearly offering a self-portrait when he describes his grandmother's mode of life as "abstract" (1993 *BB/AH* 12) because she was always simultaneously "in the world and not of the world" (7) assessing her own experiences from a wider perspective that enabled her to see herself in humanly meaningful terms. Wright at one point in "Memories of My Grandmother" claimed that she embraced "a way of life that is lived *distantly* from the environment, even though it subsists on the environment, a way of living that allows or enables or forces the organism to superimpose judgments and values upon their experience borrowed from somewhere else" ("Memories" 10). The "somewhere else" that Margaret Wilson drew from was her religious faith and her inner psychic strength, just as the "somewhere else" that Wright drew from was his iron will and his commitments to humanist values, political action, and his own art. Both Richard Wright and his grandmother were able to triumph heroically over brutally deterministic environments because they were able to envision a world that was a life-giving alternative to the racist societies into which they were born (12).

As this study has attempted to demonstrate, Wright's attitudes toward women in his life and work were much more complex and nuanced than has been generally recognized. Over his entire career, he presented a wide variety of women in his stories, novels, and autobiographical writings, ranging from the stereotyped figures of *Lawd Today!* and *Savage Holiday* to the heroic women who could be found in "Bright and Morning Star" and *12 Million Black Voices*. We should not, therefore, conclude that Wright was a misogynist incapable of understanding and fairly representing female experience.

Even *Native Son*, the work most cited as an example of his brutal portrayal of women, can be rescued from this charge. As Wright stressed in "How 'Bigger' Was Born," his careful, nearly Jamesian use of point of view committed him to filtering the entire book through Bigger's highly pressured, often disoriented consciousness, not his own personal perceptions and convictions: "Throughout the story there is but one point of view: Bigger's. This, too, made for a richer illusion of reality. I kept out of the story as much as possible, for I wanted the reader to feel that there was nothing between him and Bigger; that the story was a *première* in his own private theatre" ("How 'Bigger'" 459). Because Wright wanted us to *become* Bigger and experience directly the terrible damage that a racist environment had inflicted upon him, he kept himself "out of the story." But he clearly does not want us to endorse Bigger's attitudes about women and violence toward women. Quite to the contrary, he wants us to be chilled and terrified by such inhumanity. More importantly, he wants his readers to see the sources of such brutal misogyny in the social environment that has made it nearly impossible for Bigger to see *anyone* in human terms.

It is time now that we revisit gender issues in Wright's work, freeing ourselves of preconceptions that force us to oversimplify his vision. We must also be careful not to focus our attention only on *Native Son* and *Black Boy/American Hunger* but also examine carefully lesser-known pieces such as *12 Million Black Voices* and *Rite of Passage,* which provide strongly affirmative readings of feminine experience. Moreover, we must scrutinize important unpublished texts like "Memories of My Grandmother" and *Black Hope,* which reveal surprising new insights into Wright's vision, particularly as it applies to gender.

Toward the end of *Rite of Passage,* Johnny Gibbs's mind is "full of the running and invisible woman" (109) who pursues him and calls him to a more humane life centered on the feminine values that animate home and school. In the same way, we now need to make stronger efforts to see the positive female portraits in Wright's work that to date have been all but "invisible" to scholars and critics. This will enable us finally to gain a richer, more balanced understanding of Wright's deeply humanistic vision.

Notes

1. Several other studies explore Wright's treatment of women. Nagueyalti Warren's "Black Girls and Native Sons" argues that Wright "embraces wholly the Western attitudes of male chauvinism," going well beyond the construction of stereotypes and becoming "pathological" (71) in his representation of women. Trudier Harris's "Native Sons and Foreign Daughters" claims that Wright in *Native Son* fails to create female characters who are "complex individuals" (82) but instead reduces all of his women characters to negative stereotypes. She sees Mrs. Thomas "as an emasculating black woman" and Bessie as a "simpering, weepy woman" (79) and argues that both are portrayed as "grubbing around in the racial cages constructed for them" (64). Sherley Anne Williams's "Papa Dick and Sister Woman: Reflections on Women in the Fiction of Richard Wright," likewise, takes Wright to task for imagining women in roles

that are demeaning and stereotypical while his male characters are given the opportunity to become heroic rebels.

2. This short novel has an interesting and revealing history. It was begun in the spring of 1945. Titled *The Jackal*, it focused on a group of black male adolescents who kidnapped a woman and were afraid to release her for fear that she would report them to the police. He was unable to publish the story. It languished until the summer of 1959 when he revised it substantially, converting it to a seventy-page novella, *Leader Man*. The plot and character developments are the same as *Rite of Passage*, except the protagonist is age fourteen. Wright continued to work on it but died before he could find a publisher; it was published as a short novel in 1994.

3. After completing *Native Son* in 1939 and before he began work on *12 Million Black Voices* in 1941, Wright started to write a novel titled *Little Sister* that was consciously focused on what Wright called "the woman question." The book was intended as a sympathetic portrayal of a mulatto domestic worker that would explore the pressure of a racist environment on a working-class African American woman. In this sense, it perhaps may be seen as kind of companion piece to *Native Son*. In 1941, Wright submitted a 961-page manuscript of the book to his agent but was advised to make substantial changes. Wright then retitled the novel *Black Hope* and worked on it intermittently for the next four years. He received a $7,500 advance for the book from Harper and Brothers in 1945 and came close to completing it but, for reasons that still remain unclear, was unable to do so. The manuscript of *Black Hope* remains in the Wright Collection, Beinecke Library, Yale University. *Little Sister* and *Black Hope* are Wright's only examples of extended fiction that center on female protagonists. They may be seen as Wright's attempts to broaden his vision beyond the narrowly male perspective required by the first-person point of view of *Native Son* and give fictional form to the positive rendering of black women's experience in *12 Million Black Voices*.

4. The one clear exception to Wright's generally positive images of feminine experience in the photographs of *12 Million Black Voices* is Russell Lee's "The Black Dancer." It features eight scantily clad mulatto women engaged in a choral dance to the pleasure of well-dressed white men and women. Their saddened masklike faces and joylessly mechanical body language strongly suggest that they are engaged in a dehumanizing ritual very similar in some ways to the battle royal in Ellison's *Invisible Man*.

5. For a full discussion of Wright's complex responses to his grandmother's Seventh-Day Adventist religion, see my article: Robert J. Butler, "Seeking Salvation in a Naturalistic Universe: Wright's View of His Southern Religion in *Black Boy/American Hunger*," *Southern Quarterly* (Winter 2009): 46–60. Although Wright rejected the dogmas and liturgical practices of his grandmother's religion, he was deeply stirred by its dramatic vision of life and made extensive use of Adventist imagery, symbolism, and themes in his writings.

6. This important essay is located in the Wright Collection, Beinecke Library, Yale University, and is undated. Michel Fabre and Hazel Rowley were unable to determine an exact date of its composition. Jerry Ward's research suggests that it was probably written in 1944 or 1945 after Wright completed *The Man Who Lived Underground* published in *Accent* in 1941 and while he was completing *Black Boy*. The essay makes strong connections between his grandmother and the protagonist of *The Man Who Lived Underground*, Fred Daniels. Both experience reality surrealistically and both live lives that are "in this world but are not of this world" ("Memories" 7).

Part 2

Writing America from Abroad, 1947–1960

Richard Wright and the Dilemma of the Ethical Criminal: Can One Live beyond Good and Evil?

—FLOYD W. HAYES III—

He damned the day he had met the man who knew so well the spiritual malady that had plagued and undone him—the dilemma of the ethical criminal, the millions of men who lived in the tiny crevices of industrial society completely cut off from humanity, the teeming multitudes of little gods who ruled their own private worlds and acknowledged no outside authority. Hating that part of himself that he could not manage, Cross must perforce fear and hate Houston who knew how close to crime men of his kind had by necessity to live.
—**Richard Wright,** *The Outsider* (346)

In our civilized world, we learn to know almost only the wretched criminal, crushed by the curse and the contempt of society, mistrustful of himself, often belittling and slandering his deed, a miscarried type of criminal; and we resist the idea that all great human beings have been criminals (only in the grand and not in a miserable style), that crime belongs to greatness (—for that is the experience of those who have tried the reins and of all who have *descended* deepest into great souls—). To be "free as a bird" from tradition, the conscience of duty—every great human being knows this danger. But he also desires it: he desires a great goal and therefore also the means to it.
—**Friedrich Nietzsche,** *The Will to Power* (390)

The situation of blacks in the United States of America has always been complex, complicated, and often contradictory. The long historical nightmare—from enslavement to the present—has created a crisis of black existence: the "psychic alienation" of being black in an antiblack world (Fanon, *Black Skin* 48). To be sure, white supremacy historically has operated as a global system—of imperialism, colonialism, annihilating wars, enslavement, and racism (Mills 41–89). Significantly, following the official termination of enslavement in the United States of America, African Americans found themselves the objects of continued cultural domination as white elites constructed criminalized images of them. In the mid-nineteenth century, industrialized cities developed and established police forces that buttressed systems of criminal law. Simultaneously, urban blacks made the transition from being slaves to being always already guilty of some crime in the white imagination. Legal codes—upholding racist segregation, which might be more accurately characterized as (il)legal codes—throughout the developing nation allowed, and perhaps even encouraged, increasing forms of antiblack police control and violence (Monkkonen 141). As a result of being largely excluded from formulating the laws that govern American society, many black Americans have held as suspect a criminal (in)justice system that has historically worked against them (Hahn and Jeffries 103–21; O'Brien 7–55). Most assuredly, Richard Wright was among those black Americans who experienced the pain and anguish of social injustice and who dared to write resentfully, indicting the political hypocrisy of a nation that was democratic in theory but not in practice.

The historical and contemporary reality, and the resulting brutalizing experience of black people, has constituted the occasion and catalyst for the emergence and articulation of Africana existential thought in America. Because white Americans refused to treat blacks as fellow human beings, the consequential dehumanization produced a people whose existence and ideas have both challenged and embraced European and white American ideas. Through the pain, anguish, and desperation caused by the historic struggle to extricate themselves from what revolutionary Caribbean psychiatrist Frantz Fanon referred to as the "zone of nonbeing," (Fanon, *Black Skin* 10; Gordon, "Through the Zone" 3), blacks have raised questions designed to give full expression to their identity and desire for liberation. Consequently, it is perhaps correct to avow that black thought always has been framed by existential distress (Gordon, *Existential Africana* 8).

Into this existential vortex stepped Richard Wright, who articulated the anguish, suffering, anger, desperation, and resentment that gnawed at the lived experience of African Americans. Wright was acutely aware of the *culture of pretense* that was firmly embedded in modern Western, especially American, civilization—given the apparent bad faith and hypocritical pronouncements of democracy and equal justice under the law, but realistically coupled with the practices of white supremacy and antiblack injustice. Here was a disjuncture more extreme than contradiction that simultaneously included and excluded blacks. As a radical black intellectual warrior, Wright sought to overthrow the orthodoxy of the European American conception of existence and, in the process, assert the validity and complexity of the black experience. From perspective of Africana theorist Anthony Bogues, Wright was a black heretical thinker who had the courage to expose dangerous truths about the West (Bogues 12–16).

Wright remains one of modern America's most influential writers and political thinkers. His attempts to unmask the motives underlying Western civilization's violent, antiblack racism and black people's existential struggle for meaning and liberation in an absurd world have deeply affected subsequent generations of philosophers, literary critics, psychologists, historians, political scientists, sociologists, and activists. Indeed, it has been argued that Wright's work constitutes a discourse on racism and culture that is unparalleled in world literature (Hakutani, *Richard Wright* 368). That is because Wright was able to think through the pretensions and consequences of racist and capitalist Western culture in a way that helped to shape the content and fashion the contours of global black literary and postcolonial expressions long after his death in 1960.

An abundance of scholarly and critical literature has focused on Wright's novel of ideas, *The Outsider*. Much of this literature has examined various themes in the novel, such as French existentialism, double consciousness/double vision, Kierkegaardian dread, the Nietzschean overman, Marxism, the Communist Party USA, God's death, images and roles of black women, nihilism, resentment, racism, man's search for freedom, Wright's use of Dostoevsky, antiblack violence, and the threat of death.[1] However, a neglected theme among Wright scholars is his concept of the ethical criminal, which Wright mentions only once in *The Outsider*. The present discussion attempts to fill that void.

This essay examines Wright's construction of the figure of the ethical criminal in his powerful novel of ideas, *The Outsider*. The novel centers on the lived experience of the existential-nihilist hero, Cross Damon, who is the embodiment of the ethical criminal. Conscious of the negative view of blacks in the white imagination, perhaps Wright sought to explore the meaning of this kind of existence but from a different perspective—that of philosophical criminals whose crimes have their bases in ideas. These outsiders are dangerous to the social order, in Wright's view, because they had become cynically disillusioned about their society's values. As Wright's early biographer, Constance Webb, stated:

> These were the men dangerous to the status quo, for the outsider was one who no longer responded to the values of the system in which he lived. Communists and Fascists sought to share in the wealth and power of the nation by substituting themselves but without essentially changing its structure for governing. The greatest danger to the government stemmed from those millions of individuals who held no dreams of the prizes the nation held forth; in them . . . a revolution had already occurred and was biding its time until it could translate itself into a new way of life. (313)

The Outsider is Wright's most obvious fictional display of philosophical ideas, manifesting as it does the author's major contribution to Africana philosophies of existence (Gordon, *Existential Africana* 13). As Gordon indicates, Africana existential thought emerges as a result of the "lived" experience of being black in an antiblack world. It is this historical and contemporary encounter with the pathology of racism that gives rise to the anxieties of blackness, which constitute the seminal subject matter of black philosophers of existence. *The Outsider* is philosophically significant, among other things, because its narrative reveals unique philosophical concepts and problems often challenging received philosophical perspectives (see Gooding-Williams 12). In what follows, I pursue a phenomenological description of Wright's ethical criminal; I explore the structure of his everyday life world, seeking to reveal what lies at the core of his alienated human experience in the modern industrial world. That is, I attempt to elucidate the meaning of the ethical criminal's being in the world (see Jung, *Existential Phenomenology* 62; Natanson, "Phenomenology" 15); Yancy, *Black Bodies* xxi). This article also shows how literature opens us to the domain of possibilities and how metaphor proffers philosophical power for thinking about the black struggle for liberation and change (see Natanson, *Erotic Bird* 20).

Since God had been the natural genesis of Western values and the origin of all of their meaningfulness, the concept of God's implosion only hastened the expansion of a smoldering culture of nihilism, an anxiety of the soul, a contamination of despair (Keiji 56; M. Warren 40). God's demise, for Dostoevsky and Nietzsche, meant that everything was possible because there were no longer any prohibitions on human conduct (Dostoevsky 115–16; Nietzsche, *Beyond* 48; Nietzsche, *Thus Spoke* 41). This is the conclusion of all outsiders—human beings who are conscious of and therefore do not deny the barbarism, inhumanity, and savagery of modern Western civilization (Glover 5; Wasserstein 793; Weinstein 49). Modern white European and American thinkers have spilled considerable ink discussing civil society, but few, if any, explore the meaning and practice of civility as the main ingredient of civilization (see Cohen and Arato 345; Forni 5; Goldfarb 141).

Richard Wright understood this contradiction, and he embraced the resulting paradox in the construction of his central character, Cross Damon, the powerful African American and figure of the ethical criminal. Damon is the criminal type, one who stares into the abyss of desire, wrenched by moral nihilism. For Wright, there is little, if any, actual justice in the American (il)legal system; from his perspective, the rational-legal perception of modern civilization is a veil of illusion. Barbarism and savagery, not civility and justice, are deeply implanted in the heart of modern Western civilization and specifically American society. Damon declares: "You call this *civilization?* I don't. This is a jungle. We pretend that we have law and order. But we don't, really. We have imposed a visible order, but hidden under that veneer of order the jungle still seethes"

(1991 *Outsider* 171). The ethical criminal's motto is: Everything is possible, nothing is necessary. One can do whatever one pleases. For Wright's ethical criminal, all of modern society's ethical laws are suspended. He is a man who acts like a God; he tries to live beyond good and evil. But is he successful?

> Cross had to discover what was good or evil through his own actions . . . because it was he alone who had to bear the brunt of their consequences with a sense of absoluteness made intolerable by knowing that this life of his was all he had and would ever have. For him, there was no grace or mercy if he failed. (156–57)

Wright's antihero, Cross Damon, is overwhelmed by a fear of the dreadful. The first section of the novel, titled "Dread," contains the epigraph from Walter Lowrie, the translator of Soren Kierkegaard's text, *The Concept of Dread*: "Dread is an alien power which lays hold of an individual, and yet one cannot tear oneself away, nor has a will to do so, for one fears what one desires" (xii). Kierkegaard expresses the same idea in slightly different form in the body of the text, and the context surrounding it there helps us to understand the dialectical manner in which Cross Damon must be viewed.

In *The Outsider*, a black man in urban America in many respects transcends the assumed limitations of his blackness. As such, Wright fashions a conception of blackness as a complex system of meanings, and consequently proffers a new paradigm of the black hero (or antihero) for modern, crisis-ridden America. He proposes the ethical criminal as the black hero of a nihilistic age—an atheistic and morally destitute world—and introduces the paradox of the avid pursuit of greatness when no transcendental standard exists.

As the novel opens, Damon is suffused with feelings of alienation and self-loathing. As a post office employee, he has developed a friendship with several fellow workers; yet his personal readings, intellectual autonomy, and persistent search for the meaning of things separate him from them. Similarly, his relationships with black women are alienating and discomforting: Alas! Wright does not harbor positive views of black women. Damon drinks heavily—perhaps to alleviate his loneliness. Having bequeathed him a curiously paradoxical name (godlike but demoniacal) that seems to have rendered him always guilty of something and engulfed by a sense of dread from birth, Damon's mother constantly berates him for his sorry performance as a husband and father. His wife appears antagonistic and conniving; Damon suggests that she entrapped him into the marriage. Finally, he is entangled with a minor whom he impregnates. She and her friends set out to get Damon by taking legal action against him. In essence, Damon's blackness is significant because it constitutes the cultural matrix for understanding his predicament as an outsider in modern American society; it embodies the moroseness of black existential dread.

Yet, as a result of a freak subway accident, Damon is enabled to escape his situation and to (re)create himself in familiar existential terms. Thinking he is dead, his relatives and friends hold a funeral for him, as Damon watches in godlike fashion. Following the event, Damon finds it necessary to kill a talkative friend who discovers that Damon is not dead. He leaves Chicago for New York City. On the way, he tries to master his dread and control his guilty thoughts and feelings. It is during this journey that Wright complicates even more his representation of black existential life. He chooses this occasion to demonstrate how the ordinary experience of black people in the United States of America enables them to see with a special clarity of vision—dreadful objectivity—the same constellation of problems that existentialist thinkers had identified in more lofty and abstract arrangements.

In this way, Wright creates an almost superhuman (clearly Nietzschean) black antihero whose alienation and dread place him both outside of and yet very much inside modern American—that is to say Western—civilization. By now responsible for four murders, Damon is the ethical criminal who is highly knowledgeable and deeply perceptive. In contrast to (but recalling) Du Bois's representation in 1903 of the double consciousness as a horrifying burden in *The Souls of Black Folk* (3), Wright's complex image of blackness as double vision is a source of strategic power, freedom, and knowledge. Here is an intellectually powerful figure, a philosophical criminal, who struggles to find some meaning in his complex existence (Hayes 174). The philosophical criminal is a criminal, not so much because of what he does, but because of what he feels and thinks. What characterizes him, Wright tells us, is that he thinks through multiple layers of illusionary veils—for example, Christianity, law, racism, ideology, Fascism, Communism, and traditional family relations.

Perhaps the deepest intuition of the ethical criminal is that life is filled with adversity. His firmest judgments are that adversity itself is evil; evil is in the world and not merely in the self; evil cannot be rationally justified. In some respects the ethical criminal internalizes evil into his spirit as he makes war upon the world, himself, and other selves. Human existence may not be good, for it is hardly that, but depravity is more bad than imprudent; nothing is really necessary, it's just unfortunate. As adversity becomes self-loathing, it precipitates a loathsome world. Here we have nihilism writ large, the single attitude toward human existence that the ethical criminal embraces; it becomes quintessential to his being. From this perspective comes the affirmation of struggle that drives the ethical criminal's life. Wright indicates of Damon: "He had the kind of consciousness that could grasp the mercurial emotions of men whom society had never tamed or disciplined, . . . men who were wild but sensitive, savage but civilized, intellectual but somehow intrinsically poetic in their inmost hearts" (1991 *Outsider* 342).

Significantly, the ethical criminal rejects the legitimacy of the American criminal (in)justice system. Wright tells us that the law is one of America's numerous veils of illusion. In his view, the (il)legal system and its laws are established by lawless people. "Only men full of criminal feelings can create a criminal code," declares Wright (378). As a careful and clear-eyed examination of American history would disclose, those who historically have formulated United States laws often have been lawless people themselves. They and their descendants created a body of societal rules that had very little to do with justice and more to do with the self-interests of ruling-class whites. In their social relations of power and racism with people of color in America, white Europeans and their American descendants have exhibited criminal behavior. European colonialists' treaties with Native Americans, slave codes, the original proslavery United States Constitution, racist Supreme Court decisions (e.g., *Dred Scott* [1857] and *Plessy v. Ferguson* [1896]), segregation laws, or the inequitable application of contemporary law are glaring examples of the lawless contradictions within the system of American law (Bell 15).[2] It was the American (il)legal system and its laws that condemned Damon merely because he was black, making his ordinary existence criminal. When one's normal everyday existence is defined as criminal, a great amount of resentment can be the result. Cross Damon, the ethical criminal, embodies this attitude.

For Wright, the distinguishing element of the ethical criminal is that in breaking the laws of society, he is guilt-free. This attitude emerges from his view that the criminal (in)justice system is bankrupt; the law in modern American society is shrouded in illusion. According to Wright, even those sworn to uphold the law disbelieve its veracity. During the train ride to New York, Damon and New York district attorney Houston engage in a perceptive exchange about American law and those who break the law. Although Damon is cautious in discussing these matters with Houston, himself an outsider as a result of physical deformity, Damon's outsider consciousness compels him, as it does Houston, to scrutinize the law and assert the consciousness of the ethical criminal. Due to social and economic oppression, black Americans are outsiders, but fear of white supremacy forces them to conceal their anger and resentment. Yet there are those who overcome their fears of legal condemnation and act out their resentment, essentially rejecting the American system of criminal (in)justice. Significantly, it is the district attorney—a man sworn to defend and enforce the law but also a man with criminal impulses—who understands and acknowledges the manner in which the (il)legal system has oppressed African Americans; Wright then articulates through Houston the ethical criminal's philosophy of self-conduct. When Damon asks if Houston is sympathetic to those who break the rules of civilization, the district attorney responds: "In a way, yes. . . . But it all depends upon *how* the laws are broken. My greatest sympathy is for those who feel that they have a *right* to break the law" (1991 *Outsider* 171). But how and where does the ethical criminal exist?

The ethical criminal dwells in the crevices of postcivilized modern industrial cities (Weinstein 89). An existential-nihilist rebel, he believes that human existence is pointless and absurd. It leads nowhere and adds up to nothing. Existence is completely gratuitous in that there is no justification for it, but there is also no reason not to live. The outsider/ethical criminal is a man who has embraced a pessimistic philosophical outlook, a philosophy of self-fortification and self-conduct, that does not deny the ugliness of the world, but takes it as it is (see Dienstag xii). He attempts to become a free spirit, perhaps godlike, who has rejected all of the expectations and restraints that have characterized human existence since the emergence of the Christian era. Yet, as a modern man, he is a person absent of the moral and ethical controls of Christianity. He is an intellectual who has all the unique benefits of being no stranger to modern Western knowledge, but he has either renounced it or has somehow succeeded in avoiding its oppressive power and minimized the degree to which he has been victimized by its tentacles. There is no doubt that he is an atheist, but he has transcended it as well. Wright describes him as a civilized savage who feels no requirement to worship any god. He is a modern intellectual with the mind, consciousness, and behavior of a pagan; he has not been subdued by modern society.

The ethical criminal/civilized savage is a demystifier of Western culture. He thinks through the illusory aspects of modern Western civilization—myths that Europeans foisted upon all of us in order to forestall their fears, and thus pacify their dread. Yet the ethical criminal concludes that these very myths are dying in the West's intellectual and emotional consciousness. These myths no longer possess utilitarian value; Western Europeans and their white American descendants have jettisoned them. A growing cynicism now smolders in the soul of an increasingly decadent and morally destitute Western civilization. Wright's ethical criminal, perhaps reminiscent of the Nietzschean last man (Nietzsche, *Beyond* 41), rebels against those myths, as they constitute a culture of pretense in postcivilized modern American society. Since modern America represents the devaluation of its most sacred political values (e.g., legal freedom, justice, and equity), the ethical criminal breaks the laws of an increasingly decadent society sans remorse. Cross Damon is a criminal; yet, he thinks of himself as innocent.

The ethical criminal believes that the world has no intrinsic meaning. He can try to live with meaninglessness, he can try to create his own meaning and impose it on the world, or, more realistically, he can try to impose his own meaning and values on a small part of the world, in particular on his own microcosm and those with whom he interacts. The collapse of the idea of objective meaning leaves him free to create his own life. Self-creation is how the "will to power" expresses itself in human life. Wright's antihero attempts to create his own values and laws by which he will live. The ethical criminal tries to stand beyond God and the human, becoming a little secular god himself. That is, he seeks to live beyond good and evil. He is an atheist in whose heart and mind religion has no meaning. In the wake of God's death, the molds for the formation of the human were broken. Now the ethical criminal's highest elevation is the embodiment of his own philosophy of conduct, which would be based on his own individual desires. He is self-possessed. He seeks to become autonomous. He is the personification of Nietzsche's heroic individualism (Thiele 43).

In one of the most intriguing episodes in the novel, Damon encounters and overwhelms members of the Communist Party. Since the party cannot discover Damon's true identity, members are frightened of him. As one party member says:

> "Lane, what the hell ghastly joke is this you're pulling? Who the god-damn hell do you think you *are*? What are you *doing* here? When we try to check on you, we run into a maze that leads nowhere. That's no *accident*. Are you a spy? Frankly, we doubt it; . . . but you've not been close enough to us to get hold of any information. Don't you think, now, that we are scared of you. If we were, you'd not be breathing now. . . . But we want to know . . ." (1991 *Outsider* 472–73)

Damon's superior intellect puts him in possession of the patent duplicity of the Communist Party nihilists' will to power. Employing a cold-blooded Marxian analysis of capitalist industrialization, he mocks the Communists' quest for power, suggesting that they are similar to Western imperialists:

> "Now, during the past thirty-five years, under the ideological banner of Dialectical Materialism, a small group of ruthless men in Russia seized political power and the entire state apparatus and established a dictatorship. Rationalizing human life to the last degree, they launched a vast, well-disciplined program of industrialization which now rivals that of the United States of America in pretentiousness and power. . . . Again I say that what happened in Russia . . . could have happened under a dozen different ideological banners. . . . If you lived in Russia and made such a statement, they'd shoot you; and if you lived in America and made such a statement, they'd blacklist you and starve you to death. . . . Modern man still believes in magic; he lives in a rational world but insists on interpreting the events of that world in terms of mystical forces." (476)

Damon's power of erudition provides insight into the systematic lies of his Communist Party adversaries. He pierces the veil of the party's illusions, pointing out the organization's contradiction between idealism and naked power. To one of its functionaries, Damon declares authoritatively:

> "I'm propaganda-proof. Communism has two truths, two faces. The face you're talking about now is for the workers . . . not for me. I look at facts, processes. . . . You did what you did because you had to! . . . You use idealistic words as your smoke screen, but behind that screen you *rule*. . . . It's a question of *power*!" (476–77)

The ethical criminal Damon is a product of Wright's urgent mission to challenge the decadence of postcivilized modern Western society's barbarism and savagery, especially the lived experience of black people forced to "live in but not of'" American society. Wright seems to be arguing that a decadent social order with a bankrupt legal system brings into existence a philosophical criminal. The ethical criminal is a lawless man inhabiting a lawless and decadent social order. For various reasons, he does not believe that his victims have a right to exist. Yet he attempts to rein in his lawless impulses, which forces him to live in a subjective prison. This requires self-mastery and lucid intellectual power. But the ethical criminal has a certain self-possessed callousness that allows him to break modern society's rules without feeling guilt, because he considers himself innocent.

The ethical criminal's dilemma is that he still lives in the wake of modern civilization, even though his death-of-God decree is succeeded by the realization that modern culture has become dehumanized at the same time that it remains all too human. At the novel's end, Wright seems to suggest that a nihilistic-existential approach bears its own chaotic and suicidal logical illogic, which, tragically, is the ultimate irony of a philosophy dependent upon ambiguities. Wright seems to be saying that the path of the complex, knowledgeable, powerful, yet cynical ethical criminal ends in destruction. In what appears to be Wright's rejection of existential nihilism, the ethical criminal Damon cannot transcend human existence; he cannot exist as a god beyond good and evil. The human cannot be concerned only with the self, its fears, and desires. Wright seems really to be suggesting that people must be responsible not only for the self, but also for others. Individualism, heroic or not, is inadequate. Shot by a Communist Party operative and dying, Damon's quest has been necessary but not sufficient. He declares weakly:

> "I wanted to be free. . . . To feel what I was worth. . . . What living meant to me. . . . I loved life too much. . . . I wish I had some way to give the meaning of my life to others. . . . To make a bridge from man to man. . . . Starting from scratch every time is . . . is no good. Tell them not to come down this road. . . . We must find some way of being good to ourselves. . . . Man is all we've got. . . . I wish I could ask men to meet themselves. . . . We're different from what we seem. . . .We're strangers to ourselves." He was silent for a moment, then he continued, whispering: "Don't think I'm so odd and strange . . . I'm not. . . . Man is returning to the earth. . . . For a long time he has

> been sleeping, wrapped in a dream. . . . He is awakening now, awakening from his dream and finding himself in a waking nightmare. . . . The myth-men are going. . . . The real men, the last men are coming. . . . Tell the world what they are like. . . . We are here already, if others but had the courage to see us. . . ." (585)

The ethical criminal Damon has searched in vain for the meaning of life. He has found neither meaning nor values—or so it would appear. His apparent predicament is complicated when, after he has committed four murders and has been directly responsible for another death, he whispers in his dying moment, "In my heart . . . I'm . . . I felt . . . I'm innocent. . . . That's what made the horror" (585). Again, the significance of Damon's dying statement is contextualized by Kierkegaard's observation: "The qualitative leap is outside of ambiguity, but he who through dread becomes guilty is innocent, for it was not he himself but dread, an alien power, which laid hold of him, a power he did not love but dreaded—and yet he is guilty, for he sank in the dread which he loved even while he feared it" (39).

Significantly, the contradiction is that in fighting other little gods, the ethical criminal becomes the very thing against which he has struggled—a little god. Yet Wright demonstrates that the black man, as ethical criminal, cannot step outside of history—to become a little god, create new values, and live in accordance with those values—and survive. Wright seems to be suggesting that the black man (or black people, as such) cannot become a free spirit in the existing American social order, even if he becomes as lawless as his white oppressors. His quest for freedom, knowledge, and self-mastery is not enough.

Wright also seems to be arguing that the oppression of blacks, especially in the absence of God, makes their lives hopelessly meaningless. At the novel's end, ethical criminal Damon does not find meaning in his life through the lived experience of heroic individualism. His new ethics have demanded the thoroughgoing stripping away of his attachments (to family, friends, employment, ideologies, religion, political organizations, laws, and other human beings) so as to purge his creative will of every trace of necessity. However, he is murdered by one of his white Communist adversaries. Wright seems to be saying that the struggle for black liberation cannot be an individual project; rather, it must be a collective vocation.

Even so, freedom is unobtainable. The ethical criminal is the response to the emergence of the uncivil savagery and barbarism of modern culture, which flourishes in an environment shaped by increasing decadence and nihilism. He has sought to be creative—to create new values by which to live. But the ethical criminal cannot successfully create a new self; nor can he create new values and the meaning of his life. Ultimately, he cannot achieve authentic self-mastery as a little god. Realizing this, perhaps all the ethical criminal can do, Wright suggests, is to collect himself and employ his knowledgeable vision in order to help others to pierce the many illusionary veils that characterize the horror of an oppressive postcivilized modern society.

> "Knowing and seeing what is happening in the world today, I don't think that there is much of anything that one can do about it. . . . He can look bravely at this horrible totalitarian reptile and, while doing so, discipline his dread, his fear and study it coolly, . . . note down with calmness the pertinent facts . . . these facts can help a man to save himself; and he may then be able to call the attention of others around him to the presence and meaning of this reptile and its multitudinous writings." (1991 *Outsider* 492)

There is no final overcoming or transformation for the individual or the social order. The ethical criminal Damon cannot live beyond good and evil. Perhaps beyond good and evil there is nothingness.

Notes

1. For example, see Adell; Brigano; J. Davis; De Genova; Fabre, *Unfinished Quest*; Gayle; Gilroy; Hakutani, *Richard Wright*; Hayes; JanMohamed, *Death-Bound Subject*; Lynch, *Creative Revolt*; McMahon; Robinson; A. Singh, "Richard Wright's *The Outsider*"; Tate, "Christian Existentialism"; Walker, *Richard Wright: Daemonic Genius*; Webster; Widmer; and S. Williams.
2. See also Domanick; Feagin; Garland; Higginbotham; Nelson; and O'Brien.

Keeping Secrets: The Cold War and the Politics of Un-Belonging in Richard Wright's *The Outsider*

—JOSEPH KEITH—

> I have a taste for the secret, it clearly has to do with not-belonging; I have an impulse of fear or terror in the face of a political space, for example, a public space that makes no room for the secret. For me, the demand that everything be paraded in the public square and there be no internal forum is a glaring sign of the totalitarianization of democracy. I can rephrase this in terms of political ethics: if a right to the secret is not maintained, we are in a totalitarian space.
> **—Jacques Derrida,** *A Taste for the Secret* (59)

Feeling unsettled and more than a little homesick, especially given the struggles and deprivations of France in the aftermath of World War II, Richard Wright and his family returned to the United States at the start of 1947 after having lived in Paris, France, for the previous eight months (1946–47). The country to which Wright returned, however, was in the midst of profound and, in his eyes, profoundly troubling changes. The Cold War had come to dominate the political scene in America. Wright was struck by the increased nationalism ("Americanism," he declared, "had become a kind of religion") as demonstrated by the radical break with New Deal liberalism; in particular by antilabor policies; and by what he saw as the profound resurgence of racism. The latter was evidenced no more cruelly on a national level than by the numerous lynchings of ex-servicemen that took place in 1947,[1] and, on a personal level, by what he described as the "daily, petty humiliations" to himself and his family. By the end of July of that same year, Wright not only decided to return to France, but this time the move would be permanent. And indeed when Wright left again for Paris, he would spend the last thirteen years of his life abroad, never again setting foot on American soil. "I was relieved," Wright wrote, inverting the traditional American narrative, "when my ship sailed past the Statue of Liberty" (Wright, "I Choose Exile").

But while Wright might have been "relieved" to leave the United States behind, very few other people, it seems, felt the same way. Wright bore the brunt of a great deal of criticism about his self-exile. Ralph Ellison and James Baldwin took Wright to task for having lost his political and literary way. After Wright's premature death in 1960 at the age of fifty-two, Baldwin looked back and wondered if Wright had not made a mistake by being away from "home" so long and lamented that Wright had perhaps "cut himself off from his roots" (Baldwin *Nobody Knows* 203). A 1953 *Time* magazine article titled "Native Son Doesn't Live Here" declared, "While Wright sits out the threat of totalitarianism in Paris, an abler Negro novelist sees the problem of race differently. Says Ralph (*Invisible Man*) Ellison, 'After all, my people have been here for a long time. . . . It's a big wonderful country'" (qtd. in Singh, *Black* 161).

In respect to his writing, critics also overwhelmingly judged that Wright's move away from the United States had been a mistake. In particular, Wright's novel *The Outsider* was read, and often continues to be read, as evidence that Wright had become overly invested in European philosophy in general and French existentialism in particular. Reviews at the time overwhelmingly took Wright to task for his "misguided experimentation with European intellectual traditions" (Rugoff 4).[2] "Dick Wright . . . I think he made . . . a very bad mistake," Nelson Algren observed in a *Paris Review* interview in 1955. "I mean he writes out of passion, out of his belly; but he won't admit this, you see. He's trying to write as an intellectual, which he isn't basically" (Algren 54). Lorraine Hansberry, in her first writing assignment for the leftist African American journal *Freedom*, was even more scathing. "*The Outsider* is a story of sheer violence, death, and disgusting spectacle, written by a man who has seemingly come to despise humanity. . . . Wright has lost his own dignity and destroyed his talents. He exalts brutality and nothingness" (Hansberry 55).

Contemporary critics have been far less dismissive of *The Outsider*. Indeed, Wright's long-neglected novel is perhaps finally beginning to receive the level of critical attention it deserves. At the same time, analysis of the novel has remained, with a few exceptions (most notably Paul Gilroy's analysis in *The Black Atlantic: Modernity and Double Consciousness* and Abdul JanMohamed's reading of the novel in *The Death-Bound Subject: Richard Wright's Archaeology of Death*), focused upon its engagement with (either as an espousal or critique of) the "profoundly individualistic" philosophy of European existentialism (Fabre, "French Existentialism" 182–98).[3] And while these readings have been extremely rich and varied, in this essay I resituate Wright's deeply philosophical novel within and against a different and neglected historical and theoretical context; namely, that of the Cold War—or, more specifically, Cold War domestic racial politics and their connections to the consolidation of US empire in the years during and after WWII. Reconsidering *The Outsider* in this context allows us to read the novel as an important and neglected intervention into the *global* politics of race in the period—one of many such African American critiques that have been suppressed or rendered marginal by Cold War historiography.

In resituating *The Outsider* within the context of the early Cold War, I center my reading of the novel in the first part of the essay on the concept of *secrecy*. I argue that the secret, around which the novel's narrative revolves—while indicative of a profound individualism and retreat from the social—also represents a crucial mode of dissent within the repressive context of the early Cold War, and the Cold War's decimation of the black public sphere in particular. Specifically, I argue that the secret enables a mode of "un-belonging" from which the limits of hegemonic thought can be questioned and out of which other forms of knowledge can be preserved or secured. In the second part of the essay, I resituate *The Outsider* within the context of Wright's effort in his later work to develop a critical global perspective on the meaning of black struggle during the early Cold War. I argue that in theorizing black subjectivity through the "secret" of "un-belonging," Wright uses his own self-exile to fashion a specifically "non-national" historical agency and epistemology—one capable of challenging the dominant narratives of the early Cold War and of fusing and linking an indigenous form of black dissidence within the United States with an international anticolonial Third World political consciousness.

Secrets

As is common in the detective/noir genre, *The Outsider*'s narrative revolves around a series of secrets: there is the secret of the main character, Cross Damon's "true" identity; the secret of the many crimes that he then commits in order to preserve his new identity; Eva's secret diary that Cross reads, and so on. I am, though, less interested in examining the meaning of the individual secret, or whatever social exigencies exist for keeping one or another of the secrets in particular. Instead, I want to explore the nature of secrecy itself. In other words, instead of examining the meaning of the *content* of the specific secrets, the more compelling question to ask of *The Outsider* is: What is the meaning of the *form* of secrecy itself?

In the case of Cross Damon, for instance, the secret of his specific crimes is less telling than the very life of secrecy he leads. Or rather, what is most important about his "secret" (what he refers to at one point as his "black secret") is not that it enables Damon to avoid recrimination in the crimes, but critically, secrecy is an index of his inaccessibility to the culture as a whole—culture that would otherwise work to entirely determine him. That is, in a world where the explicit exposure of the subject would ostensibly manifest how thoroughly he has been inscribed within a social given totality, secrecy establishes a boundary across which its far-reaching discourse does not reach; that is, it marks the limits of hegemony.

Early in the novel, for instance, Cross—the novel's deeply alienated and intellectual African American main character—is mistakenly presumed dead in a subway train accident. Instead of coming forward, however, Cross resolves to use the mistake as an opportunity to break free from his life and the various burdens that have him pinned down: debt, a pending accusation of statutory rape by his ex-girlfriend, and blackmail. He decides to let the world think that he has died so that he might disappear from Chicago to fashion a new identity for himself in New York City. Soon after, he anxiously ponders the profound implications this choice will have for how he must now conduct his life.

> He took a northbound trolley on State Street and pushed his way apprehensively into the packed crowd and stood swaying. Was there anything in his manner that could attract attention? Could others tell that he was nervous, trying to hide a secret? How could one act normally when one was *trying* to act normally? . . . He began to see that this project of deception . . . was much bigger than he had realized. It was a supreme challenge that went straight to the very heart of life. (1993 *Outsider* 109)[4]

Damon's specific secret is of course that he was not one of the casualties of the recent train crash, as reported. But cast more broadly, and more significantly, Damon's "secrecy" represents the subjective practice by which he establishes a boundary between his public and private self—a distinction that Wright underscores by staging his very private reflections in the very public context of the crowded trolley. Secrecy is thus the mode of operation by which Cross can maintain his self-described "freedom" within society by remaining illegible to society. Damon comes to quickly understand that "secrecy" is not in this respect specific to his unusual circumstances, but that this "project of deception . . . went straight to the very heart of life." In other words, secrecy does not so much describe the particular life of the criminal. Instead, this particular form of criminality reveals a broader truth—the extent to which this "project of deception" bespeaks a fundamental social condition or "challenge" for living in but not belonging to the existing social order. Indeed, it is actually this very disidentification from the social order that defines Cross's greatest "crime."

Insomuch as secrecy appears to establish an implicit distinction and opposition between society and a more "authentic" individual self, we might certainly read the existential traces of Cross's "project of deception." His presumed death in the train crash, after all, enables him to bring into critical consciousness his alienation from a society whose values and whose purposes he does not share.

"Others took their lives for granted," Cross thinks to himself, "he would have to mold his with conscious aim" (110–11). But while Cross's project clearly engages the terms and logics of existentialism, as many critics have pointed out, it also has another source—less attended to by critics—that far preceded Wright's involvement with European philosophy; that is, a tradition of black dissidence that had engaged Wright from his earliest life and writings. It is perhaps useful here to keep in mind an oft-quoted anecdote recounted by C. L. R. James, about an exchange he had with his friend Wright. James recalls the time Wright brought him into his house in the south of France, pointed to a row of books by Kierkegaard on his bookshelf, and declared, "Look here, Nello, you see those books there? . . . Everything that he writes in those books I knew before I read them." James concludes that "what there was in Dick's life, what there was in the experience of a black man in the United States in the 1930s that made him understand everything that Kierkegaard had written before he had read it . . . is something that . . . has to be studied" (James, "Black Studies" 196).

In response to James's injunction to trace or "study" the source of Wright's preknowledge of Kierkegaard's existential ideas, I turn to Wright's earlier work, *Black Boy*. Specifically, I want to incorporate Abdul JanMohamed's reading of Wright's autobiography in which he indirectly describes the role "secrecy" plays in Wright's successful attempt to survive the rigors of a racist Southern hegemony and to resist Jim Crow society's attempt to limit his subjectivity to that of a "black boy" (JanMohamed, "Negating" 245–66). Wright, he argues, finds himself continually subjected to violence designed to "teach him to assume 'voluntarily' the subservient place" reserved for blacks in the South (255). But with each incident this pressure for emotional submission increasingly conflicts with Wright's desire for intellectual understanding. "I could not make subservience," writes Wright, "an *automatic* part of my behavior. I had to feel and think out each tiny item of racial experience in light of the race problem, and to each item I brought the whole of my life" (qtd. in JanMohamed, "Negating" 258). JanMohamed argues that Wright's imperative here (quite like that of Damon's existential "project") is to overcome an unthinking or "automatic" obedience to the authority of the existing social order by bringing "each tiny incident" into critical consciousness, situating it within the broader social, political, and economic context of the "race problem as a whole" and bringing his whole life to bear on it. Writes JanMohamed, "Thus, whereas ideology demands an emotional unconscious acquiescence, Wright's project entails becoming perfectly aware of the unconscious pattern of behavior" (258). Or to put it again in Cross's quite similar language, "Others took their lives for granted, he would have to mold his with conscious aim" (1993 *Outsider* 110–11).

Interestingly, Wright, in *Black Boy*, describes this critical subjectivity as a "secret burden": "Many times I grew weary of the secret burden I carried and longed to cast it down, either in action or resignation. But I was not made to be a resigned man and I had only a limited choice of action, and I was afraid of all of them" (qtd. in JanMohamed, "Negating" 259). Wright makes the "choices" that are available painfully clear. On the one hand, as JanMohamed explains, Wright can express his critical subjectivity; he can openly rebel against the hegemony of the Jim Crow South and face physical violence or death—most notoriously in the form of lynching. On the other hand, he can "resign" himself; he can acquiesce to the limited and subservient subject position of the "black boy" inscribed within the hegemonic social order. The choice is either to "voluntarily" comply with (and make "automatic") the limited view that the "ideological apparatus" has constructed for him or to have that compliance enforced by the explicit use of brute *force*.

Thus, in order to maintain his critical subjectivity, Wright must keep it hidden; "it can never be displayed in public or be recognized by most whites who surround him" (JanMohamed, "Negating" 261). Just as with Cross Damon, it must remain a "secret burden." As such, secrecy can be understood as an example of what Frantz Fanon has described as a form of counterhegemony. Challenging totalizing theories of domination and subjugation, Fanon claims that "the procedure through which subaltern or marginalized subjects are asked to identify with dominant discourses enables practices that make possible forms of resistance" (Fanon, "On National" 206–48).[5] "Secrecy" is one such strategy; it is a method by which Wright in *Black Boy* (and Cross in *The Outsider*) can at once live *in* but not be a "member" *of* the social order. It is a way to reconstitute his subjectivity outside the social hegemony–a way to establish and maintain a tenuous space of *un-belonging* where that subjectivity and his potential humanity might remain intact.

In *The Long Revolution*–published only a few years after *The Outsider* in 1959—Raymond Williams distinguishes various relationships of "conformity" and "non-conformity" between individuals and societies (72–100). Initially, he differentiates between what he calls the "subject" and the "servant" (a distinction that parallels in many respects Wright's "choice" between direct confrontation and feigned acceptance in *Black Boy*). A "subject" defines a relationship like that of the colonial subject or slave in which conformity is enforced through the naked exercise of brute force. The "servant," on the other hand, is an object of ideology; he is "given the illusion of choice, and is invited to identify himself with the way of life in which his place is defined. It is an illusion, because again, like the subject he has no obvious way of maintaining his life if he refuses. Yet the illusion is important, for it allows him to pretend to an identification with the society, as if the choice had been real" (*Long Revolution* 87). Williams describes modes of resistance or "non-conformity" (e.g., "the rebel," "the exile," "the vagrant") to this type or interpolation or identification embodied by the servant; that is, when the discrepancy between "the role the individual is playing and his actual sense of himself becomes manifest" (88). One of these modes is worth quoting at length, because it provides a wonderfully succinct model for the type of dissent expressed by and through the "secret" in the "outsider" in Wright's work.

> We have been used to thinking of exiles as men driven from their society, but an equally characteristic modern figure is the self-exile. The self-exile could . . . live at ease in his society, but to do so would be to deny his personal reality. Sometimes, he goes away, on principle, but as often he stays, yet still, on principle, feels separate. The Bolsheviks had a useful term for this, in 'internal émigré,' and . . . we can use it to describe a very important modern relationship. This kind of self-exile lives and moves about in the society in which he was born, but rejects its purposes and despises its values, in terms of alternative principles to which his whole personal reality is committed. . . . There is great tension in this condition, for theoretically, at least, the self-exile wants the society to change, so that he can start belonging to it, and this involves him, at least notionally, in relationships. But since . . . his personal dissent has remained fixed at an individual stage, it is difficult for him to form adequate relationships. . . . He may support the principles of dissenting causes, but he cannot join them: he is too wary of being caught and compromised. . . . He has become or remained his 'authentic self,' but this authenticity cannot be shared with or communicated to others. . . . Whatever he may come to say or do, he continues, essentially, to walk alone in his society, defending a principle in himself. (90)

The name itself, "internal émigré," evokes the contradictory subject position of Wright's "outsider"—the condition of being, as the district attorney defines it, at once "inside" and "outside" the nation. Williams's depiction also reiterates the importance and function of the secret as I have been suggesting: the "project of deception" represents a strategy for living and moving about in society while maintaining a difference, while maintaining "the individuality which is the term of his separateness" (90). But what I want to focus on in particular is Williams's suggestion that this mode of dissent remains at an individual stage for fear of being "caught" (an image itself of the hunted criminal, such as Cross). What this points to is what we might call the double bind of secrecy; it at once enables not only a degree of freedom and dissent, as I have argued, but it is also an index of curtailed freedom and repression. If the "secret" represents a kind of reserve subjectivity outside of the ability of society to interpolate it and where alternative knowledge can survive, it also testifies to the fact that in order for this illicit knowledge and subjectivity to endure, it cannot, as Williams describes it, be "shared with or communicated to others." And indeed throughout *The Outsider*, Cross is plagued again and again by this very dilemma. "He who had a secret to hide loved talking" (1993 *Outsider* 165). "He yearned to talk to someone" (211). "He had witnessed a scene about which he could never in his life talk with anybody. And yet he *did* hanker to talk about it. When men shared normal experiences, they could talk about them without fear, but he had to hug his black secret to his heart" (128). "He had to cope with his impulse to confide" (147). "But what was he to do with this conflict of his? This urge to confide and the fear of the danger of confiding?" (148). "He had to talk to somebody! But to whom? No; he had to keep this crime choked in his throat. He, like others, had to pretend that nothing like this could ever happen; he had to collaborate and help keep the secret" (345). "If only he could talk to somebody! To wander always alone in this desert was too much" (428).

In the end, *The Outsider* is haunted by this communitarian strain—this unfulfilled possibility of some social community, some social formation in which Cross's "way of knowing" might be recognized in intersubjectivity. The novel is in fact bracketed by this desire. Cross's very first line in the novel is "Booker let me rest this tired old body on you hunh?" To which his friend replies, "Hell naw! Stand on your own two big flat feet, Cross!" (1). And at the very end of the novel, as he lay dying in the street, the district attorney asks him what he has finally learned, to which he responds, "The search can't be done alone. . . . Never alone. . . . Alone a man is nothing." (585). Cross's persistent desire to "confide" suggests finally that as much as we might read Cross (and the novel) as *embracing* a profoundly individualistic, or for some critics nihilistic, philosophy—whose tragic limits the novel reveals—we might also read it equally as a testament to an *enforced* isolation—namely, we might find in his isolation and radical autonomy a damning testimony to the closing down of any viable alternative public sphere within the context of the period: the early Cold War.

State Secrets

While secrecy provides a conceptual and thematic link between Wright's later novel *The Outsider* and his earlier work, such as *Black Boy*, it is also true that the meaning of secrecy takes on a unique cast and significance amid the early Cold War. After all, during the early Cold War, secrecy becomes not only a strategy of dissent but also a prevailing anxiety of the state and a central mode of governance—whether in the form of state secrets, foreign espionage, or domestic surveillance. Ann Douglas writes:

> The U.S. Government stepped up its surveillance of its citizens to unprecedented levels in the 1940s and the early 1950s . . . for the first time, it compiled

> psychological dossiers on everyone inducted into its military forces (sometimes sharing the information with the ever expanding FBI) . . . federal housing agencies were making maps of every neighborhood in the United States, ranking each according to its racial ethnic homogeneity, social stability, and earning potential, and granting federal funds accordingly . . . the nation was tightening its drug laws and defining a host of beliefs and activities, most notably communism and homosexuality, as criminal, even treasonable. . . . The Cold War administration had decided the personal was political long before postmodernism made the discovery. (32)

To put it in terms of the present discussion, we can say that in making the "personal" "political," the Cold War administration employed a variety of methods to make the individual subject visible to power and to the existing social order. In compiling psychological dossiers, it sought to expose and criminalize or pathologize the potentially unnerving disconnect between the public and private self; in so doing it served to manage dissent and nonnormative beliefs and activities by playing on rising fears about domestic subversion.[6] And as in the case of Truman's Federal Loyalty Program, which required a loyalty investigation for federal employment and was in many respects an extension of the military psychological testing to root out homosexuals and Communists, there was increasing pressure on individuals to account for their beliefs and their pasts—to "prove" that their personal values fully coincided with those of the nation. In only a thinly veiled reference to the climate of the period, Cross, for example, wonders hypothetically: "Spies spying upon spies who were being spied upon! Imagine a society like that! It would be an elaborate kind of transparent ant heap in which the most intimate feelings of all the men and women in it would be known, a glass jailhouse in *which the subjective existence of each man and woman would be public each living moment*" (my italics; 1993 *Outsider* 453).

As I have been arguing, the meaning of Cross's "secret" lies in its formal insistence that he is inaccessible to the culture that would otherwise entirely determine him. Conversely, it is precisely that border, which again his secret both assumes and maintains, that makes Cross such a disruptive figure. He becomes a kind of secret agent, but with no affiliations; instead he bears subversively within himself the undercover limits of Cold War authority. His secrecy becomes a disruptive counternarrative to a prevailing Cold War culture of state secrets. Douglas points out earlier that increased domestic surveillance during the early Cold War was accompanied by a redefinition of criminality, in which a crime did not depend upon what one had done necessarily, but instead upon one's identity and/or beliefs (e.g., homosexuality and Communism). Similarly, Ely Houston's entire investigation into the crimes hinges upon trying to apprehend (in both senses of the word) Cross's way of knowing. That is, Cross's "guilt" is not dependent upon evidence or empirical proof of the murders, but on the ability to affectively imagine and render visible his perspective, which remains outside and unseen by the existing social order. The climactic interrogation scene, for instance, is less criminal inquiry and more part psychological testing and part McCarthy trial. (e.g., "Were you ever a member of the Communist Party?") Ultimately, the district attorney's ambition is to make Cross's "private" self "public." "We've proof," he says, "of who you are" (508). In so doing, he lays bare Cross's secret, which is not the content of his crime but rather that very boundary between public and private that makes him inscrutable and as such provides a precarious space of "un-belonging" out of which he can fashion his own narrative. What in fact finally proves Cross's guilt is his unwillingness or inability to show proper affect when Houston tells him of his mother's death and when he brings his former friends and family into the room. Cross's refusal to acknowledge—to "make public" in the "glass jailhouse"—his emotions proves that he is beyond the reach of society's values and as such provides "evidence" of his criminal guilt. The very nature of Houston's test cleverly bears witness to how separation from normative national life was being criminalized and pathologized during the Cold War. It also reveals the tragic limits of Cross's dissent. Confronted with his family, he has ultimately only two choices—choices that echo across a different historical and political context than those that Wright grapples with in *Black Boy*. On the one hand, he can give up his "secret" by making visible his past and thus making himself accessible once again to the hegemonic social order by reassuming the various normative social roles of father, husband, and son that bind him to society. Or, as he does, he can continue to rebel by retaining the freedom not to answer; he can refuse to make himself legible, maintaining his "project of deception" but in so doing be categorized as a criminal and psychopath, and finally be killed. Either way, the secret is out.

Black Secrets

That Cross is forced to keep this alternative knowledge a "secret," that his rebellion must remain at an "individual stage" for "fear of being caught" (to put it back in Williams's terms), might finally be seen also in this context as a profound allegory for the political pressures placed upon him and the silencing of independent black political perspectives and alternative black public spheres during the early Cold War. Again, Cross's "black secret" is on the one hand a strategy of resistance, but it also is an index of repression. That is, it is increasingly *only* in the realm of secrecy where these other knowledges and social imaginaries might endure. And indeed, under the ideological crucible of anti-Communism there was an aggressive decimation during the period of the more vibrant and global black radicalism of the war years. In an essay published in *Life* magazine soon after the war, Arthur Schlesinger, for one, directly linked Communism to black struggles, arguing that the Communist Party was "sinking its tentacles into the NAACP" (qtd. in Singh, *Black* 162). During the 1950s, charges of Communism and of challenging the existing racial order served as the basis for the FBI's increasing surveillance of organizations and individuals. Richard Wright was cognizant of being monitored and lived under a continual threat of having his passport revoked under the Smith Act.[7] And indeed, as intelligence reports have since confirmed, Wright remained on the National Security Index (the list of individuals deemed most dangerous to the government) for the entire period he lived in exile.

Several historians have recently examined how anxious the US government was in particular about efforts by various black activist intellectuals to establish *transnational* links between the struggle of African Americans for domestic racial justice within the United States with those fought against colonialism elsewhere. Penny Von Eschen, Nikhil Pal Singh, Thomas Borstelmann and Mary Dudziak have traced how the government's eye to the international stage not only helped lead to certain progressive domestic racial reforms—most notably desegregation—but also how it severely limited the forms of "acceptable" political discourse and racial politics. Mary Dudziak writes:

> Civil Rights groups and activists had to walk a fine line, making it clear that their reform efforts were meant to fill out the contours of American democracy, and not to challenge or undermine it. . . . Under the strictures of Cold War politics, a broad international critique of racial oppression was out of place—the narrowed scope of acceptable protest during the early years of the Cold War would not accommodate criticism of colonialism. . . . For that reason outspoken critics of colonialism found themselves increasingly under siege. (11)

A number of these "critics" who did not keep their radical dissent a "secret," like Paul Robeson and W. E. B. Du Bois, would find themselves under explicit state sanction. In *Black Is a Country*, Nikhil Pal Singh recounts how Robeson's claim at the Paris Peace Conference in 1949 that blacks would not fight in a war against the Soviet Union led to accusations of treason and the revoking of Robeson's passport for most of the 1950s (Singh, *Black* 164). W. E. B. Du Bois also had his passport revoked and was denied the possibility of traveling abroad for a number of years. C. L. R. James and Claudia Jones were designated "subversives" and therefore subject to deportation under the McCarran Internal Security Act of 1950, which gave immigration officials the unprecedented authority to arrest without warrant, hold without bail, and deport for an action that was legal when committed any of the 2.5 million aliens residing in the United States.

"The silencing of giants like Du Bois and Robeson," Singh writes, "along with the voluntary and involuntary exile of anti-Stalinist leftists like Richard Wright, Chester Himes, C. L. R. James, E. Franklin Frazier, and others, completed a purge of the black activist intelligentsia that had come of age a little more than a decade prior" (Singh, *Black* 169).

Wright understood his own eventual self-exile from the United States as in part a result of this broader effort to silence figures and forms of black radicalism during the early Cold War. "My un-Americanism," he declared in his essay "I Choose Exile," "consists of the fact that I want the right to hold without fear of punitive measures, an opinion with which my neighbor does not agree" (Wright, qtd. in Fabre, 1973 *UQ* 369).[8] Wright later suggested that the "opinions" that proved most threatening to the United States at the time were not in fact those related to Communism but to his growing critical engagement with the colonial world and with a broad international or transnational critique of racial oppression. "So far as Americans are concerned," Wright argued, "I'm worse than a Communist, for my work falls like a shadow across their policy in Asia and Africa" (Wright's 1960 letter to Margrit de Sablonière, qtd. in Julia Wright, "Introduction," *Haiku* x). In the end, Wright interpreted his self-exile not only as a turning point in his life and career, but also as an effort to continue and further develop his commitment to a radical global or transnational perspective on the meaning of black struggle. "My break with the U.S. was more than a geographical change. It was a break with my former attitudes as a Negro and a Communist—an attempt to think over and re-define my attitudes and my thinking. I was trying to grapple with the big problem—the meaning of Western civilization as a whole and the relation of Negroes and other minority groups to it" (qtd. in Fabre, 1973 *UQ* 336). The final part of this essay reexamines *The Outsider* as a crucial part of this effort.

The Global Secrets of Modernity

Returning to *The Outsider*, Cross's rebellious secrecy, as I have argued, renders visible the limits of the existing social order to know; but what his rebellion also ultimately attempts to do is to reconstitute that border into the site of an alternative authority. That is, through the figure of Cross, *The Outsider* can be read as staging a struggle to articulate an alternative way of knowing to both sides of the Cold War's Manichean divide, an independent philosophical and political standpoint that represented neither a vindication of American ideals nor of Communism, but of a third perspective. As Ely Houston declares during the course of his investigation, the murders were the product of a "third set of ideas." Ultimately, this "third set of ideas" is borne out of what I call an *epistemology of un-belonging*, which Cross fashions through the form of secrecy. This epistemology of un-belonging enables him, on the one hand, to bring into critical consciousness his individual (existential) alienation from society—that is, the "outsider." But this epistemology of un-belonging also enables the theorization of the broader stated social location of African Americans as both "inside" and "outside" the nation.

> "Negroes are outsiders," explains Ely Houston to Cross in the novel, "and they are going to know they have these problems. They are going to be self-conscious . . . they are going to be both inside and outside of our culture at the same time. They will not only be Americans or Negroes, they will be centers of *knowing*, so to speak. . . . The political, social and psychological consequence of this will be enormous. . . . Now, imagine a man inclined to think, to probe, to ask questions. Why, he'd be in a wonderful position to do so. . . . A dreadful objectivity would be forced upon him." (1993 *Outsider* 163–64)

Secrecy, in this respect, not only serves to protect this illicit way of knowing; it is also its very mode of operation. That is, it describes the very process by which the distinction between being both "inside" and "outside" the nation is brought into critical consciousness. This standpoint, in turn, bears witness not only to the uneven enfolding of blacks into the promise of citizenship, but it also conversely enables Wright to fashion a different way of knowing that held out the possibility of transcending the deep ideological allegiances and limits imposed by national culture and belonging. This way of knowing is not an essentialist notion of a black perspective—thus, the narrator repeatedly emphasizes that Damon's reactions and understandings to events are not racially determined. Rather, it is through theorizing this social location, which leads to privileged forms of knowing—to becoming a "center of knowing." Ultimately, the epistemic status of this cultural identity does not then only expose the limits of national knowledge, but it also fills that slip in authority with the alternative agency of Cross, a figure for the black intellectual ("to think, to probe, to ask questions"), whose way of knowing could provide not only a politically empowering narrative of black experience but also an alternative, more universal political and ethical account ("a dreadful objectivity") of the common social situation.

Wright develops similar ideas in *White Man, Listen!*, a collection of essays based on speeches Wright delivered across Europe between the years 1950 to 1956 (overlapping with his writing of *The Outsider*), which address issues of the Third World and the politics of decolonization. Interestingly, the book is dedicated to Eric Williams, the West Indian statesman and author of *Capitalism and Slavery* and "to the tragic elite of Asia, Africa, and the West Indies—the lonely outsiders who exist precariously on the cliff-like margins of many cultures—those who are distrusted, maligned, criticized by left and right, Christian and pagan—who carry on their frail by indefatigable shoulders the best of two worlds" (Wright, 1957 *WML!*).

Wright's dedication evidences, first of all, his deep admiration for these new elites. Wright invested a great deal of political faith in their ability to lead and govern their decolonizing nations, advocating in his essay "Tradition and Industrialization" that the West should "abet the delicate and tragic elite of Asia and Africa" by allowing them carte blanche to bring their countries into the modern age, "even at the cost of autocratic and dictatorial methods" (Wright, 1957 *WML!* 66).[9] But beyond a political endorsement, Wright's dedication to this tragic elite is also an effort to articulate and claim coherence for an alternative way of *knowing* (a "third set of ideas"), one that could draw together a radical black and anticolonial intellectual orientation that moved beyond the emerging antinomies that defined the Cold War period. In describing these anticolonial leaders as "outsiders," bearing on their shoulders the "best of two worlds" and who are "misunderstood" and "distrusted" by both "left and right," Wright invokes the precise language he uses to describe Cross in *The Outsider*. Both subjectivities are critically constituted on the border. Here, however, that subjectivity is unfolded beyond the nation and on to the global borders of "the West." And just as the epistemic status of the cultural identity of Cross Damon—located on the borders of the nation and its constitutive outside—had enabled him to become an alternative—and threatening—source of knowledge to the existing social order within the United States, so the epistemic status of this location on the borders of "the West" engendered a different knowledge about the global transformations and conflicts taking place during the early Cold War. In this respect, Wright's dedication is not merely descriptive or politically prescriptive, but it is also *performative*; Wright is calling into being a community into which he can locate himself and through which he can more broadly imagine an alternative historical agency and epistemology capable of challenging the hegemonic narratives of the period and their prevailing signification of liberation.

In particular, Wright saw in this shared condition and consciousness of "unbelonging" a frame for a material and epistemological analysis of modernity that was being elided or kept secret by the dominant narratives and ideologies of the Cold War. Near the end of the fourth book of *The Outsider*, for instance, Cross gets into a lengthy confrontation with Communist Party leadership, in the process of which he finally reveals his understanding of what he deems to be the true underlying historical conflicts of the age.

> The ravaging scourge that tore away the veil of the myth-world was science and industry; science slowly painting another world, the real one; and industry

> uprooting man from his ancestral ritualized existence and casting him into rational schemes of living in vast impersonal cities. A split took place in man's consciousness; he began living the real world by the totems and taboos that guided him in the world of myths. . . . But that could not last long. Today we are in the midst of that crisis. (480)

Cross's prognosis about the "crisis" of modernity is one that Wright reiterated throughout his subsequent nonfiction writing, in particular in his political analysis of the decolonizing world. Wright repeatedly argued that modernity was defined by the collapse of a religious or "mythic" understanding of the world precipitated by economic modernization and industrialization (i.e., an "uprooting" of man "from his ancestral ritualized existence" [480]). In turn, Wright cast the various antinomies that framed the early Cold War as strategic obfuscations of this more fundamental and underlying "crisis" of filiation by offering new systems of what Edward Said terms *affiliation*[*s*]—that is, panaceas providing new, "more complete visions that do away with complexity, difference, and contradiction" (Said, *The World* 16, 21). The challenge for Wright, which he is working out through the character of Cross Damon (and which he thematized formally in his turn to the genre of travel writing), is to vigilantly disavow the temptation of these various affiliations and instead transvalue the condition of un-belonging into an analytic opportunity—an unassimilated and un-co-opted "angle of vision" that could serve as an emergent model of critical consciousness.

From this standpoint of un-belonging, Wright developed a deeply dialectical and radical counternarrative to Euro-American modernity. This is captured quite poignantly in Cross's discussion with the party, in which he points out that modernity and modernization are "uprooting man from his ancestral ritualized existence and *casting him into rational schemes of living in vast impersonal cities*" (my italics; 1993 *Outsider* 480). On one hand, Cross's depiction closely mirrors the logic and promise of modernity and modernization to overcome the irrationality of tradition and the "myth-worlds" of "ancestral ritualized existence." At the same time, however, Cross's portrayal evokes an "impersonal" urban landscape characterized not only by the grand designs and orderly progress of "science and industry" but also by an economic and racial logic of stratification and segregation. Or rather, it is an image that subtly intimates both simultaneously and that suggests, as such, the inextricable link between the two. In other words, rather than the progressive narrative of modernity and modernization merely overcoming the "irrationality" and traditions of race and racism, Cross's analysis here suggests—as does Wright throughout his later writing—that race and racial subordination are also *produced by* the social and economic progress of modernity.

It is in this context that Wright comes to increasingly define the meaning of blackness outside the nation in his later work, instead theorizing black racialization as part of an *international* history of labor power and imperial capitalism—that is, one that extends beyond national borders linking the United States to Europe and its empires. Wright, thus, repositioned race as a site of communal investment and political action that exceeded US political discourses and boundaries. Cross's definition, for instance, of "industry uprooting man from his ancestral ritualized existence and casting him into . . . vast impersonal cities" is not meant solely to describe the vast black migration to Northern cities within the United States (480); it also provides a language through which to reimagine or reconnect that urban migration to a vaster, more international or global frame of racialized migrations under capitalism, which in turn establishes important links between the racial subjugation and underdevelopment of blacks under American modernity with other racialized groups under that same modernity and to European colonial modernities to colonized populations globally whose experience was similarly illuminating of the shadow—or secret—of capitalist (under)development.

In the end, Wright moved the people uprooted and "cast" into the racialized landscapes of "vast impersonal cities" into the focal point from which to rewrite the history of the period and critically remap the United States into the world. "The changing physical structure of the world," declared Wright in a letter to Nehru in 1950, "as well as the historical development of modern society demand that the peoples of the world become aware of their common identity and interests. . . . Their solidarity is essential, not only in opposing oppression but also in fighting for real human progress" (qtd. in Fabre, 1973 *UQ* 387). Wright's model of un-belonging represents an effort to respond to this "demand"; it generated a subject position from which, in the context of the Cold War, Wright set out to fashion a "third way of knowing." Rather than an expression of Wright's turn away from the particular struggles of African Americans, Wright's *The Outsider* can be seen as an effort to articulate a figure of the dissident black intellectual who brings into critical consciousness (through secrecy) this shared material and psychological condition of un-belonging precipitated by a racial or imperial capitalism whose standpoint, as such, has a double address: to critique the US nation-state and its practices and to establish a "non-national" mode of belonging both "inside" and "outside" the nation through which struggles for racial justice within the United States might be recast within a broader global antiracist, anticolonial frame.

Notes

1. Wright closely followed the story of the brutal murder of the African American ex-serviceman George Dorsey in Georgia, which received a great deal of national and international attention. In her book *Cold War Civil Rights: Race and the Image of American Democracy*, Mary Dudziak writes that "in the years immediately following World War II, a wave of violence swept the South as African American veterans returned home. Lynchings and beatings of African Americans, sometimes involving law enforcement officials, were covered in the media in this country and abroad." She quotes Oliver Harrington, former war correspondent for the *Pittsburgh Courier*: "Lynchings were only part of the highly organized conspiracy to 'put the returned Negro veteran in his place'" (20).

2. See also Bontemps 16–17; Reddick 213–14; and Redding 15–16.

3. See also Hakutani, *Richard Wright* 134–54; Davis, *Black* 275; Baraka 145–47; Fabre, *Unfinished Quest*; Hazel Rowley 400–415; Lynch, "Haunted by Innocence" 255–56; Adell 379–94.

4. All references are to the restored text established by the Library of America, introduction by Maryemma Graham (New York: HarperPerennial, 1993), 109.

5. Fanon discusses counterhegemony and the role of culture in his theory of national consciousness; see "On National Culture" in *Wretched of the Earth.*

6. In *Parting the Waters*, Taylor Branch writes, "FBI agents spotted white Communists by their ease and politeness around Negroes, or by the simple social fact that they socialized with Negroes at all." (This "clue" also suggests how connected commitments to racial justice had become with political subversion.)

7. Passed in 1940, the Smith Act, also known as the Alien Registration Act, made it an offense to "advocate or belong to a group that advocated the violent overthrow of the government." Aside from revoking passports and the threat of prison sentences, the act also required registration of all aliens living in the United States.

8. Cross will make virtually the same point in his response to Ely Houston's claim that it is not a crime to "believe that something or other ought to be done in society." "I beg your pardon, sir. In my opinion, it is right *there* where the real crime is. . . . A man today who believes that he cannot live by the articles of faith of his society is a criminal and you know it, even though Congress has not gotten around to making such into law" (1993 *Outsider* 517).

9. Reference is to "Tradition and Industrialization," *WML!* \This is the very class, of course, that Fanon will continue to denounce (see his "Pitfalls of National Consciousness," *Wretched of the Earth* [New York: Grove Press, 1961]).

Lying, Deception, Truth-Telling, and Self-Negation: Ironies and Failures of Nation-Building in Wright's African Parody *Savage Holiday*

—VIRGINIA WHATLEY SMITH—

America has never been far from the thoughts of Richard Wright, even in the most distant parts of the world. In fact, one can say that he consistently postulates through narrative techniques the question, "What if those American civic rules have been built upon lies, deceptions, and untruths—especially for racially advantaged whites or racially disadvantaged blacks?" This query strikes at the heart of American nationalist discourse. In his preexile American-based writings, Wright has placed the subjects of lies and deceptions as focal topics in his crime fictions. He uses irony in the titles *Uncle Tom's Children* (1938) and *Native Son* (1940) to signify upon the anticitizenship treatments that American whites have parceled out unequally on a daily basis to African Americans.

The subject of Western, nationalist discourse and its underlying corrosive elements arises again in Wright's exile publications, starting with his travel books *Black Power* (1954), and then *The Color Curtain* (1955) and *Pagan Spain* (1957) (see Wright, *Three Books from Exile* 611–812). However, he begins to interconnect his nonfictional and fictional works and shifts the racial perspective while writing from his European base and also treats a peripheral theme of "whiteness discourse" commonly in his black-centered writings and as a central topic in *Savage Holiday*. He probes and exposes its semiotic ambiguities and contradictions by means of Erskine Fowler, the white male protagonist. Fowler discovers his protective status of belonging to a brotherhood of professional, nationwide insurance underwriters to be fraudulent, meaningless, and absurd once he becomes useless and forced into retirement. The reversed racial perspective is a prescient move by Wright, for he parodies intratextually the stock tropes, themes, and scenes relational to the "blackness discourse" embedded in *Black Power*. The parodying enables him to expose the contradictory meanings of "paternalism" in the American insurance industry, for once Fowler is deposed in an in-house coup and disconnected from his masculine base, his world suddenly collapses, and he feels as if he has become an involuntary, Derridean "citizen of the world"—a man without a country and a refugee without a nation (*Savage Holiday* [*SH*] 4). Ultimately, Fowler's suppressed guilt and fear over a haunting mother figure force him into a new game of nation-building that, in contrast to Kwame Nkrumah's actions in Africa, impels Fowler to craft a social alliance founded upon deception, lies, and criminal activities in order to reestablish a predictable, fixed, and certain identity in America's destabilizing, postmodern world.

White Power versus Black Power: The Art of Salesmanship and the Gullible Consumer

Consistently in his fictions and nonfictions of the 1930s and 1940s, Richard Wright has written about the economic struggles of black Americans living in an empowered, white-majority society. Readers who approach Wright's productions of the 1950s will still discover the author's stock rhetorical devices and themes embedded in the crime fictions or autobiographical writings of this decade, even though Wright had been in voluntary exile from America and living in France since 1947. As before, his subject focus and plot narratives are typically male-centered, patrifocally governed, fraternally oriented, and masculine-revolutionary driven, thereby following the styles of other masculinist writers of the 1920s and 1930s whom Wright studied as an apprentice writer. *Savage Holiday* fits these patterns, but with a major difference. Similar to the occasion of Richard Wright's explication of the words, images, and meanings of the term *Negro* in his 1941 photographic text *12 Million Black Voices: A Folk History of the Negro in the United States* (*12MBV* 30), he again engages in interrogating racial semiotics but this time relational to the term *Caucasian* in *Savage Holiday*.

To illustrate, in *Savage Holiday* as well as in his other works, Wright sets out to prove that racism is transcendent; it acquires ambiguities of meanings across time and space. Take, for instance, his magnification of blackness discourse in his 1954 nonfictional travelogue *Black Power* and then, by means of parody, writing and publishing in the same year its obverse side as the whiteness discourse in his 1954 novel *Savage Holiday*. A number of significant themes in *Black Power* function as related experiences of the white protagonist in *Savage Holiday*. In the words of James Snead, "the very model of linear development—and the physical plane upon which life unfolds, [are] characterized by general recursiveness and repetition" in one's life or culture (59). As Wright illustrates, themes of linear development in life and culture also recur in the lives of people separated racially, temporally, and globally. Readers need to recognize the shifts and transformations from Africa to America.

A key theme in *Black Power* is Kwame Nkrumah's efforts at building a unified nation-state in opposition to the existing, splintered tribal-run governments in the Gold Coast. His task is huge, and Wright inserts his salesman-consumer trope to illustrate its politicized nature. Nkrumah must act as a salesman to convince his people—the consumers—about changing their allegiances from a kinship group ruled by a tribal chieftain to that of one man—potentially him—as the new president of the Gold Coast, to be renamed Ghana. Wright's alter ego Richard is the central intelligence of *Black Power* and eyewitness to history who does not spare quoting others while inserting his own reactions to events. Nkrumah, Richard notes, is very perceptive about how he and his Convention People's Party (CPP) officials can persuade Gold Coasters to adopt his platform. Over the next few days at day and night meetings in Accra and outlying districts, Richard witnesses Nkrumah's potent ability to persuade the masses.

Having fully engaged in self-studies of psychology since the 1930s, Wright, in the 1950s, had continued to broaden his knowledge about human behavior arising from his contacts with French intellectuals. An excerpt from Sigmund Freud's work *Totem and Taboo* in the "Part 1: Anxiety" section of *Savage Holiday* partially accounts for the novel's title and the protagonist's behavior. It says that "in the very nature of a holiday there is excess; the holiday mood is brought about by the release of what is forbidden" (*SH* 9). These references to "holiday," "excess," "release," and "forbidden" also suggest the heightened tension that arises when humans like Nkrumah and his allies stage illegal activities against the British.

Indeed, Wright the master craftsman is writing about "nationhood allegiance" as a weapon of power in *Black Power.* And again he is revisiting history by alluding to, undermining, and contradicting one of the most popular, post-Columbus, European psychological studies on mind-body theories published by John Locke in his 1695 "Essay Concerning Human Understanding." The philosopher explains how humans become inscribed with knowledge by means of "experience" derived from signals of the senses. He considers the lower-order "SENSATIONS"—sight, touch, smell, hearing, taste—associated with responses of the body as being subordinate to "REFLECTIONS" or the rational principles of the mind that organize singular or repeated experiences and teach one how to judge good or bad behavior (635). Following Locke, other white philosophers and statesmen seized upon his theories to classify the "national characteristics" or physical differences between Caucasians, Africans, and Mongolians. The most biased statements that claimed the nonwhite groups to be intellectually, biologically, genetically, and physically inferior to whites were published by David Hume of England (49); Immanuel Kant of Germany (53); Georges Leopold Cuvier of France (54), and Thomas Jefferson of the United States (45). They took Locke's mind-body theory to categorize races and classes of people in order to enact social, class, religious, and political policies regulating the behaviors of citizens and noncitizens. Always the "Negro" Africans on the Great Chain of Being would rank just one rung above the animals. Nkrumah, however, has cleverly seized upon the cultural practice in Africa of oral argumentation to reach his audiences and to correct untruths spread by colonizers.

Having witnessed how potent blackness discourse can be wielded, Wright reprises Nkrumah's salesman-consumer strategies as the primary methods utilized in *Savage Holiday,* with the setting now being in America. In this fictional parody of *Black Power,* Wright also inserts a detached, outside narrator who reflects all activities through Fowler's point of view. By means of Fowler's limited perspective, Wright then explores the semiotic ambiguities of whiteness discourse and how the stereotypical meanings of "savage" and "civilized" repeat and/or transform when factors of Caucasian heritage, philosophies of nationhood, and principles of citizenship become intertwined. Additionally, having set *Savage Holiday* in the West and specifically America's New York City, Wright utilizes irony to illustrate how the top level of white patriarchal power in a putatively "civilized society" operates more ruthlessly than does the bottom tier of black patriarchal leadership that Nkrumah is inaugurating on the Gold Coast.

For example, Wright portrays Fowler's America as being a developed country; his is already industrialized and on the way to becoming technologically advanced in the 1950s. The disparate competitive corporations forming the giant insurance industry exemplify how the chain of power would descend from top to bottom in an African corporate structure. It would be similar to Nkrumah's becoming the president of the newly forged nation-state of Ghana (which actually did occur) and then his delegating power to those subordinate-level officials whom Wright had met and then discussed in his chapter in *Black Power* called "The Brooding Ashanti." Nkrumah's campaign strategies to unify disparate, competitive Gold Coast entities—the Ashanti Empire, the Akan states, and the other subordinate provinces or districts—actually mimes the pyramidal structures of American corporations (*Black Power* [*BP*] 291). His nation-building efforts have placed him in the role of a salesman, according to Wright, but not only that of selling a product called "freedom under Nkrumah" to ordinary citizen-consumers but also to those tribal chieftains whom Nkrumah has disempowered, but yet to whom the people maintain their allegiances owing to birthright. As Wright shows, each structural level of a tribal government overseen by a chief corresponds to a large corporation overseen by an American president who must perform supervisory tasks to ensure that nothing endangers the business's infrastructure inclusive of the lower-level unit managers who are responsible for meeting the company's goals.

According to Wright, Richard, the admitted westerner, logician, atheist, and skeptic, sees one obstacle for Nkrumah, which becomes a central argument in

Savage Holiday. If Nkrumah sticks to political ideology guided by "reason" and avoids the pitfalls of "irrational" appeal based upon religious-oriented ancestral traditions—the very heart and passion of birthright identity for Gold Coast Africans—the leader could succeed in his nationalist endeavors. Richard, with great boldness and even audacity, issues such a warning to Nkrumah at the end of *Black Power* by suggesting that Nkrumah should adhere to a stoic, "militarized" form of leadership (415, 419). Moreover, to prove Richard's point, Wright deliberately writes a fictional parody about the pitfalls of such "passion"-driven, errant thinking to illustrate in *Savage Holiday* how the mixing of reason and passion or mind and body oppositions can destabilize fixed identities.

Liars and Deceivers: White Power and the Pitfalls of Nationalism and Patriarchal Allegiance

Stephen Hunsaker supplies some working definitions of *nation* as it is being reconceived in contemporary discussions. He states: "There are myriad academic definitions of 'nation,' but the importance of territory, history, and some shared meanings of self-definitions (whether linguistic, religious, or ancestral) are common to all" (2). This sense of belonging experienced by people with a shared history or common cause is exactly how Fowler in the 1950s had conceived of his identity and totally associated it with his employment. The opening setting of *Savage Holiday* at the Jefferson Banquet Salon in one of New York's finest, midtown hotels is festive like Nkrumah's rallies on the Gold Coast. And like Nkrumah, Erskine Fowler is the honoree but with a difference. Wright contrasts Nkrumah's voluntary, upward career move with Fowler's downward, forced retirement/termination at age forty-three from Longevity Life Insurance Company. Contrary to Nkrumah's all-black participants, all of Fowler's are white. Wright also repositions Nkrumah's seat of power as being held by the company president Warren, who is leading the festivities. He even addresses the celebrants in paternalistic language as if all belonged to the same tribal collective like that of Africans: "Brothers and sisters, . . . Erskine Fowler looked upon Longevity Life as his family!" (12). And, "Brothers and sisters . . . as . . . head of this family, . . . Erskine Fowler has served us well" (13). Similar to Nkrumah's Westend rally, Wright portrays the president's action of establishing a bond of intimacy with the crowd by his inspiring all members to rise as if "one man," one collective, and "vent to prolonged cheering" (14). He calls for no oath of allegiance to a human as did the Africans to Nkrumah, but their unified responses suggest their undivided loyalty to their company leader.

Wright positions Fowler's platform speech as a success because Wright utilizes his strange/familiar oppositional tropes to compare Richard's reception from an African audience with Fowler's reception from an American one. Instead of being a stranger, he is a familiar face and displays emotion when he half-whispers, "'Thank you, Mr. Warren'" (14). In addition, he receives a burst of applause, shouts, and whistles of encouragement, contrary to the audience's silent reception of Richard's stoic body posture and overintellectualized speech. Fowler, like Nkrumah, bonds intimately with his "brothers and sisters," and reacts emotionally like Africans: "Truly, my heart's full to overflowing" (16). His "family" ties to Longevity Life have provided him with a collective identity like that of Gold Coast Africans to their tribes (2008 *BP* 119; see Mbiti 78). Never, until now, has Fowler felt alone since, in the words of President Warren, Fowler had grown "up with a growing company, becoming a Mason, a Rotarian, a Sunday School Superintendent . . ." (*SH* 12). Fowler had felt connected to a kinship group, from which his corporate links reached into the community as well as into national, state, city, and local political units, educational entities, fraternal organizations, and religious groups. His affiliation with a nationwide corporation also had netted him capitalist gains: his rise from lower to middle class, his acquisition of property, and his regard by society as a man of high moral standards. His is the ideal blending of politics with religion, which Nkrumah is striving to attain.

As usual, however, Wright complicates matters by illustrating the contradictions between appearances and reality. Contrary to Richard's peaceable, eyewitness meetings with Nkrumah and his aides or allies at their offices, Fowler earlier had faced a closed-door frontal assault without witnesses. Nkrumah had informed Richard that five years previously, such a public gathering would have been implausible because of fears of retaliation from the British. Fowler, too, would never have fathomed the nature of his backdoor meeting with the president and vice president as being plausible and resulting in his being verbally denounced and then dethroned of his position. Rage causes Fowler to perceive the public festivities to be no more than an orchestrated performance, which, more on a positive note, Richard had watched Nkrumah repeat over and over again at rallies. And Fowler, like Nkrumah being surrounded by emblems of national unity (flags, streamers, paraphernalia, etc.) connoting meanings of "insiderism," "patriotism," "loyalty," and "fraternalism," contrarily considers them to be signs of hypocrisy. In Nkrumah's Africa and Fowler's America, such words have suddenly become destabilized, arbitrary, and contradictory in their meanings. A totally negative experience at Fowler's backroom meeting, the president had informed him that he was "deadwood," "old fashioned," a "washout" and "no longer useful to the company" (22).

Wright clearly stresses in both works the psychological reactions of groups or individuals to life-altering changes. Fowler's feeling of being destabilized because of a life-changing action is akin to Gold Coasters facing a new form of government. The transformation of old ideas and/or acquisition of new values are difficult tasks for them after having practiced thousand-year-old traditions on a regular basis. Altering and "stripping away" fixed ideas and customs are difficult tasks for Nkrumah, the agent of change, but he does so initially by disempowering the tribal chiefs, starting first with himself. Altruism, according to Wright, is not the Nkrumah-type position taken by President Warren when he makes a selfish decision to make his company more technologically progressive by hiring his own son. Thus, the "stripping" of customs had been staged more viciously in America, and caused Fowler to experience a pernicious side effect of rage. His had been a Nkrumah-type character assassination similar to the occasion of Nkrumah's public, verbal attacks upon the qualifications of his opponents. As Hunsaker notes: "Although national unity is an act of imagination, there is no guarantee that a group of potential compatriots all will imagine the community uniformly" (4). Clearly, Nkrumah, Busia, and Danquah have different views on how to achieve national unity, but Fowler is totally eliminated from the conversation. His is not so much of "us" (the three African elites versus "them" (the British colonial empire) as it is "he" (Fowler) versus "them" (the president and his corporate ally).

As Wright indicates, this polarizing event has epochal proportions. It is the historical moment when Fowler consciously becomes aware that a memorable occasion has taken place—a paradigm shift in his worldview that words and meanings may be binary oppositions—especially when the meaning of "compatriot" had suddenly undergone a hermeneutic fracturing and recodification. All things formerly "familiar," routine, and certain had become "strange" and destabilized in that back room. But has Fowler been gullible about progress in a changing world? As Wright depicts in opposition to Nkrumah's case, Fowler appears to be clueless about the vulture-type competitiveness now being acted out at the upper level between and among old executives and new employees. Rules have obviously changed in the company's policies that have escaped Fowler's notice and/or foresight over their priorities. It was the president's secretary, in fact, who, in a verbal blunder, had conveyed a company "secret" to Fowler that he was being retired in order to make room for President Warren's twenty-three-year-old, newly engaged, Harvard-educated son. What Fowler has lacked in youth and formal education, the son immediately possesses. He is bringing modern "scientific theory" to the art of salesmanship—the kind of postmodernist education and vision that, like Nkrumah's, are requisite for nations and corporations to advance in the technologically competitive world of the 1950s.

In this opening scene, there are two value systems colliding: "nationhood" discourse pertaining to job security for the loyal, Longevity Life worker such as Fowler, and "birthright" discourse relational to personal family and community beliefs akin to the tribal values of Nkrumah's Gold Coast people. Here, Wright is delving into new theories because of his alliances with Jean Paul Sartre and other French existentialist thinkers during the 1950s. In his essay on "The Bad Faith of Whiteness," Robert Birt provides some basic explanations about the distinctions between lying and truth telling. Birt paraphrases the statements of Jean Paul Sartre in *Being and Nothingness*: "'The human being,' according to Sartre, is 'the one who can take negative attitudes with respect to himself.'" And building upon Sartre's ideas, Birt advances his own theory of selfhood: "This is a possibility inherent to human consciousness. Consciousness may direct its negation towards others, as in the form of resentment or lying" (55–56).

Obviously, Wright is exploring the gray area between lying and truth telling, both dependent upon an individual's perspective. The transposing of values occurs in Fowler's conscious responses to events of "negation towards others . . . in the form of resentment or lying" because of his forced retirement. The president had subtly but skillfully recodified the semantics and the traditional meaning of "family" that Fowler and other Longevity Life employees had always parroted. It formerly meant upholding personal allegiances to work-related strangers as opposed to blood-lineage allegiances like those of Africans to their clan families. Nkrumah, in fact, had been attempting to introduce a new nationalist concept of family akin to President Warren's that would require specific tribal units to bond with nonrelated tribal groups. His nationalist platform would classify everyone on the same level. As far as Longevity Life, the cross-tribal blending has been the operating mode of the family's infrastructure and its conception as the bonding of strangers in a nationwide conglomerate. But suddenly the president has rescripted codes and devised a new meaning of family according to blood kinship ties by hiring his own son. In the corporate world, such a process is known as *nepotism*, a term that Fowler has not grasped.

Kwame Anthony Appiah in his chapter on "Rooted Cosmopolitanism" from his book *The Ethics of Identity* provides some cogent points on distinctions between "nationalism" and "cosmopolitanism" that will help to explain Fowler's bifurcated identity problems. Suddenly, nepotism, birthright, and blood lineage have become the company's modern-day hiring policies. Until now, Fowler's work relations have had no biological connections; it has been a different experience for Africans who have been shaped by their collective tribal governances relating to blood kinship relations. But now Fowler has plunged from his nonbiological nation-state collective and seemingly been cast asunder to fend for himself. He is not a sophisticated global traveler aware of the ethnic diversity of the world. To the contrary, he finds himself grouped in the category of a rootless man or involuntary, "cosmopolitan" citizen of the world unbound to any cause other than his own selfhood. This solitary distinction would be conceived as a compliment for well-traveled statesmen such as the African American ex-slave Frederick Douglass who, in celebrating Emancipation Day yearly held in the West Indies, applauded his self-determined identity as a freethinking, unencumbered former American slave. Like most worldly cosmopolitans, he could fight for global humanism and freedom for all oppressed people, but still express some personal allegiance to a special group—in this case, oppressed African Americans (*Life and Times* 505).

Wright implies that, as a company leader, President Warren has been exposed to global travel, if not global capitalism. If he were to be considered a "cosmopolitan," he would be more like what Appiah calls a "biased cosmopolitan" (224). Thomas Jefferson, for instance, presented himself as a statesman and globally conscious humanist, but he could not tolerate "Negroes" whom he considered to be inferior to whites (47). President Warren, in Wright's depiction, has not expanded his corporation to include blacks since none are noted in the novel. For certain, he is more of a "nationalist" than a cosmopolitan. In this nationalist grouping, he has, without warning, blended what Appiah calls the "moral partiality" associated with a person who belongs to a nonbiological group of strangers with the cosmopolitan mode of "ethical partiality" associated with a person who belongs to a tribal group because of blood kinship ties. Like Nkrumah in his synergizing of politics with religion, President Warren has synergized "moral partiality" with "ethical partiality." In the former case, one feels that one "ought" to protect a national cause; in the latter, one feels that he or she "should" protect blood kinship affairs (Appiah 224). President Warren no longer feels a moral obligation that he "ought" to protect Fowler.

Wright stresses that the president has bypassed the old traditions of self-education or field experience for the new-age criteria of formal education. His biological son is a member of the new, elite corps of young, educated executives who are equivalent to the super-educated, African elite of which Nkrumah is a member. Fowler's "moral partiality" to Longevity Life had driven all of his actions for thirty years; it had worked successfully until his showdown with the president. Unfortunately, Fowler has suffered from class-limited short-sightedness because he had not been regularly exposed to the sophisticated thinking of the corporate elite. He, like Wright's other myopic characters, has maladjustment problems and new fears of death from living in a vacuous world. The opening scene reflects his disorientation. And Wright has expressed Fowler's fear as that of Freudian "Anxiety"—the title for part 1 of *Savage Holiday*. Owing to his sudden state of becoming a refugee without a nation, he is more akin to the type of cosmopolitan whom Jacques Derrida in "Cosmopolitanism and Forgiveness" attributes to refugees in/from war-torn countries in postmodern societies whose lives as rootless, stateless people are bleak and meaningless (27–30, 306).

Wright is writing America in current times. Like Nkrumah's, Fowler's life is being acted out in the post–World War II era of the 1950s when Russian space travel, technologies, and Communist policies are supportive of Africa but threatening to America. And somehow Fowler, unlike Nkrumah, has not kept abreast of global changes or new corporate practices because of Fowler's limited position of being a lower-level, field salesman. It takes all of Fowler's energy and willpower not to scream to the audience that the banquet is a "farce, a put up job!" (20). Instead, Fowler does what Nkrumah's rally participants do not. He breaks his oath of allegiance to the president that he would stay for the entire ceremony and flees through a side door (20).

The flight scene is a typical rhetorical device in Wright's crime fictions and nonfictions in which his criminal hero flees from a misdeed. But in the first few pages of *Savage Holiday*, Fowler does not appear to have committed a misdeed or hard-core criminal act other than being blind about the corporate world. Yet, in attempting to avoid another confrontation with his associates, Fowler takes a "side stairway" out of the hotel, and in exiting, he "[creeps] down the stairs like a criminal" (22). Why the guilt of criminality when no murder has been committed? Or has Fowler acted criminally? Certainly Nkrumah is acting criminally by blatantly opposing the British at his rallies. But Fowler has done nothing but to abet the side of the insurance industry in dealing with his lying and deceitful customers. In some respects, he even has held contempt for them and even considered his personification of "Insurance" as a "sluttish woman," "a greasy-faced Italian," or a murderous old woman (28). None of these are positive images of clients, which suggests that Fowler has felt repugnance for his customers. Female, male, young, old, sensual, sadistic, white, or ethnic, Fowler secretly has perceived "Insurance" as being a lying, immoral, androgynous, and chameleonlike personification.

Fowler's consciousness-raising, to follow Birt's theory of lying and self-deception, reveals some darker sides of his character contrary to his self-constructed pious public image. He has managed to outmaneuver deceptive customers, but at the same time, he has been complicit in corruption since he never reported any illicit practices to law-enforcement agencies. But in this consciousness-raising session of finding fault and casting blame, Fowler does exactly what Birt asserts about human behavior: "Consciousness may direct its negation towards others, as in the form of resentment or lying" (55–56). Fowler sees no fault in himself, but readily casts blame on President Warren, who not only hired him but now has literally retired him and figuratively "fired him." He sees the president as a potent opponent who, similar to Nkrumah's callous action of dethroning useless tribal chieftains, has cast him asunder like a voided insurance policy.

Again, Wright portrays environmental conditions in the sales industry to be as predatory and savage in the 1950s as it had been throughout society in the 1930s at the start of his own career. Fowler's experience is just a continuum of the vicious, competitive, and carnivorous nature of American capitalism and the nonprofiting, victimized poor. A difference in the new conflict involving

Wright's protagonists in his exile writings is their ascensions to middle-class levels. In Fowler's specific case of being among Wright's class-elite protagonists, he has climbed the ladder to economic success at the high price of becoming trapped in the exploitative tactics of American capitalism to generate sales continually and to make money for the corporation. His industrial-era sales tactics requiring human contact have been discarded in favor of young Warren's Lockean-type rational and technologically advanced methods of salesmanship.

Wright parodies other elements of rudimentary psychology occurring in *Black Power* to show distinctions between Western and Southern thoughts on good and evil. Again, it involves human nature and issues of epistemology, or how one knows the good or evil inner workings of the human heart in terms of selling a product or philosophy. Africans do not engage in Freudian psychology, but Nkrumah, a native-born Gold Coast African, easily understands the human hearts of his people, their sufferings, and their desires for freedom. He is selling new ideas to his disciples that blend tribal religion with modern technology; his platform of progress includes uplifting their economic conditions as the country becomes capitalistic and more globally competitive. On the other hand, Fowler, a native-born American and a member of the dominant, privileged Caucasian racial group, has never had to struggle with developing a sales strategy to win over customers. As an elementary-school-educated white man akin to sparsely educated or illiterate Gold Coast Africans, he, starting out at age thirteen, had cultivated a Freudian notion of the uncanny—an "intuitive" knowledge of how to "read" a customer's actions—and then developed a mantra on his philosophy: "You just couldn't learn out of books, [no] matter how thick and profound they were. You just had to know in your heart that man was a guilty creature" (30). His mantra echoes Nkrumah's remarks castigating Busia and Danquah for possessing too much book knowledge and too "many degrees" for their simplistic, illiterate audiences to grasp. Fowler at the grassroots level has relied on his Lockean intuition as his method of understanding the behavior of his clients. However, he never thought deception would include those white men at the top level of the corporation—a basic knowledge that a formally educated person like Nkrumah would have learned from sociology courses.

No matter how intelligent or educated Wright's characters become, they still possess acute sensory/intuitive skills and a few even become super-intellectuals like Nkrumah. However, they all brood and/or meditate. As Wright clearly illustrates, these periods of introspective musings involving a moral dilemma for the black Wrightean hero most often occur at night. Certainly, Nkrumah speaks openly in his daytime speeches and nighttime rallies about the problems and fears of defying the colonial enemy. However, it is Richard the eyewitness who is recording and translating events for the reader through his consciousness. This is the reason that Wright calls the work's subtitle *A Record of Reactions in a*

Land of Pathos. Examples are Richard's numerous interior monologues or asides throughout the travelogue. Instances include his meetings with Justice Thomas and statesmen Busia and Danquah. Moreover, his long subsection titled "The Brooding Ashanti" exemplifies how Wright likes to illustrate the arbitrariness of a word and its contradictory meanings throughout his texts or full body of works. Fowler's conscious "brooding" takes place at 11:00 p.m. at night because, like Nkrumah's Cape Coast afternoon rallies, Fowler's late-afternoon showdown, evening banquet, and then sudden departure had lasted until late at night. Now as a rootless man, Fowler meditates on his situation, which normally occurs in the blackness of night for Wright's black protagonists. But being suddenly socially "tarnished," Fowler the nightwalker does acquire some clarity about his misguided appraisal of the president. However, his own tarnished past causes a greater religious, moral dilemma to await Fowler.

Nation-Building Contravened: Gender Equality as Matriarchal Revenge

A politically motivated religious, moral dilemma about the status of women in the new Ghana has not been a problem for Kwame Nkrumah in his nation-building efforts. By contrast, Erskine Fowler has made a major blunder by repeating policy, and has deliberately avoided elevating women in the workplace or allowing them into his life. His recent fall from grace has mentally cast him to a moral low after being denationalized, de-tribalized, and detached from an established insurance clan. His condition is worse than disempowered tribal chiefs; at least they still have roots. But Fowler, now without any employment base, feels shorn of an ontological identity and has no idea of how to fill the void in his life until a series of mishaps involving a child and mother demand that he attach himself to a network of people for self-serving purposes.

Robert Birt's comments on the distinctions between acts of "bad faith" and bald-faced acts of lying help to describe Fowler's dilemma as an involuntary retiree. Says Birt: "Bad faith is self-deception, a lie to the self." Fowler has been engaging in intentional self-deception, even while working at Longevity Life. Birt further elucidates on this matter: "The intent of bad faith is precisely to deceive oneself while also denying that intention. The person 'who practices bad faith,'" continues Birt in his paraphrasing of Sartre, "'is holding a displeasing truth or presenting as truth a pleasing untruth.' *In bad faith it is from myself that I am hiding the truth*" (56; emphasis mine). Earlier, Fowler had crept down the stairs of the hotel as though he were a criminal. Now, Wright has employed Freudian psychology and new theories of French existentialism to reveal the "truthful" reasons motivating Fowler's ontological crisis and stealthy behavior.

Readers should wonder why, after the first nineteen pages, Wright's novel goes on for 193 pages more to complete part 1, and then parts 2 and 3? The reason is that Wright delves deeply into Freudian psychology to expose the hypocrisy of American religious principles and moral claims by means of Fowler. But, Wright does not stray far from his archetypal themes or plot devices, either. The transformation of the central male character into a criminal is typical in Wright's fictions and nonfictions, especially in terms of sociological and psychological events involving race, gender, sexuality, religion, and morality, and their interconnections. Nkrumah, a male, is not innocent in *Black Power* as he blatantly engages in breaking British laws in order to sever their imperialistic stranglehold over his people. *Savage Holiday* repeats the threat of prison that Nkrumah is facing as the darkening moral issue for Fowler, another male, but his outcome differs. To demonstrate the complexity of Fowler's trajectory, Wright deconstructs and entangles the socioreligious and moral aspects of "whiteness" discourse in order to expose its "tainted," "stained," "darkened," or "blackened" components within its infrastructure. Gradations of shading difference are exemplified when Richard had examined the varying hues of brown in the palms of Africans to destroy assumptions that their melanin coloring is a monotone.

Hence, an exterior marker can connote covert meanings associated with an interior moral flaw. Nkrumah, a black man, has presented himself overtly to his people as having a tarnished, lawbreaking moral base, for he positions his anticolonial actions as having a paradoxical, purist motive—to free his people. As a West African, he does not accept Western definitions of good or evil that the British colonizers have foisted upon Africans to subjugate them by claiming that their dark skin coloring marks them as being holistically "bad," "savage," "inferior" people. By dismantling these demeaning British color and moral codes, Wright equally demonstrates the same kind of negativity existing in Anglo-American whiteness discourse. Fowler's loss of his employment identity causes him inner turmoil over some deep-seated, dark, "monstrous and hoary recollection" that he has long suppressed. His consciousness awakening indicates that Fowler, in the words of Birt, has been morally deceitful by hiding a "displeasing truth" about himself. The narrator states:

> Work had . . . made him a stranger to a part of himself that he feared and wanted never to know. At some point in his childhood he had assumed toward himself the role of a policeman, had accused himself, had hauled himself brutally into the court of his conscience, had arraigned himself before the bar of his fears, and had found himself guilty and had, finally and willingly, locked himself up in a prison-cage of toil. (*SH* 32–33)

Fowler's thoughts are replete with impure, "criminal discourse"—"policeman," "court," "arraign," "bar," "guilty," "sentence," and "prison-cage." Now that his metaphorical Longevity Life safety barrier is gone, "the reality that had so frightened him was so completely himself and his own past life that he could only feel it, suffer it; he couldn't know it, master it" (22). He has been practicing "bad faith" and lying to himself, but now his dark secret about his childhood has begun to surface in his consciousness.

Wright titillates readers with a few references to suggest that Fowler's psychological problem is related to his Freudian, Oedipal feelings for his own mother. But Wright clouds that full revelation with a number of impediments and digressions related to gender, sexuality, and nudity—all interconnected to moral issues—that Fowler must surmount because life no longer is following the linear plane that he had so carefully plotted. The night scene at home in bed illuminates all of Fowler's contradictions, hypocrisies, and lies to himself. While he feels pride at never having "dishonored" his virgin bed with a "stray woman of pleasure," his body sends another signal as his libido becomes aroused. He feels both attraction and repulsion for little Tony Blake's mother, known in the building to be sexually licentious, after once seeing her clad in sparse underwear. On Fowler's puritanical scale, Mabel Blake does not qualify for the label of *virgin* in the virgin-whore paradigm, so it is clear that he has set that bar for himself.

However, forthcoming incidents reveal Fowler's self-delusions about his virtuousness. Wright's characters normally experience two to five minor blunders before they commit their gravest infraction and fall into hard-core criminality. Fowler makes two errors in judgment that end up having grave consequences. The first concerns the incident of his stepping naked into his hallway the next morning to retrieve his Sunday paper, only to have the door slam firmly shut behind him. The second concerns his attempt to resolve his nakedness quandary by scaling his balcony. He frightens little Tony Blake because the child had never seen a hairy naked man, causing the boy to accidentally fall backward over his balcony to his death twelve stories below. Both of these scenes Wright extracts from incidents involving Richard's phobias and fears about sexuality and nudity en route to or land-based in Africa as partial aspects of Fowler's character. The first relates to Richard's visit to a house of prostitution in Las Palmas, the Canary Islands, with Judge Thomas and Mr. Togoland, another African. Richard, a married man, is technically sexually impure; however, he seems to be the most virtuous of his tarnished companions, and thus the symbolic Virgin between and among the literal Whores—the lecherous males and the solicitous Spanish prostitutes (2008 *BP*). Fowler shares similar opinions about sluttish women, especially Mabel Blake, and complements Richard's prudishness in this area. Additionally, Richard's phobia about sex, disease, and nudity as forms of impurity surface again once he arrives in Accra when, time after time, he witnesses the natives openly displaying themselves in various states of nudity or seminudity in public. Fowler's phobia arises when he finds himself in a state of public nudity in the hallway of his apartment building. Wright's obfuscating, encoding, and decoding assumptions about the morality of gender, nudity, and sexuality in private and public spaces are the reasons that critics have attacked Wright's representations in *Black Power*. Critic Ngwarsungu Chiwengo charges Wright with prejudicial reporting since his alter ego Richard continually looks at Africans through a tainted "Western gaze" (Chiwengo 23, 27). The location is near the equator, and the black inhabitants cope with the tropical heat by dressing in light or no attire. They feel no embarrassment about exposing their bodies except when Westerners like Richard gaze at them. On another occasion, Richard is amazed at seeing a young girl bathing nude in public (2008 *BP* 70).

Richard's assessments on nudity stem from his overall perception of Africans as being natural people close to the earth. These are the reasons that Richard often compares their skin colorings, the palms of their hands, or their dirt-covered bodies to the various hues and tones of the African soil (91). They seem to be part of nature. While Chiwengo perceives this latter comparison and many others of being exemplary of Wright's offensive views of Africans as being "savage" people in the mode of many racist, white Westerners (33), scholar Yoshinobu Hakutani has another perspective. He construes Richard's descriptions in the scene of dirt-covered bodies, as well as Richard's other remarks about body discourse, as being examples of Wright's "primal" theory about human beings who live in rural areas as having remained in the most pure, natural states of existence because they have not been corrupted by social, educational, or political policies (Hakutani, "Richard Wright's Haiku" 5–6).

Wright modifies his primordial trope in *Black Power* as Fowler's experience in *Savage Holiday* to illustrate Western hypocrisy, false racial labelings, and skewed morality. Fowler's body is massively covered with black hair on his head, torso, arms, and legs, which makes him appear like a carbon copy of early *Homo sapiens* as they evolved into primitive, modern man in southern Africa. Wright, here, is actually vindicating Africans. Placed in a Western setting out of time and space, African history and culture collide in a civilized world. Fowler appears to embody apelike characteristics that European Americans have cast as aspersions against black people since the claims of eighteenth-century French naturalist scientist Georges Leopold Cuvier (54). And, without doubt, Fowler the Virgin does not appear to be virginal in the hallway scene. He knows that Westerners are morally intolerant of illicit sexuality. It is a tabooed practice—Mabel Blake being the example—and the reason that Wright has invoked Freud and his ideas from *Totem and Taboo* to illustrate Fowler's hypocritical thoughts about nudity and sexuality. Previously, Fowler had expressed his condescension of women by characterizing his personification of "Insurance" as a "sluttish woman" (*SH* 28) and associating the two-dimensional thing with Mabel Blake.

She, too, is in the sales industry, but her product for profit is her body. But now in the hallway scene, Fowler, the naked, primitive-looking, Bible-espousing Christian, knows that if he is spotted by any of the tenants, his nakedness would be grounds for his arrest on morals charges and being labeled as a homosexual and religious hypocrite.

Wright the Marxist has continually condemned religion as a form of "irrational thinking" and a false panacea deluding black culture. *Savage Holiday* is no exception. Fowler is in a moral dilemma; his nakedness quandary is about as "irrational" an action that any Sunday-school teacher could conceive. Fowler has now caused an accidental death and is, therefore, an actual criminal. And as he descends deeper into criminality, he demonstrates the art of "bad faith" through lying and self-deception in the hope that he can escape detection. Nkrumah does place his rebel followers at risk to criminal charges, but Richard reports no loss of life attributable to the leader. For this reason, Wright begins to signify intratextually upon materials from his other criminal works for scene developments in *Savage Holiday*. He selects Bigger Thomas in *Native Son* who accidentally kills a white heiress for rescripting that portion pertaining to Fowler's accidental killing of little Tony Blake. This blunder is why Fowler's whiteness discourse collapses and blends in with blackness discourse to illustrate the common gray areas of shared human experiences. Like Bigger Thomas's nighttime epiphany, Fowler has a daytime epiphany that propels him to devise a scheme that will divert the blame for Tony's accidental death from himself to anything or anyone else. Again, he is clearly exemplifying Birt's definition of "bad faith" by lying. He is not intellectually sophisticated like Nkrumah, nor does he have Bigger Thomas's *Real Detective Magazine* to use as a guide. For, thinks Fowler, "nothing he had ever heard of could offer him any guidance now" (*SH* 57). However, Wright shows that Fowler, having come from the grassroots level like Bigger, also has some street knowledge of human behavior from self studies. He knows that he can practice "bad faith" in front of his neighbors and community members by using his insurance tricks to cover up his role in the boy's death: telling half-truths, lying blatantly to people, and casting blame on another—namely, Mabel Blake. In vacillating spates of calmness and fear, Wright shows how Fowler begins to playact deceit by retracting his condemnation of Freud and engaging in wish fulfillment: that little Tony is really dead and unable to expose him as the balcony culprit, and that Mabel Blake has been acting predictably and sleeping off a night of "carousing" when the boy had fallen (58).

In essence, Fowler acts somewhat like Nkrumah and starts to build a nation of supporters by manipulating familiar religious and cultural practices that would appeal to the emotions of his followers (2008 *BP* 247). He is successful in his performances. Unlike Nkrumah, he does not have to stage a public rally; his neighbors do so in the hallways. Their impassioned outcries assist Fowler in his cover-up scheme as he engages in stealthy actions of hovering behind their backs, eavesdropping on conversations, and/or providing select, terse comments. While the people invoke Nkrumah's name as their new god, Fowler's neighbors invoke the name of their Christian God as a way of expressing shock and sadness over Tony's tragic death. Unknown to them, Fowler remains self-centered and maniacally frightened about his own safety (*SH* 71; 2008 *BP* 148, 168). In body posture, he adapts Nkrumah's poised demeanor and stage-acting skills. But, more like Bigger, Fowler deliberately feigns ignorance of the situation when talking to neighbors and an inquisitive police officer about Tony's death. He also allows his neighbors, unknowingly, to abet his own cause; two women verbally cast aspersions on Mabel Blake or convey derisive eye signals toward her door so as to indict her for criminal negligence of her child.

However, America's civic lessons on human subjectivity and the culture's promotion of individual agency, male empowerment, and female subordination are the subliminal factors that dismantle Fowler's attempts to rebuild a tribal collective of support that mimes, on a smaller scale, Longevity Life's operating principles. From the start of his career, Fowler has hidden behind a masculinist world where they practiced gender subordination of women. Fowler took the practice of sexism even further into misogyny because of his own maternal past. Nkrumah has been attempting to elevate women and break down rigid patriarchal laws keeping them silent. His new African mode of gaining male and female collective support as opposed to the American mode of promoting gender bias and male-driven individualism through collectivism within a group are diametrically opposed. Fowler's sexist perspective is a major blunder in the ensuing gender war between Fowler, a male, and Mabel Blake, a female. Since both are white, race is not an issue but class and gender are relevant. Female gender is the reason for Fowler's defeat when Fowler the Virgin engages in verbal and/or stealthy combat with Mabel Blake the Whore and Matriarch. Both are skilled salespeople and Fowler discovers that he has a formidable opponent similar to Richard's discoveries of Nkrumah's opponents Busia and Danquah. Fowler assumes that Mabel Blake is a two-dimensional female abstraction without depth or intelligence. But his errors in judging her resilient nature are catastrophic: she is a three-dimensional woman and a mother. This is the reason that Wright titles part 2 "Ambush" after an episode experienced by Richard in Africa. On a street in Accra one day, Richard is ambushed by a "tall, well-dressed black girl" who runs "wildly" toward his taxi (2008 *BP* 200). He staves off her sexual propositions and learns from the taxi driver that his assailant was just another two-dimensional "type"—a "Mary" figure or common street prostitute (205).

Fowler's inbred misogynist views cause him totally to miscalculate Mabel's superior street skills like her model Mary in Africa. Even Fowler's "bad faith" efforts of "nation- building" by recruiting tenants as allies dissolve after he receives a telephone call from a mysterious person claiming to have "seen someone on the balcony." He instinctually knows that he has a formidable nemesis in the guise of Mabel Blake (*SH* 142), and accelerates his campaign of "bad faith" lying by resorting to Nkrumah's nation-building strategy of smearing his opponents. Besides his tribal allies of neighbors, Fowler extends the outreach of his blame game to sympathetic church members. However, his self-serving overtures of paying for Tony's funeral costs, courting Mabel, and then proposing marriage to her all flounder. Instead, they work in favor of Mabel's counterstrategies to extract the truth from Fowler by using her sexual power. She playacts the scene from *Black Power* when a woman pretends to be Mrs. Nkrumah by pretending to become Mrs. Fowler. Like Mary the African, Mabel is very cunning. She, unlike Richard's response, manipulates Fowler into a greater state of emotional passion and jealous rage by advertising her male clients while in Fowler's presence (see 2008 *BP* 147).

Wright's final episodes in the part 3 "Attack" sequence are rife with Freudian allusions as Fowler becomes reduced to the level of an individuated, psychically deranged child-man owing to his blind, misogynist views of women, starting with his biological mother. Her image colludes, collides, disjoins, and emerges from his subconsciousness in the guise of Mary–Mabel Blake. All of his efforts of lying and self-deception to bury his mother's image go awry in an emotional gush of his pent-up "psychic energy" as he reverts to or reengages in his childhood state of "cathexis." According to Dr. Charles Brenner, a Sigmund Freud Fellow and psychoanalytic specialist:

> The accurate definition of "cathexis" is the amount of psychic energy which is directed towards or attached to the mental representative of a person or thing. That is to say, cathexis refers to a purely mental phenomenon. It is a psychological, not a physical concept. Psychic energy cannot flow out through space and cathect or attach itself to the external object directly. What are cathected of course are the various memories, thoughts, and fantasies of the object which comprise what we call its mental or psychic representatives. (18)

Indeed, Fowler's bad-faith action of casting blame on Mabel Blake has only served to exacerbate his "various memories, thoughts, and fantasies of the [real] object": his mother (Brenner 18). He could not control Mary-Mabel no more than he could control his own prostitute mother. After Mary-Mabel confronts him about the bloodstains on her newspaper, Fowler totally loses emotional control: his passion rises to "excess," his psychic energy turns to rage, and he deliberately stabs Mary-Mabel to death. Their levels of violence and accusatory remarks simulate Jake and Lil's death battle in Wright's posthumous novel *Lawd Today!* (1963).

The final "Attack" sequence also derails whiteness discourse about masculine superiority. Wright's portrayal of Mabel Blake is commendable, for she is smarter than Fowler and is a prelude to the more positive images of black and white women to follow in *A Father's Law* and *Eight Men*. Fowler's efforts at nation-building fail because of female power, female sexual astuteness, and matriarchal self-reliance that are well beyond Fowler's intelligence because he had been sired on false claims of white male superiority over women. Stripped of his former beliefs, he consciously awakens to the truth behind his repressed sexuality: his Freudian Oedipal feelings for his mother and his incestuous guilt over her so-called death. Freudian psychology is for Westerners, not Africans, and this is the reason that Wright turns to European American culture to locate patterns of the tabooed practice. After he deliberately murders Mabel Blake, Fowler has a second epiphany of truthfulness. His mother had been a Whore like Mabel Blake and also had favored her male clients over him (*SH* 38–40). To paraphrase Brenner, she had become the source of "many important" moments of Fowler the small child's "instinctual gratifications." And having continuously met her rejection, he became obsessed with her acts of betrayal. Says Brenner, "The child's mother is an important object of his drives, and . . . this object [becomes] cathected with psychic energy. By this we mean that the child's thoughts, images, and fantasies which concern its mother, that is her mental representative in the child's mind, are highly cathected" (18). Fowler's obsession with his mother had caused him to fantasize his matricide of her. His jealous rage or psychic energy eventually cathected to a mental phenomenon—a doll that Fowler the child had drawn with its head bludgeoned by a brick in mimesis of Bigger Thomas's head-bludgeoning Bessie Mears to death. By means of transference, he acted out his fantasy upon an inanimate object that he had drawn with his coloring pencils. This Jungian creative act of matricide was his small measure of power, and totally passion driven and irrationally based. Those sharp, phallic instruments had been used symbolically to "kill off" his mother. But Fowler, as a psychically deranged child, could not distinguish fantasy from reality. The four colored pencils consistently housed in the adult male's vest pocket had somehow neutralized his unbridled psychic energy for years. But they also signified his own self-deception as well as Fowler's ability to dupe people by stealthy acts of lying until he lost control and used another phallic object, a knife, to kill another mother-whore figure deliberately.

How does Fowler make sense out of a nonsensical, postmodern world no longer familiar or certain to him? Truth telling, Fowler concludes, is the reason that Fowler the double murderer embarks upon a final, nation-building venture to enter a static prison environment. There he would know with certainty that his amoral behavior and psychic derangement will remain steadfastly fixed in a masculine-controlled world behind bars. Indeed, Fowler believes that he is coming out of a black hole when he finally takes this third step of truth telling and turns himself into the police at the end of *Savage Holiday*. "Irrational" is Fowler's state of mind and body, thereby confirming Richard's prediction of Nkrumah's fate should he continue to mix politics with religion. Fowler miscalculates how postmodernism destabilizes previously fixed meanings, especially as it has begun to operate in the new, technologically advanced world of the 1950s. His sudden abandonment by his symbolical father, President Warren, is the second cause that sends Fowler spiraling into an abyss of passion-driven, irrational thinking.

Because of his childhood emotional scarring, the suppressed first cause of matriarchal betrayal ultimately destroys Fowler's "bad-faith," self-deceptive lifestyle. Mary-Mabel strips Fowler of his false moral core and thus forces Fowler into his final stage of Oedipal truth: his desire for his mother. He attempts to stabilize his mental disarray by divulging both an epistemological and ontological "truth" to the police about his prehistory and crimes as only he understands them to mean. His props, the colored pencils, had always been emblematic of his insane, fractured childhood that he had attempted to suppress. At the ending, Fowler knows that he must use his Lockean instincts to make sense of his nonsensical world by joining another nationalist fraternity—the state's prison system. By his returning to his familiar bottom tier of nation-building only with men, unlike Nkrumah, Fowler chooses voluntarily to cease linearity, reenact circularity, and reinstate masculinist tradition in order to restore his sanity. He literally achieves the affirmation of his Freudian wishes when he confesses his macabre crimes to the police and presumably is locked up indefinitely, unlike white society's immediate reactions of "killing off" Wright's black criminal protagonists. His confessional is cathartic; it literally results in Fowler's self-liberation, self-incrimination, and self-incarceration.

Psychoanalysis as Self-Reflection in Richard Wright's *Savage Holiday*

—TORU KIUCHI—

Richard Wright's *Savage Holiday* was published in 1954 and it was dedicated to Clinton Brewer, then a prisoner at Trenton State Prison in New Jersey. In fact, the events that inspired Wright to go back to a much earlier period around September 1940 concerned a letter that he had received from an elderly white woman who implored him to use his influence to obtain the prisoner's release—a man whom she described as "a talented Negro musician who is now serving a life sentence." This woman's request immediately aroused Wright's curiosity. He met Brewer at the Trenton State Prison in mid-March 1941. He says about his visit:

> On my visit to the Trenton State Prison, Colonel Selby was kind enough to allow me to examine Brewer's prison record, and I was struck by two facts which I feel should mitigate his punishment. First, when Brewer committed his crime, he was 18 years of age, that is, not legally a man, but merely a boy emerging from his adolescence. I am now convinced that Brewer has, through the medium of the artistic expression, worked out an organic and social relationship to the world in which he lives and that a repetition of his crime would be most unlikely. Secondly, I was impressed by the record of good behavior which has characterized his prison life. (Wright to Edison, 30 March 1941, Richard Wright Papers [RWP])

Wright rather quickly became committed to aiding Brewer's cause.

Wright's renown as a national and international writer helped Brewer's case. By the end of March 1941, in order to prove his talent for music, Brewer sent Wright a copy of "Stampede in G Minor"—an instrumental piece of jazz music that he had composed. The latter immediately forwarded the work to his friend John Henry Hammond Jr. of Columbia Recording Studios in New York (Fabre, 1993 *UQ* 236). Meantime, on March 30, 1941, Wright sent a letter to Thomas A. Edison Jr.,[1] governor of New Jersey, "to enter a plea for clemency on behalf of a Negro prisoner, Clinton Brewer," a sensitive and intelligent man who apparently had succeeded in maintaining contact with the outside world by means of books, periodicals, and music. Wright also thought that through art, Brewer would be able to establish a wholesome relationship with society, and he asked that Brewer be released on parole (Fabre, 1993 *UQ* 236). On April 6, 1941, Wright again met Brewer at the Trenton State Prison, this time with his friend Hammond (Ross 19). Thanks to Wright's efforts, Brewer was eventually paroled on July 8, 1941.

As a result of Wright's interest, Brewer seemed to have become positively renewed and self-actualized after his parole. At that time, Brewer was planning to work on musical arrangements for Count Basie on a regular basis (Fabre, 1993 *UQ* 236). Basie recorded and released "Stampede" in 1941 along with his other big-band, swing-era jazz pieces. Nonetheless, the release of his music did not cause Brewer to forget his benefactor. In mid-August 1941, after serving a nineteen-year sentence at Trenton State Prison, Brewer, the paroled musician, paid a visit to his benevolent defender at the latter's three-room apartment on Revere Place in Brooklyn, New York (Fabre, 1993 *UQ* 244). Brewer simply wanted to express his gratitude to Wright for everything that the latter had done to acquire Brewer's release.

Yet Brewer's freedom seemed more daunting to him than Wright had anticipated. This became apparent since it was short-lived. Brewer's criminal mindset apparently was only dormant briefly outside the prison walls; it became suddenly reawakened after his parole. Although Brewer "took up a new career as an arranger for CBS and Count Basie's band, . . . his new career ended abruptly." According to media accounts, Brewer "was locked up again because his lady love, Wilhelmina Washington, was found dead, all cut up with stab wounds" (Anon., "People"). On September 25, 1941, some eighty days after being released on parole, Brewer had stabbed another woman in her home in New York City under circumstances similar to those of his first crime (Anon., "Murder"). The news was both shocking and disappointing to Wright.

Needless to say, Brewer's true-life story of crime deeply affected Wright. In fact, he had not forgotten the case even ten years later. Wright permanently left the United States in 1947 and assumed residency as an expatriate in Paris, France. From his European base, he set about writing a psychoanalytic novel partially based on the data that he had collected years earlier during interviews with Brewer. The outcome eventually became the novel *Savage Holiday,* which was published in 1954. Not only is Brewer's criminal history utilized to explain why the protagonist Erskine Fowler commits a crime, but also Wright's own past is embedded in the novel. *Savage Holiday* is not only a novel based upon true-life criminal cases, but also is a self-reflective text that illuminates the tragic events that occurred during Wright's own childhood, youth, and adolescence. These personal incidents additionally account for the character traits and psychological problems of Wright's protagonist Erskine Fowler.

The 1940s to 1950s: Wright's Involvements in Psychological Studies

Wright began to take a keen interest in psychoanalysis during the decade between 1940 and 1950 when the Brewer case concluded and Wright started to produce *Savage Holiday*. Wright's biographer Michel Fabre confirms that there are "purely autobiographical touches" in *Savage Holiday*. These personal references were the reasons that "Wright was anxious to have the critics' opinions on this last novel [*Savage Holiday*], of which he was particularly fond" (Fabre, 1993 *UQ* 503). Fabre also thinks that these autobiographical elements account for two things; namely, why Wright originally took such a great interest in Brewer's case, and why he attached so much importance to the publication of *Savage Holiday*. As he was working on *The Outsider* (1953) and recalling his childhood memories, Wright was forced to confront his own conflicted feelings about his grandmother and mother (Fabre, 1993 *UQ* 378). The outcome of his initial plan to write a detective novel turned out to be a psychological interrogation into his own past. As critic John Reilly observes, Wright utilizes a dual-narrative style in the work—especially in the "final scenes: One level is constituted by overt action represented by dialogue and the author's description of character behavior . . . [and] another narrative, vividly present in Fowler's mind but evident to [readers] only" ("Curious Thriller" 221). This dualistic framework means that Fowler converses with others in dialogue and with himself in interior monologues.

Although Erskine Fowler was partially modeled on Clinton Brewer, the novel's protagonist is also an "unconscious" reference to Wright himself. According to Claudia Tate:

> Throughout Wright's unpublished manuscripts ("Memories of My Grandmother," "Personalism," and "On Literature," for instance), Wright also explicitly refers to the discursive power of the unconscious—or what he calls, in the context of *The Man Who Lived Underground*, "the recurring motif of the *strangely familiar*," a phrase that Wright repeatedly uses in his fiction and that clearly invokes Freud's "Uncanny" ("Memories" 17; emphasis mine). In "On Literature" for example, Wright speculates that "all writing is a secret form of autobiography" (6). By "secret," Wright is referring not to a deliberate intention of concealing information but to an unconscious purpose, uniquely personal and inscribed in all language use by every individual. This secret marks the text with distinctive characteristics as much as an individual author's signature would. (Tate, "Rage" 94)

While Brewer's motive for repeating his crime did not fully preoccupy Wright's thoughts, a series of important events did occur during the 1940s that kept Wright's interest in psychoanalysis alive.

Having moved from Chicago, Illinois, in 1937 to Harlem, New York, and then to Brooklyn in the 1940s, Wright cultivated friendships with several renowned psychologists and psychiatrists. On October 14, 1941, almost at the same time as the Brewer case was ongoing, German-born psychiatrist Frederick Wertham sent Wright a complimentary copy of his case study *Dark Legend*. The non-fictional book rekindled Wright's layman's interest in psychoanalysis since the studies had become increasingly popular all over the world after World War II. Certain fields flourished such as medicine and its specialized areas of pediatrics and nursing, education, and justice science—especially studies on the criminal behaviors of juvenile delinquents. Psychoanalysis, with its interdisciplinary connections to anthropology and sociology, enabled scientists to study the environmental and hereditary conditions in American culture affecting formation of a person's ego identity as well as the role of parents during an individual's growth into childhood.

Wertham's case study is an example of Freud's theories about how good or bad parenting shapes a child's ego identity. According to Bart Beaty's summary of *Dark Legend*, Gino, the Italian American case study, grew up as the oldest of three children of a male New York resident who died when Gino was only six years old—a crucial stage of identity formation and a child's bonding with his or her parents. Shortly thereafter, Gino's mother relocated the family to Borda, Italy, where she began to neglect her children while spending time with their father's married brother Aiello. Such a flagrant, illicit kinship relationship outraged Gino, who prayed to his father for the strength to avenge his family's honorable name by killing his uncle. But Gino was never able to fulfill his wish to carry out the deed. Years later and at the age of thirteen, Gino relocated to New York with his family. His mother again began to carry on a series of illicit relationships with different men. Again, Gino despised these men as well as feared the transient males who never fulfilled his father's role. However, Gino eventually was forced to assume his father's responsibilities. As finances waned, he became his family's sole financial supporter. Although he felt unable to disobey his mother by leaving the family or quitting his job, Gino still felt an overwhelming urge to restore his family's honor that his promiscuous mother had tainted. Finally, Gino carried out his mission. He murdered his mother as she slept—an act of matricide for which he told Wertham that he never felt remorseful (Beaty 28).

Dark Legend, the book about Gino's act of matricide, fascinated Wright, especially since it involved a male's murder of a female similar to the Brewer case. After reading the text, Wright quickly wrote to Wertham and asked the psychiatrist which factors, motives, or psychological abnormalities had provoked Gino to commit murder (Fabre, 1993 *UQ* 236). According to Wright:

> My reactions to Gino, his plight and his crime were so many and varied that it would be futile to attempt to set them down in a letter. It is enough to say that I think it is the most comprehensive psychological statement in relation to contemporary crime that I have come across. Indeed, it is as fascinating as any novel. (Wright to Wertham, 14 October 1941, RWP)

The cases of Brewer and Gino had many parallels. For these reasons, Wright decided to meet with Wertham on November 3, 1941, at Wertham's office in Harlem to talk about the Brewer case. They also decided to visit him in prison (memo attached to Wertham's letter, 1 November 1941, RWP). Moreover, Wertham hired a lawyer, James D. Dempsey, to assist Brewer. Wertham also agreed to provide testimony in the hope that his expertise as a psychiatrist would save Brewer's life. On his part, Wright sent a letter to Brewer, urging him to write immediately to Dempsey (Wright to Brewer, 9 November 1941, RWP). Brewer's legal proceedings continued to move ahead. He pleaded guilty on December 2, 1941, in general sessions "to second-degree murder in the stabbing of a Negro woman in Harlem" (Anon., "Murder"). Because of the Brewer case and the shared interest of both men, Wertham and Wright developed a close friendship. It led to Wright's continued interest in psychoanalysis from then on.

Wright gleaned many ideas from Wertham's case study *Dark Legend* that recur in *Savage Holiday*. For example, Erskine Fowler starts to work for the Longevity Life Insurance Company in New York at the age of thirteen, not unlike Gino, who returned to New York at the same age. In New York, Gino's mother developed a series of illicit relationships with different men, all of whom Gino grew to despise and fear because of his own Freudian Oedipal desires for his mother. Similarly, the child's Oedipal rage against his mother is similar to Fowler's anger toward Mabel Blake, a next-door neighbor, whom Fowler views as a mirror image of his own mother. Like Gino's mother, Mabel Blake has a series of illicit sexual relationships with different men while neglecting her own five-year-old son Tony. Fowler experiences a psychological transference of jealousy and rage on behalf of little Tony, the victim, because Fowler had experienced the same kind of negligence from his own sexually promiscuous mother at a similar age. After Gino stabs his mother to death, he never feels any remorse for committing the heinous crime. Similarly, Fowler has no regrets after stabbing Mabel Blake to death because he believed that, under the circumstances, she alone was responsible for her own demise. Additionally, Fowler, like Gino, conveys his narrative to officials in a dispassionate manner. Gino tells Wertham: "I never slept so well like I sle[ep] now. . . . I did what I thought was right. . . . I am sorry I didn't do it a long time ago. I don't believe in forgiving. . . . I can forgive anybody who would give me a slap, but not one who dishonors my family. . . . About my honor I don't forgive" (*Dark*

Legend 120–21; qtd. in Beaty 28). This confession prefigures Fowler's terse but dispassionate remarks to the police after he murders Mabel Blake: "I just killed a woman—her body's in my apartment" (*SH* 217). Clearly, *Dark Legend* functioned as a resource for Wright while he was working out character traits of his protagonist in *Savage Holiday*.

A valid reason for Wright's broadened knowledge of psychoanalysis derives from his own studies as well as his extensive involvement in Wertham's professional life. For instance, Wright chaired a panel during which Wertham gave a speech on "The Psychological and Social Significance of Juvenile Delinquency" on January 3, 1942, in New York. The conference was convened under the auspices of the Saturday Forum Luncheon Group (invitation card featuring Wright, RWP). On another occasion, Wright gave a talk before a group of psychiatrists at the invitation of Dr. Helen V. McLean with the Institute for Psychoanalysts in January 1942 (invitation card, RWP). In addition, on April 3, 1943, Wright addressed the Institute of Psychoanalysis in Chicago at a meeting arranged by his friend, the esteemed sociologist Horace Cayton. The latter had asked Wright beforehand to speak about problems affecting the "Negro" family. Because Wright's novel and play *Native Son* were both nationally and internationally renowned at this time, Cayton asked Wright specifically to stress how hostility, as exemplified by both Bigger Thomas and his mother, plays a central role in the psychological problems of African American families (McLean 706–13). Furthermore, Wright received an invitation to speak before students and the faculty at Howard University in Washington, DC, on May 14, 1943, and then also lectured that same day on "Reflections of a Psychiatrist on Humanity and the World Crisis" at the meeting of the War Problem Study Group chaired by Abe Harris (Karpman to Wright, 14 May 1943, RWP).

Certainly during the 1940s, Wright received a substantial amount of training in psychological theory by reading widely, learning from specialists, applying his knowledge by means of activities, and speaking on the subject at public forums. Because of his friendship, Wertham also helped Wright to broaden his knowledge of psychoanalysis as a means by which to interrogate his own past. He began in-depth analysis with Wertham, who probed and exposed Wright's submerged memories. Wertham stressed to Wright that Jungian therapy endorses creative outlets as the means by which to uncover subliminal issues. Wertham also reminded Wright that an author is more successful at representing psychoanalytical problems as a tension in his works only if the artist himself has undergone psychoanalysis (Wertham 111–15).

The clinical aspect is the reason that Wertham and Wright began to discuss the latter's childhood experiences, with Wright functioning as both subject and object. They also could explore other fantasies that Wright was planning to implement as incidents in his stories. Out of these one-on-one discussions, some of the case studies from earlier times and incidents from Wright's own personal history became apparent resources for constructing the life story of his alter ego Richard in Wright's autobiography *Black Boy,* which he published in 1945, and also for his novel *Savage Holiday,* which he published in 1954. Erskine Fowler is emblematic of how Jungian psychotherapy probes the unconscious and how it plays an important role in the activities of creative writing, drawing, and playacting (*New York Times,* 24 December 1944; qtd. in Kinnamon, *Richard Wright Bibliography* 177). In *Black Boy,* Wright illustrates how he, as a child, literally fulfilled his father's command to kill a cat as a form of creative play. He knew that his father's order was a figurative expression, but young Wright did so as an act of spite in a father-son clash (Wright, *BB/AH* 12). Wright continually makes these psychoanalytical distinctions between the literal and the figurative, the real and the fantastic, and the awakened state and the dream state in his works. In *Savage Holiday,* Fowler figuratively playacts the interested lover and suitor of Mabel Blake, and then literally kills her because of her flagrant actions of planning sexual trysts with other men while in his presence.

Wright additionally began to stock his library with many books on psychology and its related fields arising from gifts from friends, their recommendations, or his own interests. In mid-August 1944, Benjamin Karpman, then a doctor at the Washington Medical Building in Washington, DC, sent an inscribed copy of his *Case Studies in the Psychopathology of Crime* to Wright (Fabre, *Books* 85). Wright had increased his efforts to become more informed about psychoanalysis by obtaining specialized books on the subject after World War II ended. In one interview with *L'Express* in 1955, he conveyed his familiarity with the writings of a number of authors: "For the past few years most of my reading has been the works of Freud, Malinowski, Theodore Reik, Nietzche, etc." (Wright, "I Curse the Day" 163–64). By means of his character Erskine Fowler, Wright also reveals his current reading habits. At one point, Fowler thinks about his disdain for Freud: "Yes; these days everybody was talking about 'complexes' and the 'unconscious'; and a man called Freud (which always reminded him of *fraud!*) [who] was making people believe that the most fantastic things could happen to people's feelings" (emphasis original; *SH* 61). Freud, regarded as the father of psychoanalysis, had many disciples. Wright bought copies of Carl G. Jung's *Psychology of the Unconscious: A Study of the Transformations and Symbolisms of the Libido* in February 1945 (Fabre, *Books* 84) and Theodore Reik's *Psychology of Sex Relations* on October 13, 1945 (diary, RWP). By reading these books, Wright was able to gain an in-depth knowledge of psychology, psychiatry, and sexuality from Freud, his disciples, and his opponents.

Another training method for Wright derived from invitations to engage in firsthand observations of deprived children of troubled juvenile delinquents. On April 8, 1946, Wertham opened his LaFarge Clinic in Harlem where poor

African American children could be provided with free health care. It was based out of the parish at St. Phillip's Church in Harlem (Fabre, 1993 *UQ* 292). A few months later, in September 1946, Wright published "Psychiatry Comes to Harlem." Produced by *Free World*, the copyright earnings were to be allocated to Wertham's clinic. While extolling the value of psychiatry in thwarting untreated mental illnesses, Wright stated:

> Psychologically, repressed need goes underground, gropes for an unguarded outlet in the dark, and, once finding it, sneaks out, experimentally tasting the new freedom, then at last gushing forth in a wild torrent, frantic lest a new taboo deprive it of the right to exist. As with the human personality, so with human institutions which seek to administer to human needs. Social needs, too, go underground when they have been emotionally or morally rejected, only to reappear later in strange channels and in guises as fantastic as the images of a nightmare. (49)

Erskine Fowler's actions confirm how repressed need "goes underground, gropes for an unguarded outlet in the dark." But once he retires from the insurance company at which a demanding workload had helped him to control his Oedipal desires, and once he begins to interact with Mabel Blake because of her son's death, he drops his guard. His conscious awareness of Mabel Blake's womanliness fuels his desire for her and "sneaks out, experimentally tasting [his] new freedom" to feel emotions after he sees her scantily clad in her underwear from his side window. Finally, Fowler's emotions become so intensified that, at last "gushing forth in a wild torrent," he first proposes marriage to Mabel Blake to stave off her suspicions about his role in little Tony's death, and then, in a fit of rage, he murders her. According to critics, Wright appears very faithful to psychoanalysis "when he wants to apply it to his novel," with "every situation involving different aspects of psychoanalysis [that] has its foundations in Freudian theory" (Gounard and Gounard 348). In the novel, Mabel Blake seemingly represents a second self of Fowler's mother in disguise. She, too, treats Fowler like her own child, saying phrases such as "you and Tony," which lumps them together like children, and "come here; let me wash that blood off your hand," similar to a mother admonishing and then cleaning up her soiled child (*SH* 210).

Wright, Psychoanalysis, and the Religious Tyranny of His Grandmother

Besides the fact that Wright's studies of psychoanalysis exerted great influence on him as he created his works, his own sense of personal liberation became greatly enhanced once he tasted the French flavor of freedom. In 1947, he moved to Paris, France, to live in exile from the United States. Nonetheless, distance did not negate his thoughts about America or reflections on the constant tensions that had existed in his grandmother's home in Mississippi during his childhood, youth, and adolescence. Having published his autobiography *Black Boy* in 1945,Wright, once living abroad, did not desist from recounting his childhood experiences in other forms of narratives. He wrote "Memories of My Grandmother" around 1944 or 1945. The work proves that Wright began to examine and explore the geographical as well as the spiritual significances of his independence by now being distantly removed from his maternal ties. A new sense of freedom to live without accountability or detachment from a family, however, is not welcomed by Erskine Fowler in *Savage Holiday*. Having become involuntarily forced into retirement becomes problematical for the suddenly liberated central character. Fowler is set free after working thirty years as an employee of an insurance company. Critic Gerald Early rightly argues that "simply put, the [question] that continued to be of interest to him [Wright] in this small novel, as in much of his other work, [is]: What is freedom and what is desire?" (225). Wright had earlier addressed the philosophical issues concerning freedom by means of his protagonist Cross Damon in Wright's existential crime novel *The Outsider* published in 1953.

Wright, too, had felt two bursts of freedom once he had moved from Jackson, Mississippi, to Memphis, Tennessee, in 1925, and then to Chicago, Illinois, in 1927. Twice he felt less cloistered by being away from Mississippi. Yet his financial burdens were great. He was attempting to become economically independent, but had to remain the main financial supporter of his mother and brother still living in Mississippi and of his aunt with whom he shared an apartment in Chicago. He became involved in the insurance business at this new northern base, which later Wright adapted as another autobiographical resource for plot development in *Savage Holiday*. During the summer of 1931, after assistance from a cousin, Wright found employment as an insurance agent with a funeral director. During that year he "worked for several burial and insurance societies that operated among Negroes," and he "received a new kind of education" (*BB/AH* 339). Once he had gained enough experience, Wright, in February 1932, tried to start an insurance business in Chicago with his childhood friend Joe C. Brown, who worked for the *Herald American* newspaper. They additionally worked for an African American business, the Supreme Liberty Life Insurance Company, but the company soon went bankrupt (Fabre, 1993 *UQ* 91). Nevertheless, the experience of working with heads of companies was directly instrumental in Wright's development of Fowler's relationships with the president and vice president of Longevity Life Insurance Company.

Wright's religious training as a child and youth growing up in his grandmother's household also became creative material that accounts for Fowler's character portrait as a strict, pious man. As a child, he had lived in his maternal grandmother's house in Natchez, Mississippi, and then as a youth in her second home located in Jackson. His grandmother was a devout Seventh-Day Adventist who ruled her household strictly. Margaret Bolden Wilson was born in 1853 or 1854, and was an obvious product of miscegenation; she appeared to be as white as any other white person and acted more Irish and Scottish than African American. In his unpublished manuscript "Memories of My Grandmother," Wright explains his perception of his grandmother's rigid Seventh-Day Adventist beliefs as a youth living in her home: "My mother being an invalid, I lived in my grandmother's house and ate her bread and automatically this dependence obligated me to worship her God. My grandmother practiced the Seventh-Day Adventist religion, a form of religious ritual that encompasses and regulates every moment of living" (2). His mother, not quite as zealous, attended another church. Wright was baptized in his mother's religion at the Lynch Street Methodist Episcopal Church, Jackson, in 1922, when he was thirteen years old. He recalls his inward resistance even to this religious sect and the memorable ritual performed: "Finally my turn came and I felt foolish, tense; I wanted to yell for him to stop. . . . But I said nothing. The dripping branch was shaken above my head and drops of water wet my face and scalp. . . . Then it was over. . . . I sighed. I had been baptized" (*BB/AH* 148–49).

This incident and other autobiographical and/or religious events recur in *Savage Holiday*. For example, Fowler's thirty years of employment as an insurance company agent corresponds to Wright's thirty years in 1952 of becoming baptized as a Methodist at his mother's church in 1922. The sum of thirty years has another symbolical meaning. Wright's literary agent Paul Reynolds pointed out in a letter that Fowler's retirement at age forty-three was too early, according to American customs of a person working until at least age sixty, the standard bar. In his reply dated March 21, 1953, to Reynold's query, Wright explained that the president of the insurance company wanted to get rid of Fowler in order to assign Fowler's job to his son (qtd. in Fabre, 1993 *UQ* 380). The explanation, however, may sound unsatisfactory not only because of Fowler's premature age for a retiree, but also because he could have filed a lawsuit against the company once the president told him, "WE'LL FIRE YOU!" in order to force Fowler into accepting his figurative termination (*SH* 26).

Another religious reference in the novel relates to Wright's direct conflicts with his zealous grandmother. The very first epigraph in part 1 of *Savage Holiday* reads:

> Six days shalt thou labor, and do all thy work: But the seventh day is the Sabbath of the Lord thy God: in it thou shalt not do any work . . .

These two lines refer to one of the Ten Commandments and are about the seventh day of the week—namely, Saturday. As Moses stated, the Sabbath day should strictly be observed as a day of rest and worship. This is a tenet that the Seventh-Day Adventists rigidly follow. President Warren mimes the words that echo biblical language when he introduces Fowler to the audience at the retirement ceremony: "This is the end of a perfect day!" (12). He sounds like a minister presiding at a church service or meeting. Like a preacher delivering a sermon, the Longevity Life president also adopts a moralizing tone: "But never forget, time enough for devotion, for service, for character building, for brotherly love . . ." (13). Fowler has been the personification of the president's creed. He has been a longtime member of a local church where he also has taught Sunday school. After being discarded from Longevity Life, he decides to teach Sunday school an additional six days per week in order to stabilize his now destabilized world. Religion becomes an outlet and crutch to occupy his time.

At the banquet, moreover, the president refers to his company as if it were a religious structure. He stresses the importance of family like the patriarchs in the Old Testament. He says to his employees: "Brothers and sisters of the Longevity Life Family, . . . I want simply as president, or head of the family, to make manifest to the world that if Erskine Fowler has served us well, we want him and the world to know it" (13). His references to Fowler having "served," to them as being "brothers and sisters," and to himself as the "head" of the family are phrases that one usually associates with a religious service. In the president's eyes, the company is an extension of the church. Fowler's position as a Sunday school teacher indicates that Longevity Life has power over various religious organizations in New York as well.

Wright found that religious power used as a weapon to control ordinary citizens tends to be manipulative and oppressive. He condemns religious practices for imposing beliefs on unwilling people because it seems tantamount to forms of tyranny and irrational thinking. Readers can sense Bigger Thomas's frustration, for whenever he comes home, he finds his mother singing a hymn that in no way has relieved their economic plight. Another example of religious tyranny can be found among Wright's many conflicts with his grandmother. Her rigid Christian beliefs caused the family to experience unnecessary economic oppression because she prohibited family members to work on the Sabbath Day. But as a youth, Wright became tired of feeling ashamed of having no money to eat lunch at school. As a consequence, he forced a showdown with his grandmother one morning by packing his suitcase and threatening "to leave right away if he was not allowed to work on Saturdays" (Fabre, 1993 *UQ* 42). He reports that his grandmother snatched the luggage from his hands and, weeping, she rushed from the room. Says Wright: "Her humanity had triumphed over fear. I emptied the suitcase, feeling spent. I hated these emotional outbursts, tempests of passion, for they always left me tense and weak. Now I was truly dead to Granny and Aunt Addie, but my mother smiled when I told her that I had defied them. She rose and hobbled to me on her paralytic legs and kissed me" (*BB/AH* 170). During his walk home from the banquet, one can recall Fowler, too, having become privately tearful and emotionally spent after his showdown with the president and his aides.

Religion, continues Wright, also demeans natural behaviors, especially in terms of the body relating to sexuality and/or nudity. Another religious marker of shame occurred very early when Wright was a six-year-old child and temporarily residing at his grandmother's house in Jackson. Having been abandoned by his father and left to wander the streets of Memphis while his mother worked, the child very early learned about the tawdry aspects of sexuality and nudity from having witnessed or heard the most obscene and profane incidents. However, none of his family members, including his mother, could fathom how deeply the graphic, street exposés had warped the mind-set of a six-year-old at this crucial stage of developing his ego identity. Thus, on an occasion when his invalid mother could not assist, Grandmother Wilson took over the task of bathing the two boys. As she dried young Wright with a towel, he, having witnessed similar acts of sexual expression, asked his grandmother in the most innocent way to "kiss back there" once she had finished drying him (*BB/AH* 48). Granny reacts in the form of an insane tirade by slapping Wright's body with his wet towel, and then threatening to kill him if she catches him. Wright recalls his fright: "Naked, I rose and ran out of the room, screaming" (48). In Granny's mind, any reference to the nude body or to sexuality was a sign of moral degeneration.

The scene of Fowler's debacle in the nude is a reconfiguration of young Wright's experience. The incident occurs the morning after Fowler's retirement ceremony when he, like young Wright, makes a thoughtless blunder. While stark naked, he steps outside his apartment to retrieve his morning newspaper, oversteps his boundary, and the door slams shut behind him. Fowler, like Wright, too, imagines the worst episodes that could possibly occur should his neighbors find him in his present state of nakedness. While lying nude in the privacy of his bedroom, he could cast off all pretensions of shame because "nude, Erskine looked anything but pious or a Christian" (*SH* 40). But standing naked in the public hallway of an apartment building has greater consequences, even satanic implications.

Wright's use of the "nakedness" metaphor can also be construed as a symbol of immateriality to describe Fowler's spiritual interiority. On the one hand, *naked* means shorn of material goods as well as being stripped of accountability to others. It is like being reborn anew. After his severance from Longevity Life, Fowler had felt naked and stripped of family ties. In essence his nakedness could mean his liberation from company dogma that had demanded that all employees remain socially and morally clean and untainted. As Lâle Demirtürk also observes, it can refer to race, especially since Fowler is white, and his skin pigmentation suggests that he is supremely pure according to the company's religious commandments. As a white man working for a company with all-white employees, he had blended in with the rest of the workers. But once Fowler becomes severed from his all-white world of work, he additionally becomes detached and even erased from the collective in a stroke of white power. At his showdown with the president, the term *naked,* meaning *invisible,* functions as an absent marker. As Fowler argues with the president over his sudden "white out" on the company's slate of active employees, another naked metaphor emerges. A chasm, meaning a void, opens up between them immediately: the gulf that had yawned so *nakedly* between them would never have been so glaring had he kept his mouth shut (*SH* 16). In this manner, the adverb *nakedly* functions as a spatial metaphor for a chasm.

After this reference to Fowler having become stricken from the company's roster of active employees, the word *naked* in its many variants recurs in the novel twenty-seven times.[2] Hence, the scene of his standing naked outside of his apartment is not only real, but surreal. It is emblematic of Fowler being in a state of nothingness. As Wright notes in an interview about Fowler's predicament: "The door slams shut before he has time to step back and he finds himself trapped outside of his place with *nothing* on. Such a condition brings to the surface, to his consciousness, acute feelings of anguish and utter panic which had always been latent within him and had conditioned his life although he had tried to fend them off" (Barthes, "Interview" 168; emphasis mine). Suddenly, Fowler finds himself being recodified by submerged narratives from his childhood.

Wright's childhood religious experiences again come into play as significant elements that both express and explain the traumatic events that have begun to resurface in Fowler's adult life. As it has been stated, the influence of Wright's grandmother and her strong Seventh-Day Adventist beliefs were so great that he chose to commemorate the long period of thirty years that had expired since his baptismal ceremony, itself another traumatic event in his life. As a number, it also symbolizes the awakening of Fowler's unconscious to traumatic events in his childhood that he had suppressed for that length of time. The dual shocks of suddenly being retired and then suddenly being trapped naked in a public hallway dissolve the mental barriers in Fowler's mind and, by default, the truth about his past criminal behavior. Says Michel Fabre:

> The concept of a deeply buried desire that emerges thirty years later in the form of a crime has two meanings in Wright's novel. First, it places the murder itself on

> another, almost secondary level, since the remembered reality of Fowler's childhood is revealed as the unreality of a dream. And it also supports Wright's claim that it was impossible to separate the act from the fantasy and life from the dream, which was, in fact, the theme of "The Man Who Killed a Shadow" and later, *The Long Dream*. (1993 *UQ* 378)

Readers can add *Savage Holiday* to Fabre's list of Wright's works that deal with the collision of fantasy and reality. The admixture of these two opposite states of mind illustrates the uncanniness of Fowler's vacillating thoughts now propelling his actions after his experiencing two shocking events within a twenty-four-hour period.

Wright and the Psychoanalysis of Abandonment: Locked In or Locket Out

Wright's childhood adversity draws another parallel between himself and Fowler on the occasion when his own mother had locked him, a child, out of the house, and Fowler's adult quandary of locking himself out of his apartment. While he was living in Memphis in 1913, Wright, the same age as five-year-old Tony in *Savage Holiday*, had been ordered by his mother to go out with a market basket and to conduct the shopping for his family. However, a street gang attacked Wright and took his money. He ran back home, terrified; nonetheless, his mother sent him off again and fortified him with their precious household money: "She slammed the door and I heard the key turn in the lock. I shook with fright. I was alone upon the dark, hostile streets and gangs were after me. . . . I clutched the stick, crying, trying to reason. If I were beaten at home, there was absolutely nothing that I could do about it; but if I were beaten in the streets, I had a chance to fight and defend myself" (*BB/AH* 20). Fowler's door-slamming episode is Wright's psychoanalytical reenactment of the social implications facing him as a five-year-old boy. But Wright goes forward, battles the gang leader, and earns his manhood rites of respect from them. Similarly, Fowler the naked man must respond to a slamming door: "He dashed forward toward the door and reached the sill just as the door, pushed by a strong current of air, slammed shut with a thunderous metallic bang in his face" (*SH* 43). Fowler, too, now faces a formidable opponent like Wright, but his foe is that of his fellow apartment dwellers, who, upon seeing him standing naked in the hallway, will express their consternation. Fowler manages to temper his panic and to think creatively by crawling onto his deck. Yet his decision is errant; he frightens little Tony playing on his own deck. The boy falls backward over the balcony to his death twelve stories below.

Win or lose? That is the consequence of both Wright's and Fowler's forced decisions to resolve a daunting situation. As stated, young Wright wins his confrontation with the street gang. Fowler loses his battle in an effort to avoid public exposure. His fearful experience as a child again directly relates to Wright's memories connected to his mother. In 1916, Ella Wright's health deteriorated so greatly that she had to send Wright and his brother to a Methodist orphanage located in Memphis. The director of this center asked Wright if he would like to be adopted by her, which scared him to death. Wright stayed in the orphanage for over a month: "During the first days my mother came each night to visit me and my brother; then the visits stopped. I began to wonder if she, too, like my father, had disappeared into the unknown" (*BB/AH* 30). He grew to believe that Ella Wright's desertion of him had ruined his childhood (Fabre, 1993 *UQ* 16). Says Wright, "Dread and distrust had already become a daily part of my being and my memory grew sharp, my senses more impressionable; I began to be aware of myself as a distinct personality striving against others" (*BB/AH* 30).

The trauma of abandonment with its sense of rootlessness and isolation carries over into Wright's adulthood, and he illustrates how such childhood scarring affects Erskine Fowler. At a very young age, Fowler had felt desperately afraid to be left alone because of his mother's erratic sociosexual lifestyle. On one occasion, he recalls:

> He'd been ill in bed and his mother had told him to go to sleep, that she was going out. . . . He'd begged, wept, his teary eyes intent upon the fat, bald man who stood at his mother's side. . . . But after he'd gotten well she'd gone off again, ... and he'd been left alone in the house all day and night, hating her, trying to think of the many things he wanted to do to her to make her feel it. (*SH* 39)

Like Gino, young Fowler has a desire for revenge.

The time period is approximately 1951, since Mabel Blake indicates that five or six years had passed after World War II ended when she had birthed little Tony and had become a war widow simultaneously (34). The 1951 date also means that thirty-five years previously, forty-three-year-old Fowler had been an eight-year-old boy in 1916—the year of Wright's experience at the orphanage. Like Wright's, Fowler's eight-year-old memory of experiencing his mother's abandonment has remained fixed in his mind: "Then on one cold winter day," Fowler recalls, his mother had been "hauled off to jail as a public nuisance and Aunt Tillie had come down from New York and fetched him" (39). He was not sent to an orphanage, although the absence of a father and mother symbolically, technically, and socially labels him to be an orphan.

A big difference between Erskine Fowler's and Richard Wright's life lies in the fact that Fowler's mother "remained in prison for two years [Fowler never learns the name of his mother's offense] and died only one year after she was released" (40). As for Wright's mother, she was not sent to jail but she became physically immobilized with paralysis for two years, a period during which it seemed to Wright that his mother had become symbolically dead. Thus, the absent mother/dead mother metaphors in Fowler's life are Wright's psychoanalytical restagings of his experiences as a deserted child. In the summer of 1919 in West Helena, Arkansas, three years after Wright's stay at the Memphis orphanage, his mother again became seriously bedridden with paralysis. Recalls Wright: "I was tense during the days I waited for Granny, and when she came I gave up, letting her handle things" (*BB/AH* 101). In this case, Wright yielded to his grandmother's authority by letting her take over caring for his mother and running of the household. Fowler has a different experience; he mentions nothing about the years with Aunt Tillie, but obviously he, too, had yielded to her authority after his mother went to jail. However, after her death, he, contrary to Wright, feels ashamed over his mother's tawdry past: "From that time on he felt that he had something to live down, to overcome" (*SH* 40). Abdul JanMohamed rightly argues in terms of the mother's desertion that "Fowler's uncanny exclusion from 'home' becomes the indirect route for his return to the originary object-cause of desire: the maternal body as 'home'" (*Death-Bound* 219).

Wright, Psychoanalysis, and the Mother Figure

Wright's Freudian, love-hate feelings for his mother are clear by means of his autobiographical reenactments of such contradictory feelings as aspects of Erskine Fowler's personality in *Savage Holiday*. Fowler consistently has carried in his vest pocket four colored pencils; they are sharp instruments as well as, on a sexual level, phallic symbols for "*what he'd wanted to do to his mother for having gone off*" (*SH* 220; emphasis mine). In other words, they are objects that he has used or anticipates to use to fulfill his wishes. To be more specific, he has sexual feelings of attraction and repulsion for Mabel Blake, also a mother figure. The narrator says: "His [Fowler's] desire for her [Mabel Blake] was so close to his rejection of her that he couldn't separate the two" (*SH* 138). Mabel Blake seems to Fowler to be a mirror image of his own licentious mother. In phonological language, his name, *Erskine Fowler*, when pronounced, sounds like "her skin—foul her" (or "fouler"), and when run together, the two phrases connote the "love-hate mother complex" identified by psychoanalysts (Vassilowitch 206). Wright himself also suggests the same idea: "Fowler brings to mind the notion of being 'foul,' of defining, of not behaving according to social rules" (Barthes, "Interview" 167). These binary conflicts between male sexual desire ("her skin") and female degradation ("foul her") are Fowler's Oedipal fantasies about

Mabel Blake (Vassilowitch 207). As Wright admits, "And from the beginning the protagonist is tortured by two contradictory impulses. Should he love and redeem Mabel Blake or should he hate and destroy her?" (Barthes, "Interview" 168). Fowler seems to acquire traits of mental imbalance more like Gino's than Wright's at this point.

Wright's exploration of desire in forms of Freudian wish fulfillment and/or Jungian creative play seems to be the factors driving his character's reactions toward his mother from Fowler's childhood onward to adulthood. When Fowler is forced to perform as keynote speaker on the occasion of his retirement party, he consistently touches something in his vest pocket that is mentioned for the first time in the novel: "With reflex gesture, he inserted his left hand to his inner coat pocket, as though to make sure that he had not lost something, then he continued" (*SH* 16). The narrator does not say explicitly what Fowler touches with his left hand; he only says that Fowler touches "something." But five pages later, the reader is informed about the specific kinds of objects that Fowler has been stroking: Fowler's "fingers [had] touched the tip ends of a row of four automatic pencils—black, red, blue, and green—clipped to an inner pocket" (21). Fowler touches them in the same way twenty times in the course of the novel.[3] Like the knife that he later uses to stab Mabel Blake, these pencils are sharp instruments and also symbolize phallic power that can overpower, injure, destroy, or erase a female's pictorial representation. Near the novel's ending, Fowler reveals the tawdry meaning of the four pencils by connecting them to a shameful, childhood daydream of his during which he exacts revenge against his mother. One day when he was a little boy, he had drawn a picture of his having crushed his girlfriend Gladys's doll with a brick. Symbolically, she represents his mother. He recalls:

> "*she's a bad woman . . .*"; *they'd been coloring paper with colored pencils and he'd drawn the image of a dead, broken doll and he had imagined Gladys telling on him and his mother branding him as bad. . . . He'd pictured vividly to himself what he'd wanted to do to his mother for having gone off and left that night when he'd been ill. . . . He now understood the four pencils!*" (*SH* 220; emphasis mine)

He had playacted his Freudian desire to commit matricide, and now as an adult, Fowler finally has begun to understand the differences between fantasy and reality or figurative and literal actions.

Phonetically speaking, the female character Mabel Blake or variants of her name and race recur in several of Wright's other works. "The Man Who Killed a Shadow" has a Maybelle character who is also a victim of a psychotic protagonist. In *The Long Dream*, there is a sensual African American girl, Maybelle, whose name Michel Fabre deciphers to mean "ma/belle"—that is, "beautiful mother"

(Fabre, *World* 121, n. 10). Nevertheless, the names *Mabel* and *Tony* in *Savage Holiday* may also refer to Mabel Dodge Luhan (1879–1962) and her Native American husband Tony, whom Wright visited in 1940 when the couple was living in Cuernavaca, Mexico. An American writer, Mabel Dodge Luhan moved to Taos, New Mexico, with her first husband Maurice to start a literary colony. Visitors included D. H. Lawrence. Luhan divorced Maurice in 1923 because Tony, a local Native American, would nightly drum outside her door until she came to him.[4] Wright associates the drumming sound with sexual connotations in *Savage Holiday*. One morning, Fowler wakes up to hear "*Bang bang bang* . . ."; "he knew that Tony was beating his drum" (*SH* 37). Another character's name has indirect sexual allusions. Wright may have named Mary Westerman, the superintendent of the Elmira Apartments, after Percy F. Westerman (1876–1960), a British pilot in World Wars I and II, who later gained popularity for publishing 174 novels for boys concerning air battles. Clearly, Tony associates Fowler's gift of a toy plane with sounds similar to his mother's lovemaking with clients. He becomes frightened of the object and gives it to Mrs. Westerman.[5]

Wright and Psychoanalysis: "Jazz and Desire" and Vindication for Clinton Brewer

Dedicated to Clinton Brewer, *Savage Holiday* may be viewed as a fictive jazz piece meant to honor him. Brewer's musical talent was undoubtedly an important factor because it contributed to Wright's interest in Brewer's case, which, in turn, led Wright to conduct psychoanalysis of his own life. When Brewer was placed in confinement at the Trenton State Prison, he composed "Stampede in G Minor," which Count Basie, a swing-era, big-band jazz musician, played and then included among his album's selections. The prison band even played Brewer's jazz piece for Wright when he visited the facility (Rowley 257). From that time in 1941 onward, Wright took a special interest in Brewer's musical talent. The beauty of jazz is that it can embrace all levels of tempo—fast and slow or harmonious and discordant. In an April 4, 1961, interview with Frank Tenot and published posthumously for *Cahiers du Jazz*, Wright clearly expresses that he does not like "modern jazz," but prefers the style of his era closely linked to the down-home blues and gospel music of the 1920s Jazz Age. Sometimes raw or graphic in sexual connotations, this form of jazz music was sung by Ma Rainey or Bessie Smith and played by Louis Armstrong or Count Basie. It was very erotic. Says Wright:

> The main gift that jazz has to offer the world today is an affirmation of *desire*. In spirituals and in Ray Charles . . . there's the same erotic exultation. This aspect of

> black music has been denied for too long. The faith of mystics and of most blacks has a sexual ingredient which well meaning people are too timid to dare admit, but which must be proclaimed. (Kinnamon and Fabre 243)

Wright's connecting jazz music to Freudian desire clarifies the reason for his interest in the Brewer case and his utilization of the musician's life story and musical talents as textual matters in *Savage Holiday*.

At the beginning of the novel and just before his retirement speech, Fowler has a combative meeting with Longevity Life's President Warren and "the crusty, acid-tongued vice president, Ricky" (24): "For almost five minutes the three of them had stood wordlessly in the tiny, closed room, fronting one another but avoiding one another's eyes, and in the background there was that faint, discordant plunking of a violin, the insistent sounding of the keys of A, B flat, and C on the piano . . ." (27). For Fowler, this modern-jazz piece of dissonant music being played on a piano with a violin accompaniment captures the discordant atmosphere that has been taking place in the room. It is not even a sorrowful jazz tune more like Brewer's "Stampede in G Minor" recorded by Count Basie. Brewer's piece better reflects Fowler's post-meeting, sorrowful emotional state as he leaves the banquet building. A stampede means "a sudden headlong rush often of animals" (Davies 677), which succinctly defines the beastly nature of President Warren's and Ricky's headlong attacks on Fowler's unworthiness to be a company man. A work played in G minor, like other minor chords, however, evokes a "sound [that is] a little sad" (Evans 51). Fowler's emotional state after the meeting certainly parallels the sorrowful, musical tones of the Brewer-Basie swing-era jazz piece played in G minor that, in the 1940s, earned public acclaim. As Wright says in his letter to the New Jersey governor, "The record is now being sold throughout the nation, under the title of 'Stampede in G Minor,' and Clinton Brewer is receiving royalties from its sale" (Wright to Edison, 30 March 1941, RWP). Fowler's postretirement emotional state compares to the swing-era's more harmonious jazz music that was popular between the 1920s and 1940s, rather than the discordant, modern jazz of the 1950s (the song is still available today on the Internet).[6]

Wright's remarks published in 1961 speak candidly about his preference for the blues and gospel lyrics accompanying the swing-era jazz music that Ray Charles carried over into the 1950s and 1960s. As a holistic work, many of the forms of lyrics and musical beats that are integrated into a jazz piece convey sexual allusions. Ray Charles's musical pieces are the best examples of sexually suggestive works. But Wright's enjoyment of jazz music was not always possible for him as an adolescent. Because of the Seventh-Day Adventist religious principles that Wright's grandmother stridently imposed upon her family, he says that "no piece of music ever sounded in my home save a hymn" ("Memories" 9). For the same reason, Wright adds, "she ordered me to destroy the first radio I brought into the house. She refused to believe that the music and the voices were coming over the air" (11). Since it was too difficult for Wright to override her authority, his hostility toward her religion could not "keep its influence from registering upon [his] sensibilities during [his] adolescence" (14). Despite her religious strictures, Wright still managed to attain the "ability to interpret the surrealistic theory of art by taking seemingly unrelated images and symbols and link[ing] them together into a meaningful whole" (24). When combined, blues lyrics and instrumental jazz music also could produce surrealistic art by linking them "together into a meaningful whole" as Wright has done in producing *Savage Holiday.*

Savage Holiday is Erskine Fowler's dissonant, modern-jazz/swing-era jazz refrain. The sound of clashing piano and violin modern-jazz music in "the keys of A, B flat, and C" during the office showdown symbolizes one aspect of his tragic downfall. But Brewer's swing-era jazz piece, "Stampede in G Minor," signifies the sorrowful, degenerate conditions under which Fowler grew up with his mother that became more compounded and degraded after his retirement: little Tony's accidental death and then Fowler's crazed murder of Mabel Blake. In the latter case, he became a woman-killing incarnation of Brewer, who experienced heartfelt sorrow for his criminal urges that he could not control. In essence, *Savage Holiday* is not only Wright's interrogation of psychoanalysis and his own psychoanalytical and autobiographical rendition of his childhood, but also his psychoanalytical study of music in its fictive form. Wright successfully transfers his real-life experiences as the fantastic and dramatic events punctuating and driving at a stampede pace the textual flow of Fowler's rapidly dissolving life that rushes forth in an outpouring of uncontrolled desire and rage like that of Brewer's jazz piece—itself a stampede moving at a stretch, without catching a breath.

Notes

A version of this essay appeared as "Subjacent Importance of Psychoanalysis in Richard Wright's *Savage Holiday.*" *Expressions: International Cultural Expression Studies* 9 (31 March 2013): 65–89.

1. Wright committed an error in speaking about his addressee. The actual name of the New Jersey governor was Charles Edison—not Thomas A. Edison Jr., son of the famed inventor Thomas A. Edison Sr.

2. The words *naked* or *nude* recur in variant forms on pages 26, 34, 35, 40, 41, 44, 46, 47, 49, 50, 51, 52, 54, 55, 56, 57, 58, 60, 61, 68, 71, 104, 107, 116, and 217.

3. Fowler repeatedly touches the four pencils on pages 16, 21, 27, 32, 83, 88, 116, 132, 154, 177, 219, and 220.

4. Mabel Luhan later published a memoir in 1923 about D. H. Lawrence's visit titled *Lorenzo in Taos*. Lawrence also wrote about the fraught relationship with his hostess. These books, along with Tony's interesting episode, enabled Wright to suspect that Mabel Luhan was sexually promiscuous.

5. Fowler lives on the tenth floor of the Elmira Apartment building. Wright's choice of a name for the building may have derived from several sources. The Elmira Institute was established in Elmira, New York, in 1876. The Wiltwych School for Boys may have influenced Wright since he was concerned about juvenile delinquents and the rehabilitation of offenders. He worked to solicit funding from the wealthy patrons of the Wiltwych School that was located along the Chemsung River on the west side of Binghamton and Elmira, New York.

6. "Stampede in G Minor" can be obtained from Yahoo Music or amazon.com for a small fee. It can also be listened to for free on YouTube.

Wright on Patmos: The European Refiguration of Mississippi in *The Long Dream*

—JOHN LOWE—

With the exception of Joyce Ann Joyce's unpublished dissertation, Richard Wright's 1958 novel *The Long Dream* has still not received the attention it deserves as one of the Mississippian's greatest creations. Discussions of the novel, when they occur, all too frequently relegate it as a lesser reworking, almost a retread, of the materials found in the author's earlier masterpieces set in his home state: *Uncle Tom's Children* (1938) and *Black Boy* (1945). We can all agree, however, whatever the merits of the book might be, that Wright was obviously, at this point in his life, drawn magnetically back to a South he could not forget. Indeed, the original title, rejected by his editor, was "Mississippi." I will here suggest, however, that he radically refigured that experience from the perspective of his years in Europe and his travels to Africa and Spain, the last twist of the lens of his ever-changing perspectives. As Michel Fabre's biography and subsequent books have copiously documented, Wright's life was a series of separations, flights, departures, and new visions. This had much to do with the protean nature of his work, which was always changing, and perhaps also had a decisive influence on the central characterization of Fishbelly, *The Long Dream*'s protagonist, in this bildungsroman. Wright creates a masterful portrait of Fishbelly's relationship with his powerful father, Tyree Tucker, which testifies to the fact that Wright was also returning at last to face his vexed relationship with his own father as an inevitable factor in any consideration of male identity formation in African America. Fishbelly's rebirth in the whalelike body of a silver airplane at the end of the book, en route to Paris, France, echoes Wright's own exile as well, and also sets a "type" of regeneration that was to find its "antitype" in the projected third novel of the trilogy.

In a work in progress, *Native Sons and Daughters*, I draw on my research at Yale University and my reading of the still-unpublished manuscript "Island of Hallucinations," the sequel to *The Long Dream*, to make a case for the novel as one of Wright's greatest achievements, and as a virtual laboratory for the dissection of black masculinity—a subject that has been given fascinating treatment by Jeffrey Geiger. Here, however, I emphasize the mythic aspects of these subjects by demonstrating how Wright used biblical typology, classical references, and copious doses of African American folk culture to deepen and underline his narrative strategies and thematics.

We might understand Wright's motives in this ultimate fictive return to his home state better by thinking of his sometime nemesis, Zora Neale Hurston. The Floridian grew up in an all-black rural town and was steeped in black folklore from birth, but in one of her most famous pronouncements, she claimed that it was only after her Northern education, particularly at Columbia, where she studied anthropology, that she was able to understand and truly "see" her past: "it was fitting me like a tight chemise. I couldn't see it for wearing it. It was only when I was off in college, away from my native surroundings, that I could see myself like somebody else and stand off and look at my garment. Then I had to have the spy-glass of Anthropology to look through at that" (Hurston, "Stories" 3). We are used to the argument, of course, that Wright similarly refigured his memories of Mississippi once he arrived in the North and began a massive program of reading, political action, and work with eminent University of Chicago sociologists. But after writing *Black Boy*, he put his Mississippi past aside and concentrated on other settings for his work. Subsequently, there was the move to New York, later to Paris, the trips I have mentioned, and a final reassessment of the world picture, his past, and his present. It can easily be seen that each of these changes caused Wright to recast his assessment of things; in each case, flight leads to temporary elation, a grappling with new circumstances, and, ultimately, to yet new disappointments.

In the final chapter of his last published novel, Wright replays an ending he used in his writings several times, that of flight to a "Promised Land." This had functioned most importantly in his early fiction at the conclusion of his magnificent 1936 short story, "Big Boy Leaves Home." In that narrative, the titled figure narrowly escapes the lynching and burning that he witnesses being inflicted on his best friend Bobo. Hidden inside the blackness of a truck rumbling north, Big Boy replicates the flight of slaves to the "Promised Land" of the North or Canada. Wright wrote the story, however, knowing the ironic reality of that distant realm, a grim reality he would chart in fiction in *Native Son* published in 1940 and in the second part of his 1945 biography, *American Hunger*, eventually published posthumously in 1977. In parallel fashion, this latter text similarly extended the narrative of *Black Boy*, which also ended in flight to a presumedly positive and promising Northern rebirth. *The Long Dream* reflects Wright's disillusionment, despite his happy family life in France, with his final refuge as an intellectual and artist, and a seeking, once again, for an antidote for his shattered aspirations in yet another realm, this ultimate time, in a fictive recreation of a Mississippi he in some ways never left.

The idea of Mississippi as a prison finds several expressions in Wright's books. Indeed, Fishbelly's growing sense of psychological confinement, as the social boundaries and opportunities around him paradoxically seem to be shrinking more rapidly when he inherits his father's empire, leads relentlessly to his actual incarceration in prison, a section of the book that inevitably recalls the final chapters of *Native Son*. Moreover, when asked about the European title of the book, *Fishbelly*, Wright told the interviewer that although the belly of a fish is white, "you can't actually see it"; thus, his hero, though black, looks at the world through black eyes, but eyes influenced by his absorption of the values of white society ("Interview with Richard Wright" 205). Therefore, Fishbelly's confinement is something he must learn to see by acquiring a second kind of sensory equipment.

The concept of actual flight eventually culminated in Wright's own life in his self-removal from the United States to Paris, where *The Long Dream* was written. Ironically, however, it was inspired to some extent by the story of a black youth, Ish Kelley, who was expelled from France for illicit relations with white women. Addison Gayle also suggests that Wright himself was feeling rejected by the expatriate black circles in Paris, citing Baldwin's summary of the older writer's gradual estrangement, one by one, with his peers: "Gone were the days when he had only to enter a café to be greeted with the American equivalent of 'cher maître'" (Gayle 280). Once again, he created a narrative based in the South of his youth that eventuated in flight, this time a literal one, because the final, brief chapter takes place in the belly/womb of a great silver airplane/fish, and appropriately a liminal space for the hero, Fishbelly. As he looks out the window, he feels his "yearning to be at last somewhere at home" (410).

We know, however, from a letter Wright wrote to his editor Edward Aswell, that writing this final scene in the plane gave him more trouble than anything else in the book. Why? Perhaps one answer lies in the obvious parallel in this decisive moment of transition in his character's life, the matching one in his own life, and ambiguities about the realities he knew would await Fishbelly once he landed at Orly—the beginning point for the fascinating unpublished sequel "Island of Hallucinations." In 1957, Wright was not only reassessing his past in Mississippi, but also what life in France had meant to him and had now become for him. As this projected title demonstrates, Wright's life in Paris had been illuminating and exhilarating, but disillusioning as well. The readings and experiences that he had amassed in the years preceding the composition of *The Long Dream* had a crucial effect upon the outcome of his refiguration of Mississippi and the way that he planned to expand Fishbelly's story in the sequel. Conversely, adverse American reaction to *The Long Dream* had a devastating effect upon Wright and definitely transformed his writing of "Island of Hallucinations."

To better illustrate my argument, I would like to point to a basic narrative construction that I believe is typical of Wright's entire work and is illustrated nowhere better than in this novel. Namely, in a biblically inspired prophetic mode and one that found shaping and amplification in his secular role as Communist activist, it has a basically apocalyptic vision that owes much not only to the tropes and methods of the book of Revelation, but also to its function as a completion and fulfillment of the New Testament as well as the Old. One of the key incidents in the novel occurs when Fish and Tony are unfairly arrested by white policemen for trespassing on white-owned property. Fish is terrified to realize that he has a newspaper picture of a scantily clad white woman in his wallet; surreptitiously, he swallows it. As Earle Bryant has noted, "Fish has enthroned within himself the image of the white woman, has incorporated it into his being forever" (64). I would suggest that this process began much earlier, and, ironically, in lessons taught to him by his father, who, as Bryant also points out, has been intent on teaching Fish the cardinal lesson for a black man: Never look at a white woman. Tyree, however, contradicts his own rule by preferring white-looking African American women within his own race; his mistress Gloria, whose chief glory seems to be her light skin color, dazzles Fish, and leads to his own selection of an even whiter woman, Gladys, as his own mistress. Moreover, by ingesting the photograph, Fish's action suggests a sacramentalization of white standards similar to a biblical parallel between the ingesting scene and that of Revelation 10, where an angel instructs John to seal up the things the seven thunders have revealed and "write them not." The prophet, on the other hand, is instructed to eat a little book that is in an angel's hand: "And he said unto me, Take it, and eat it up; and it shall make thy belly bitter, but it shall be in thy mouth sweet as honey. And I took the little book out of the angel's hand, and ate it up; and it was in my mouth sweet as honey: and as soon as I had eaten it, my belly was bitter. And he said unto me, Thou must prophesy again before many peoples, and nations, and tongues, and kings" (Rev. 10: 9–11).

We have already seen how Wright in many ways is reaching back to his past, rewriting scenes he had now rethought and refigured, with much more fantastical elements; this was the method of the writer of Revelation as well, for many of the passages in that text, which Northrup Frye and other biblical scholars have shown, is consciously constructed to relate back to and confirm the prophecies of the Old Testament (Frye 119). The scene where Fish eats the newspaper clipping, already established as a parallel to the eating of the book from the angel's hand in Revelation, has an almost exact precedent in Ezekiel 2 and 3, where God calls upon Ezekiel to preach to Israel: "For they are impudent children and stiffhearted . . . yet shall know that there hath been a prophet among them . . . And thou shalt speak my words unto them, whether they will hear, or whether they will forbear: for they are most rebellious." God then forces Ezekiel to eat a rolled-up book, in which is written woe, mourning, and lamentations: "Fill thy bowels with this roll that I give thee. Then did I eat it; and it was in my mouth as honey for sweetness" (Ezek. 3:3). The roll is sweet, Joel Rosenberg suggests, because of the prophet's obedience to his calling (197), suggesting that Wright has answered a call with a newly conceived "response," one based on his European experiences and disappointments.

The sequel to this novel would prove even more intent on the fantastic images inspired by Revelation, as the following passage proves:

> There's nothing on earth calculated to shatter a person's faith in the ordinary reality of life better than an atmosphere like this. When you make a person feel that what he sees and lives each day and hour is not true, then it is as though you shunted him off the earth. He is on an island and this island is himself. . . . Most of the world we live in is given to us by those around us. In order to live we must trust, in a sense, even our enemies. No man can stand absolutely alone and make any meaning out of life. When you begin distrusting the images that make your world, you're standing alone. Soon you'll begin to doubt everything. Your world turns into a dream. It is as though you were having a hallucination. ("Island of Hallucinations" ["IH"] 328; cited in Fabre 1973 *UQ* 481)

This important passage reveals that Wright's use of the word *dream* really means, in most cases, *hallucination,* which makes Tzvetan Todorov's definition of the fantastic much more applicable. We remember that the title *The Long Dream* was not Wright's choice, but his editor's. He had himself initially preferred "Mississippi," and then "The Double Hearted" or "American Shadow" (Fabre, 1973 *UQ* 453). Moreover, this passage takes us back to the parallels with the biblical book of Revelation, which details the solitary visions/hallucinations of Saint John the Divine on the Isle of Patmos, where he has been imprisoned for his Christian faith. The tone and mood of the book is persecution; many scholars have thus felt it was written in the terrible days of Nero's rule. Furthermore, the book strongly relates to the earlier imagery and language of the Old Testament rather than the New Testament, a pattern that one could find parallel to Wright's early Southern life, Northern years, and the imaginative return to the South at the end of his life in France.

We should also bear in mind that *The Long Dream* in some ways returns us to the ending of *Black Boy* and its memorable conclusion:

> I was not leaving the South to forget the South, but so that some day I might understand it, might come to know what its rigors had done to me, to its children. I fled so that the numbness of my defensive living might thaw out and let me feel the pain—years later and far away—of what living in the South had meant. Yet, deep

> down, I knew that I could never really leave the South, for my feelings had been formed by the South, for there had been slowly instilled into my personality and consciousness, black though I was, the culture of the South. So, in leaving, I was taking a part of the South to transplant in alien soil, to see if it could grow differently. . . . And if that miracle ever happened, then I would know that . . . light could emerge even out of the blackest of the southern night. I would know that the South too could overcome its fear, its hate, its cowardice, its heritage of guilt and blood, its burden of anxiety and compulsive cruelty. (*BB* 227–28; qtd. in Fabre, *World* 82)

We notice the prescient use of the plural—the affective rains, winds, and other suns—that accurately suggest that the North will be only the initial scene of transplantation. Did Wright's "part of the South," internally and externally shaping him, indeed bloom again in, and because of, France? The evidence of *The Long Dream* would suggest that it did, especially when one compares the sense of the South that the book conjures. In this novel, Wright seems to imagine a childhood that might have been, for he described Fishbelly this way: "When [a] person happens to be black and the son of a rich black father in Mississippi, then the absorption of the values of the society in which he is born assumes fantastic forms" (summary of *The Long Dream*, Richard Wright Papers [RWP]; cited in Fabre, *World* 83). The word *fantastic* is revealing, particularly when we follow Todorov's suggestion that this realm presents us with an event "not likely to occur in everyday life" (34), one that some might mistakenly term *supernatural,* a much more extensive frame of reference.

But what do we mean by "everyday life"? Richard Wright, throughout his work, forced white readers to face the eruption of grotesquely "fantastic" events in the lives of his black characters. Many times—as in the scenes in *Native Son* set in the skull-like, empty building on the South Side where Bigger hides after murdering Mary, and where he will later kill Bessie—we are situated in the realm of the Gothic. But Todorov's emphasis is not on being placed in a setting, but in the explosion of a fantastic action. These actions can have a stunting or blighting effect. Wright, in his remarks on the novel, repeated the plant imagery that concludes *Black Boy*. *The Long Dream*, he said, "deals with a black human plant that has to draw its nourishment from abnormal conditions of life" (summary of *The Long Dream*, RWP; cited in Fabre, *World* 83).

We must note at this point the trajectory that Wright intended for the projected trilogy of novels that would continue—first in "Island of Hallucinations," which details Fishbelly's dissolute life in France as a pimp and ne'er-do-well; finally, resolution in a final volume (which Wright never completed) that would take Fishbelly first to Africa and finally back to New York with his wife and child. "Island" ponders the question of why black expatriates, once situated in

France, are unable to break out of the obsessions that hobbled them in America. Wright posits:

> There's nothing on earth calculated to shatter a person's faith in the ordinary reality of life better than an atmosphere like this. When you make a person feel that what he sees and lives each day and hour is not true, then it is as though you shunted him off the earth. He is on an island and this island is himself. . . . No man can stand absolutely alone and make any meaning out of life. When you begin distrusting the images that make your world, you're standing alone. Soon you'll begin to doubt everything. Your world turns into a dream. It is as though you were having a hallucination. ("IH" 328; cited in Fabre, 1973 *UQ* 481)

The bitter satire of disillusionment that Fish experiences in this novel was parallel with Wright's, and his despair only deepened when he received news of his mother's death in January 1959. Conversations with Martin Luther King Jr. around this time did not improve his mood, as King, too, was pessimistic about racial relations in the United States. However, as Fabre points out, liberal Americans—especially white ones—felt things were changing after *Brown v. Board of Education* (1954), and were impatient with negative views of the racial impasse like those found in *The Long Dream*. Certainly early academic critics of Wright fell in this category as well. Wright clearly felt like a prophet without honor: "If they define being for America as being unable to say that America is not perfect, then they can say that I'm a bad guy . . . this makes it hard for a writer. . . . I've grown to feel that nobody, not even Negroes, wants to listen anymore. Yet I'm convinced that I'm telling some important truths" (Fabre, 1973 *UQ* 485)

Accordingly, Wright pressed on with the trilogy and sent his editor two long letters outlining the final volume. It finds Fish finally deciding to marry one of his pregnant French mistresses and to leave France with her, first to North Africa, and then black Africa, where he starts a business. His mother comes over when his son is born, and persuades Fish and family to relocate in New York. Fabre reports that the novel was to conclude with musings over Fish's son; should he return to Mississippi with his grandmother, or live in New York or France? (Fabre, 1973 *UQ* 486).

As this brief summary indicates, Wright in many ways is preceding Paul Gilroy's pronouncements in his seminal text, *The Black Atlantic*, but he also seems to be prophesying future explorations and linkages for all people of color between Europe, Africa, and the Americas. Walt Whitman once declared that the role of the prophet had been misunderstood—too many think that the role leads merely to condemnation. But as Whitman helpfully noted, the prophet always concludes by offering hope of the restoration of the covenant between

God and man. Wright's refiguration of Mississippi also came after extensive readings of Faulkner's work. When the white writer won the Nobel Prize in the early 1950s, Wright claimed that in showing the "degradation of the South," Faulkner had "affirmed its essential humanity for America and for the world. . . . Faulkner's gallery of characters will live as long as men feel the need to know themselves" (cited in Fabre, *World* 90). The statement is an indication of the importance of transcending the bonds of mere chronological time in his own work as he considered posterity.

The Long Dream begins with a re-creation of Richard Wright's childhood, but with a very different set of parents. In terms of the basic dynamic of the book, Wright sets up a fantastic, nightmare world, one framed by the unstated assumption that it may be understood only against the backdrop of a constitutionally imagined America of decency and basic rights. As Wright would claim, "In the United States, we [African Americans] fight for a real application of the Constitution (Clark, "Richard Wright" 449), underlining the *unreality* of everyday illegalities in black life. He also claimed that Tyree's encomium to Fishbelly, "Don't allow yourself to be carried away too far by your dream," really meant, "If you really believe what is written in the Constitution, you will get killed" (Clark, "Richard Wright" 451). Fishbelly, like Jonah himself, is protected for a time within the belly of his wealthy family, without understanding the peril this "whale" experiences every day, navigating among the sharks of white America. Wright said of this book's characters, "Though black, they react positively to the dominant values of the white world in which they live—that is, sex and money—and their conditioning takes place in an atmosphere charged with greed, lust, betrayal, a world in which justice is bought and sold, where money means love and love means money." This suggests that Fishbelly's father, Tyree, simultaneously engaged in the legal business of undertaking and an illegal one of prostitution, and is, as a merchant of love and death, a demonic emblemization and epitome of underlying white values. These realms become fused in the tragic nightclub fire that lies at the novel's heart, where the woman Fishbelly has both bought and loved, Gladys, is incarcerated, ironically in a building his father owns and has largely designed as a money-making honey trap with barred windows. The latter fact is important, for Wright immediately saw in this aspect of the real fire that killed 209 people in his native Natchez at the Rhythm Night Club on the night of April 23, 1940. The fire functions as a metaphor for the hopeless and ultimately fatal condition of his fellow blacks. As he stated clearly in an interview just three months before his death in 1960, "Mississippi is only an immense black ghetto, a vast prison where the whites are the jailers and the Negroes are the prisoners" ("Interview with Richard Wright" 202). Obviously, he felt the situation he had written in *The Long Dream*, although it would be attacked as out of date, was still an accurate rendition of realities, for in the same interview he stated that "unfortunately, I do not have to return there to write about the United States because the situation changes so slowly" (202).

Certainly there is more overt sexuality in this late novel than in Wright's earlier Mississippi texts. The initial nicknaming of Rex as "Fishbelly" involves a comparison of the smell of fish with female sexuality; there are scenes making comic use of condoms, and many more that detail a young boy's acquisition of innumerable signals that sex is "nasty," obscene, forbidden, dangerous, and associated with death. An early segment begins the constellation of episodes that merge death and sex, when the child Fish discovers his father having intercourse with a "customer" in a tomb-like, "fetid" storeroom in the undertaking parlor. His father, the child thinks at first, must be "working on a dead body," but when Fish sees Tyree in the throes of sex, with "red eyes" blazing, he seems to us like a vampire, and then, through Fishbelly's eyes, like a pulsing locomotive. This scene of course suggests Ham's biblical sin of looking upon his father Noah's nakedness, thereby establishing the curse of bondage. Wright seems to be signifying upon the racist assumption that this myth explains the origins of black people, cursed to bondage, by suggesting that all men in some fashion are enslaved to their father's sexuality, especially in an America obsessed with sex and money, and where, all too often, the woman is indeed "worked on," rather than lovingly caressed. The narcissistic focus on the train image causes Fish to want to go home and play with his toy trains as well, suggesting the casting of the malignant spell of sexuality's bondage on the young acolyte. Perhaps nowhere in all African American literature is there a more compelling linkage of sex and death, for the biological desires of the black male body are inevitably attracted to the omnipresent images of the white woman. And yet to embrace—or even look at—that body is to invite a violent retribution, even death and/or castration. Jeffrey Geiger has persuasively described the intricate set of images and narrative clusters that Wright plants in this novel that focus on the triangle of desire/castration/death.

The demand of the white mob for the blood of a sacrificial victim such as Chris, the bellboy who has had sex with a white prostitute, offers yet another example of the blasphemous activities of the racists who are allowed to run amok by the authorities, who know that their own power is predicated upon the enactment of these savage rites. As such, all levels of society cooperate in a replication of the act of God in the Old Testament when he demands that Abraham be willing to kill his own son Isaac on the Lord's altar. Chris, of course, *is* killed and dismembered, but we should remember that Fish himself is threatened with castration four times by the white policemen, and three times he faints at the sight of the approaching knife. Each time, the knife is sheathed, for the symbolic power of the patriarchs has been given a visible and, it seems, amusing "sign." Conversely, however, Tyree forces Fishbelly to gaze at Chris's nude, broken, and mutilated body as Doc performs an autopsy, intoning the lesson for his son that to look on a white woman is to invite this fate.

By the time *The Long Dream* (1958) appeared, Wright had been to Africa, written *Black Power* (1954), and met many African intellectuals in France. He was much more conscious of his black ancestry, and *The Long Dream* shows it in many ways, particularly in the early scene where Sam has a long argument with his childhood chums, including Fishbelly, about Africa. According to Sam's father, "black folks ought to build up Africa, 'cause that's our true home," to which Fishbelly replies, "All I know about Africa's what I read in the geography book at school," an obvious echo of Countee Cullen's poem "Heritage," which had intoned, "What is Africa to me . . . ? / A book one thumbs / Listlessly, till slumber comes" (Locke, *New Negro* 250). Sam raises the stakes, however, by dropping his argument about going to Africa by sarcastically suggesting that they go to America—although they are theoretically *in* America. As Sam says, "'Cause the white man took you out [of Africa]," he argues that they "ain't in America, 'cause if you were, you'd act like *Americans*," rather than the part of Jumpin' Jim Crow. This deeply meaningful argument, proceeding out of the verbal dueling of boys, leads to a fight between Fish and Sam because, of course, it cannot be resolved. The doubleness, directly addressed in Cullen's poem, of black consciousness in the prison house of white America inevitably leads to violence that is frequently self-destructive, as this scene and its sequel reveal; after the fight, Fishbelly stares at the mirror, spits, and hisses "Nigger" (*Long Dream* [*LD*] 34).

By this time, Wright had also met many gay writers and ordinary citizens, including James Baldwin, and had read much more psychoanalytical material, including Edmund Bergler's *The Writer and Psychoanalysis*, (1951), which he bought in 1954 (Fabre, *Books* 12). This was a continuing interest, as he would also purchase Edmund Bergler's 1951 book *Neurotic Counterfeit-Sex* on homosexuality, impotence, and frigidity in England in 1958. *The Long Dream* dramatizes the parallel between the treatment of blacks and homosexuals in a rather distanced way in the early childhood chapters, when Fishbelly and his friends brutally beat a "sissie" who wants to play ball with them. Afterward, Zeke mumbles, "We treat 'im like the white folks treat us," and when Fishbelly says the "pansy" should stay away from them, Zeke responds, "That's just what the white folks say about us" (37). In "Island of Hallucinations," Wright would feature a major gay character named Mechanical, but his life and ultimate suicide prove to be meaningless.

Wright had had an opportunity in Paris to compare and contrast the modes of black entertainment preferred in America and Europe. The success of black nightclubs, black musicians, and black dancers and singers, performing authentically in their own chosen way, rather than according to minstrelsy-derived formulas, caused him to go back to the seedy sideshows of Mississippi's fairs, which are replicated with telling effect, again in the childhood scenes. Fish and his friends attend on "colored day," but of course whites, who attend all other days, are permitted in on this day, too. The white girlie show, which seeks customers by presenting one of the white dancers in front of the tent with a barker, also presents the sign "NO COLORED." The scene begins a long pattern of examples on how black males are relentlessly acculturated to desire white woman, while simultaneously being legally and extralegally blocked from satisfying those desires. The black sideshow the boys do attend includes a boring "Mack and Jack" minstrel routine, complete with black-painted, white-lipped artists who wearily tell racist jokes. Wright brilliantly underlines the self-destructive ethos of this performance, which the boys enjoy, by following it with their attendance and participation in the "Hit the Nigger" game. While it permits the chained black human target to taunt white customers, it causes great shame on the part of the boys, who revealingly vent their rage not at the abstract system, but at the black man who has caused it: "That obscene black face was his own face and to quell the war in his heart, he had either to reject it in hate or accept it in love. It was easier to hate that degraded black face than to love it" (44), and although Fish misses, Tony hits the pathetic target, causing the white crowd to "orgiastically" rejoice, "The nigger hit the nigger!" (45). Ashamed, the boys leave, but as they pass a circus tent, a white woman, unbuttoning her blouse, offers to service them for five dollars apiece. Terrified, they flee from this "lynch-bait," but the ever-philosophic Sam muses, "She wasn't no different from that nigger who let you throw two balls at 'im" (44).

The entire sequence of events at the carnival strongly echoes the thematics of the battle royal scene of Ralph Ellison's *Invisible Man*—but, of course, Ellison had been strongly influenced, in turn, by Wright's even earlier portrayal of whites inciting blacks to fight each other in young Richard's fight with Harrison in *Black Boy*. Here, however, the carnival episode shows Wright's vastly increased consciousness of the underlying social implications of black participation in white-dominated popular entertainment.

The many initiations in pain and suffering that one finds in Wright's earlier works are frequently transposed here to psychological rituals, although these, too, are usually based in horrific violence. When Chris, a black bellboy at a local hotel, is tortured, castrated, and lynched because of his affair with a white whore, the entire black community pays a terrible price, and Tyree finds it is time to initiate his son—only twelve but still a man in white eyes—into the realm of black male survival tactics. Always, the Golden Rule is "NEVER LOOK AT A WHITE WOMAN." Later, to reinforce this lesson, Tyree, who as the black undertaker, prepares the mutilated body of Chris for burial, forces Fish to look on. This pattern follows the method of "Big Boy Leaves Home," where the title figure hides in the kiln and receives the same terrible education by watching a similar fate befall his best friend. The difference in the two texts is that Wright, by opting for a presentation of Mississippi through the eyes of a different class, seizes on the opportunity to accompany the horrific visuals with equally commanding words, as Tyree annotates the text of Chris's body, who, like the Christ who died before him, is meant to instruct all mankind, but in a terrible gospel of fear, masking, and survival. Later this scene will be echoed when Fish dissects a dead dog in order to prepare himself psychologically for what white folks might one day do to him.

As Yoshinobu Hakutani states, "Thematically, *The Long Dream* focuses on Fishbelly's creation of himself through sexual initiation" (Hakutani, *Dream* 267). The initiation, however, is inexorably linked to the theme of miscegenation and Fishbelly's fascinated location on the shores of "dread and delight" as he contemplates the forbidden temptation of the white woman's body, whether it be that of actual white women or white-appearing African American women.

Although there have always been and still are critics of *The Long Dream,* most of them have tended to echo the verdict of the first ones—something like "It's no *Native Son* or, alternately, as noted earlier, "Wright had been away from Mississippi too long." To my mind, Donald Gibson has offered the best explanation for the general dismissal of the novel; he notes that here, for the first time, in the convincing figures of Tyree and Fish, Wright had focused on characters who are virtually powerless to alter their circumstances. Tyree's life is first dominated by and then taken by the white chief of police; subsequently, Fish is unjustly incarcerated for two years. Gibson goes on to state that the book looks backward to the characters of earlier African American writers such as Charles Chesnutt and Paul Laurence Dunbar (Gibson 83–84).

In another cogent and influential critique of the novel, Edward Margolies compares it to Wright's 1938 story "Fire and Cloud," which depicts a similar moment of racial oppression, but ends in a heroic and communal stand against the powers that be. For Margolies, by 1958 there should have been even more opportunity for protest and action: "The first stirrings of the Negro rebellion had already begun to achieve results. Ironically, Wright had given up hope in a dream he had visualized so accurately twenty years before" (Margolies, *Art* 70). And yet Margolies will also say, "Oddly, Wright, now twenty-nine years removed from Mississippi, provides his readers with a more tangible sense of time and place than in much of his earlier fiction" (151). Margolies, however, wrote this in 1969, and perhaps he himself was the victim of misreading recent history. In 1958, I would submit, conditions were in fact very much as Wright depicted them, and it is simply inaccurate to think that the thousands of angry and effective protesters of the late sixties represent the late fifties. This is all the more striking because in other ways, Margolies offers one of the very best readings of the novel, particularly in the parallels that he finds between Fish and the protagonist of *Black Boy*, and in his careful delineation of what he terms the novel's "social freudianism."

One reason that critics have not taken Fishbelly more seriously surely stems from his undeniable location among the black bourgeoisie for the first two-thirds of the book. In this respect, he prefigures one of Toni Morrison's key figures, Milkman Dead, who in *Song of Solomon*, many have argued, only comes to the fore powerfully in the last third of the book. In both narratives, the authors seem to take special pains to portray the callousness of these figures in early life, perhaps to more boldly highlight their eventual transformations. As Margolies claimed some time ago for *The Long Dream*, both novels, in fact, epitomize the American genre of the search for identity and rebirth (*Art* 154). Margolies, however, ultimately claims the novel, in particular, and Wright, in general, fail to achieve greatness because their dreams—Fishbelly's and Wright's—for some reason have to be related to a particular environment. Thus, Fishbelly's flight to Paris at the end of the book—and, one presumes, Wright's expatriation—represents a kind of copout, both personally and in terms of the demands of narrative. Margolies calls this a "paradox"—that the dream of freedom and dignity that develops in Mississippi can never be realized there: "And it is doubtless because he could not resolve it that Richard Wright seldom achieved his fullest measure of artistic promise" (*Art* 167).

Again, Margolies was writing this in the apocalyptic and absolutist days of the sixties. Toni Morrison, in more measured words, later in the eighties was to suggest that a novel "should have something in it that enlightens; something in it that opens the door and points the way. Something in it that suggests what the conflicts are, what the problems are. But it need not solve those problems because it is not a case study, it is not a recipe" (341).

Fishbelly, as the projected leading figure in the third novel of the trilogy, finally becomes centered in himself and is the paterfamilias figure Wright himself tried to be within his own nuclear family. There is at least some indication that in projecting this idea of Fishbelly, Wright was seeing the character's final emergence as Rex, his actual name, king of a new order, after passing through the worlds of a racially terrorizing South, France, Africa, and then back to the South. In this sense we have witnessed yet another aspect of Wright as racial prophet, and, of course, experienced a reverse migration in the past few decades to the South, and after the period of black nationalism and the liberation of Africa that Wright did not live to see)—one in keeping with the book of Revelation. As such, Rex becomes the saving remnant, a concept crucial in both the Old and New Testament, particularly in the depiction of the seven churches of Asia in Revelation, the concluding text. As Northrup Frye has stated, "The feeling that a pure or homogeneous group, no matter how small, is the only socially effective one, and in times of crisis is the one to be kept for see, so to speak, until a new age dawns, is an integral part of the revolutionary consciousness" (Frye 119). We remember, too, that Wright kept his children away from America to keep them "uncontaminated."

Richard Wright died at age fifty-two on November 28, 1960. Although the last years of Wright's life may be read as a tragic story of increasing isolation, suspicion, and bitterness as well as increasing physical pain and disability, there is also reason to see the writer's final years like all the others—as a time when he somehow fended off these adverse conditions and found a generative fire for his creative life precisely in his exile and solitude. In this he perhaps resembles the contemporary critic Edward Said, who in his memoir, aptly titled *Out of Place*, has declared, "Better to wander out of place, not to own a house, and not ever to feel too much at home anywhere, especially in a city like New York, where I shall be until I die" (294). Indeed, just before his death Wright was planning another novel that was to be called "Celebration."

Along these lines, the negative reception of *The Long Dream* in the United States centered on the charge that Wright had been away too long, was too crudely presenting black/white relations, and was writing, as one critic said, "as if nothing had changed since he grew up in Mississippi" (Anon., "Tract in Black" 95). Michel Fabre, however, who has had access to the manuscript of the sequel, "Island of Hallucinations," asserts that it proves *The Long Dream* to be a "solid foundation for this new departure" and not just a "return to the beaten path" (1973 *UQ* 468). Wright's great predecessor in examining the dark recesses of the American psyche, Nathaniel Hawthorne, wrote tellingly of the effect of a writer's experiences abroad:

> The years, after all, have a kind of emptiness when we spend too many of them on a foreign shore. We defer the reality of life, in such cases, until a future moment when we shall again breathe our native air; but, by and by there are no future moments; or, if we do return, we find that the native air has lost its invigorating quality, and that life has shifted its reality to the spot where we have deemed ourselves only temporary residents. Thus, between two countries, we have none at all, or only that little space of either in which we finally lay down our discontented bones. (461)

Although I suspect Wright would have found much to agree with in Hawthorne's somber assessment, we can claim, on the basis of *The Long Dream*, that Wright's final refuge, even though it might be all too similar to the Patmos of Saint John, was the true isle of hallucinations, that of his fiction. Like Melville in his last years, protected by his family but isolated and out of literary favor, he found refuge in his art, refiguring his past and issuing one final, grim warning, pointing the prophet's finger at the mysteries of man's glories and iniquities.

To fully understand the significance and power of *The Long Dream,* we need to see how it reflects Wright's mature stance as racial and historical prophet, one who had slipped the bonds not just of the repressive American South, but also of any narrowly defined national identity. His projected transnational trilogy, located in all three poles of the black Atlantic, would refigure the thematics that he had charted much earlier in *Native Son* and his other Southern works, showing how issues that many Northern scholars and thinkers of the United States (and European critics too) were able to consider but not address in their own realms because of their insistence on identifying racial oppression with the American South. Wright, to his credit, exploded this paradigm, but he also went beyond race to demonstrate that it was one of the central barriers—albeit a crucial one for people of color around the globe—against the forging of a modernist identity, one in keeping with the enduring quest for dignity of the human soul.

Signifying and Self-Portraiture in Richard Wright's *A Father's Law*

—ROBERT BUTLER—

The novel that Richard Wright was trying to complete at the time of his death, *A Father's Law*, invites the reader from its opening paragraphs to connect it with Wright's first published novel, *Native Son*. By thus signifying on the two books that bracket his career as a novelist, Wright created an interesting conversation between these novels that reveals much about his overall development as a writer.

The "*Brrrrrrrriiiiiiiiiiiiiiiiiiiinng!*"of an alarm clock that opens *Native Son* shocks Bigger Thomas into an awareness of a grim problem that demands his immediate attention—a rat has entered his family's apartment and he must kill it (1998 *Native Son* [NS] 3). In a strikingly similar way, *A Father's Law* opens with a harsh, grating sound, the "*Wrrrriiiiiieeeeee . . .*" of a telephone that jars the central character awake, confronting him with a problem that could very well destroy him by the end of the novel (*A Father's Law* [*FL*] 1). Both novels, therefore, are calculated by Wright as "wake-up calls" that exhort the reader to become more sharply aware of serious problems that, if not addressed, can lead to disastrous consequences.

A Father's Law also abounds with other revealing parallels with *Native Son*, which strongly suggest that Wright at the end of his life was consciously signifying on his first published novel. Ruddy Turner's neighbor is named Mr. Britten, the name used by Wright in *Native Son* for the prosecuting attorney who badgers Bigger in court. Both novels are saturated with images of ticking clocks that create a sense of inevitable doom for the central characters and also suggest that the problems explored in each novel are veritable "time bombs" that will explode if not adequately understood and dealt with.

Images of blindness and vision are also threaded throughout both novels as a way of exploring appearance/reality themes that go to their thematic cores. The central characters in both books are initially blinded by illusions and appearances that are gradually stripped away, confronting them with harsh realities that either overwhelm them or spur them into psychological growth. In the opening scene of *A Father's Law*, for example, Ruddy's eyes are "sleep drugged" (2), suggesting his inability to see clearly the problems that threaten him and his family. By the end of the novel, his eyes are described as "sightless" (268), indicating that he is still too stunned by the light of reality to see his situation clearly. Bigger Thomas's story also begins with his eyes out of focus as he struggles to orient himself in a world of poverty, racism, and violence, but by the end of *Native Son* he has achieved a lucid vision of himself and the world as he glares ironically at Max, who is finally portrayed as "a blind man" (1998 *NS* 424).

Native Son and *A Father's Law* also focus sharply on family problems and generational conflicts as parents and children struggle to relate to and/or to teach others in a culture that changes so rapidly that real understanding between generations is difficult, perhaps impossible, to achieve. Tommy, Ruddy's eighteen-year-old son, is as much a puzzle to his parents as is Bigger to his mother. Just as Mrs. Thomas is confounded by her son and at one point exclaims, "Boy, I sometimes wonder what makes you act like you do" (1998 *NS* 7), Ruddy in desperation asks himself, "What's wrong with that boy?" (*FL* 6). Mrs. Thomas's worries about her son run so deeply that she prophesies disaster for him, warning him that "the gallows is at the end of the road you travel" (1998 *NS* 9). Similarly, Ruddy has dark suspicions that his son may be involved in a series of brutal murders that may result in his execution. Ruddy's frustrations with his son become so extreme that late in the novel he cries out, "Boy, are you crazy?" (*FL* 8). And while Mrs. Thomas becomes so exasperated with Bigger that she exclaims, "Boy, sometimes I wonder why I birthed you" (1998 *NS* 8), Ruddy wonders whether his problems with his son are rooted in his "not really wanting" (*FL* 251) any offspring.

The novels are further linked by several other significant similarities. Although the two books are set in similar parts of Chicago, Wright employs nearly identical surrealistic images to describe them. The ghetto is often described in *Native Son* as a Gothic mindscape that forces the reader to experience Bigger's psychological disorientation as he confronts a world that is an extended nightmare. Deserted houses are seen as "skeletons with snow on their bones" (1998 *NS* 173); streetlamps cast a ghastly "yellow sheen" (47), and windows of abandoned buildings are likened to "eye sockets of empty skulls" (231). The upscale suburb in *A Father's Law* is also often portrayed in Gothic terms as a way of re-creating the mental stress of the central characters as they experience the dark realities lurking beneath the apparently calm, rational nature of their ordinary lives. Streetlamps "glow . . . like blobs of shimmering gold" (*FL* 127) and cast "hazy blobs" (14) of yellow light, creating an eerie atmosphere that approximates the strange mental life into which Ruddy descends as he explores the murky world of serial killing. As he examines the densely wooded area where several murders have taken place, he thinks that "such a landscape offered criminal possibilities galore" (128). In both novels Wright abandons the standard techniques of mimetic fiction, using surrealistic settings to dramatize heightened states of mind experienced by his psychologically stressed characters, who are at various points pushed to their rational limits and inhabit what David Weimer has called "the landscape of hysteria" (52).[1]

But by far the most significant parallel between *A Father's Law* and *Native Son* is the fact that their narratives are centered on single dramatic moments that radically change the lives of the central characters by confronting them with shocking epiphanies that completely discredit their earlier assumptions about life and plunge them into a wildly irrational world that they can neither understand nor control. Bigger experiences this life-changing moment when his lovemaking with Mary Dalton turns into his killing her in irrational panic when her mother enters the room. Tommy Turner's entire life is likewise turned upside down when he discovers that his fiancée has congenital syphilis, thus destroying his hopes for a stable life centered on love and turning him into a crazed serial killer. In both cases, the impulse to love has been blocked with disastrous consequences, converting a rational desire for intimacy into a mad impulse to destroy. Although Tommy does not literally kill Marie, he admits to his father that his abandonment of her amounted to his having "killed" her because she no longer has the will to live (*FL* 175).

Ruddy will receive a similar shock of recognition on the book's final pages when he reads the newspapers and learns that his son has confessed to the wave of murders he has been investigating. Such a revelation could very well destroy his rational, stable life, plunging him into the despair and destructive behavior that have consumed both his son and Bigger Thomas.[2]

Two Different Social Works

What is extremely surprising about these parallels between *Native Son* and *A Father's Law* is the extraordinary discrepancy between these two novels in terms of the social environments that comprise their settings. While *Native Son* takes place in a hellish racial ghetto in one of the worst years of the Great Depression, an environment that explains most of the terrible violence and suffering depicted in that novel, *A Father's Law* is set in a prosperous suburb during the post–World War II American boom, which provides the Turner family with an apparently stable, loving human environment. Tommy Turner is approximately the same age as Bigger Thomas, but unlike Bigger, he enjoys a social world that gives him not only material comfort but also emotional stability and human possibility. He owns a sports car whereas Bigger can only drive a car when he assumes the subservient role of chauffeur. While Bigger has dropped out of school and has little chance of gaining further education, Tommy is a brilliant student at an elite university and can expect the life of greatly expanded opportunity that such an education makes possible. Moreover, Tommy is never depicted as being a victim of the racism that blights Bigger's life from cradle to grave. He has many white friends and moves easily through the privileged world of the University of Chicago and the upper-middle-class neighborhood that his parents have provided him with. White policemen, who hound Bigger and trick him into a confession that leads to the electric chair, are never a problem for Tommy. Quite to the contrary, they are his father's colleagues and friends, and they welcome him into their homes. His best friend is the son of a policeman.

But by far the most significant contrast between Bigger Thomas and Tommy Turner is their vastly different family circumstances. Bigger, like most of Wright's black protagonists, is victimized by the systematic destruction of the black family by a racist white society. His father has been killed in a race riot, his mother is overburdened by the bleak poverty enforced by a segregated society, and he has been given the role of breadwinner, a role that his environment does not enable him to fulfill. As a result, his life is corroded at its core by self-hatred, emotional instability, and a deeply alienated self. Late in *Native Son* he reveals to Max, "I don't reckon I was ever in love with nobody" (1998 *NS* 353).

But Tommy Turner is unique in all of Wright's fiction because he is the only young African American male who has the benefit of a family that is whole and a genuine source of material security and emotional health. Although Ruddy sometimes feels that the long hours he has spent at work have not provided him with the time he needs to develop the full relationship with his son that he had hoped for, and at times is exasperated by Tommy's "strange" late-adolescent behavior, he loves his son and has worked hard to be a responsible, caring father (*FL* 14). He has nothing in common with Wright's own abusive father as he is described in *Black Boy/American Hunger*, the absent father of *Native Son*, or the inadequate father of *The Long Dream*. Moreover, he is a loving husband who shows no signs of the misogyny that blights the relationships between men and women in *Lawd Today!* and *The Outsider*. Mrs. Turner, although only sketchily developed in the novel, is a faithful wife and a concerned mother. So the Turner family, while certainly imperfect, is unique in Wright's fiction because it provides a reasonably wholesome environment that should be a positive factor in Tommy's life.

Loeb and Leopold Again

So how is one to account for all of the human suffering and terrible violence depicted in *A Father's Law*? And why is this novel even more pessimistic than Wright's first published novel, *Native Son*? Answers to these two questions can shed some light on the arc of Wright's career, especially how his final vision was substantially different from the way he imagined human experience at the outset of his career.

One way of understanding the important distinctions between the Wright of 1940 and the Wright of 1960 is his radically different handling of the Loeb/Leopold case in *Native Son* and *A Father's Law*. As I have argued elsewhere, Wright had a long-term fascination with this "crime of the century," studying news accounts of the trial in 1924 and extensively using the entire case in *Native Son* to develop central themes and important characters.[3] *Native Son* is basically consistent with Clarence Darrow's deterministic defense of Richard Loeb and Nathan Leopold, arguing that their heinous crime was caused by their social environment, which provided them with economic and political privileges but stunted their moral growth, making them cold-blooded killers who had no feelings for their innocent victim, Bobby Franks. Darrow was able to avoid capital punishment for his clients by convincing Judge Caverly that a sentence of life in prison would provide them with an opportunity to morally rehabilitate themselves and return to society as useful citizens. While Loeb morally deteriorated in prison and was murdered in a shower-room brawl, Leopold did succeed in transforming his life in prison, was released, and spent his last thirteen years in Puerto Rico as a solid citizen, thus validating Darrow's theories.

Wright strongly endorsed Darrow's ideas about crime being a "disease" caused by toxic environments and also shared Darrow's abhorrence of capital punishment because he, too, believed that criminals could rehabilitate themselves if they willed themselves to do so and were placed in a proper corrective environment. So Wright used Darrow's defense of Loeb and Leopold as a model for Max's defense of Bigger, which is centered on the idea that a prison sentence would provide Bigger with an opportunity to reform and return to society as a useful citizen. For Wright in 1940 believed, as did Darrow and Max, that both environment and human nature were not unchangeable absolutes but were subject to positive changes. By reengineering social environment, which Wright as a Communist and Socialist believed was possible, better human lives could be developed.

Julia Wright, in her introduction to the HarperPerennial edition of *A Father's Law*, observed that her father's interest in the Loeb/Leopold case persisted to his final years, and he used it, along with Alfred Hitchcock's film adaptation of the case, *Rope*, in his last novel. Tommy Turner in many ways resembles Loeb and Leopold. Like them, he is a precocious student who attends the University of Chicago and is regarded by several people as a "boy genius" (*FL* 47). He shows some signs of having a "superiority complex" (177), asserting at one point that "a bold few" (172) could commit the perfect crime. Like his infamous predecessors, he enjoys intellectual theories that valorize certain types of crime as "something free and pure" (174). Tommy can also be compared to Leopold because of his compulsion to discuss his crimes with the police and his enjoyment of news accounts of the murder. All three killers are caught when they leave important evidence near the scenes of their crimes.

Brentwood, the place where many of Tommy's killings take place, also bears close resemblance to Kenwood, where Loeb and Leopold grew up and carried out their murder. Both locations are extravagantly opulent neighborhoods populated by wealthy people who place themselves above the law because their money and privilege give them the power to manipulate the justice system. Both places also have smarmy undersides as its inhabitants cover up histories of crimes such as wife-swapping, child molestation, and rape.

But the Wright who published *Native Son* in 1940 had a very different interpretation of the Loeb/Leopold case than the Wright who wrote *A Father's Law* in the final months of 1960. The hopeful and very rational assumptions at the center of *Native Son* that environments could be improved and human beings could be rehabilitated is altogether missing in Wright's final novel. *A Father's Law* presents us with a much darker vision centered on the facts that Tommy Turner's outwardly wholesome environment can do very little to prevent his baser instincts from asserting themselves, and his heinous crimes, in the final analysis, have no rational basis and therefore could neither be prevented nor even fully understood. The novel is without a character such as Boris Max, who can step above the action, diagnose certain social "diseases," and then prescribe "cures" in a rational way. For crime in *A Father's Law* is not a disease that can be rationally understood and remediated, but instead a malignant "poison" that has no antidote.

Tommy's father tries hard throughout the book to logically explain the causes of his son's crimes but fails miserably. As a highly trained, experienced, and successful policeman, he views crime as Clarence did, as "diseases" (180) that can be studied, categorized, and cured. When he explains his theory of crime to Professor Redfield in chapter 12, he argues that criminal behavior can be understood in terms of social class and economic background, parts of the environment that can be improved. He has a deep faith in the power and efficacy of rational investigation, which he calls "deductions and inductions" (180). But when he applies his rationalism to his son's crimes, he comes up against a "blank wall" (193), and by the end of the novel, he concludes that "he knew little or nothing of what was happening to that son and knew even less about what to try to do about it" (242).

When he looks at Tommy's social environment, Ruddy finds nothing like the moral laxness and parental failures that could explain the depraved characters of Loeb and Leopold. Nor does he find the poverty and racism that could explain the violence of Bigger Thomas. In a desperate attempt to find some logical explanation for his son's moral deterioration, he tries to blame himself, thinking, "I should have had a better, closer relationship with him. What has happened is as much my fault as his" (252). But the novel provides very little evidence for this. On the contrary, it depicts Ruddy as a concerned and scrupulous father who has a healthy, mutually respectful relationship with his son, despite certain frictions that are normal between a father who has received relatively little formal education and an eighteen-year-old son who is a precocious university student.

The deterioration of Tommy's character and his descent into horrific criminality, therefore, cannot be given the rational explanation that applies to Bigger in *Native Son*. For in the final analysis, Tommy's moral collapse is a kind of poison that simply erupts after his traumatic discovery of his fiancée's being "poisoned" (91) by congenital syphilis. While the central metaphor of *Native Son* consists of "walls" that block human development, the controlling metaphor of *A Father's Law* is the "poison" that corrupts society and destroys human life. But whereas the metaphor of walls can lead to hope because they can be removed as a way of creating a more humane and just society, the kinds of poisons explored in Wright's last novel can generate only pessimistic meanings since they cannot be understood rationally and are absolutely lethal. Tommy's fiancée, Marie, for example, has been literally poisoned by the syphilis that she has inherited but not caused. In a larger sense, she has been psychologically poisoned by the irrational shame that has led her to think of suicide and the equally irrational resentment that has motivated her to want "to kill anybody" (122).

Tommy has not been physically contaminated by Marie even though they have had sex together, but he has been psychologically sickened by the shock of the discovery of such a malignant disease in a woman he considered to be pure. He feels "unclean, polluted, contaminated, poisoned" (89) by this experience even though he realizes that Marie is in no way responsible for her condition, and he has been told by doctors that her disease may be treatable with modern medicines. He then abandons her in a fit of emotional disgust and, in the process, discards his only chance for a stable, rational life grounded in love. He also abandons his constructive sociological studies of Chicago's Black Belt because he illogically comes to the conclusion that all black people are hopelessly "contaminated and poisoned" (91). He then turns his academic attentions to a study of the outwardly attractive but morally murky world of Brentwood. Shortly afterward, he begins his mad career as a serial killer, abandoning his earlier posture as a reformer and assuming the role of a nihilistic murderer.

Although Ruddy tries to reasonably explain Tommy's insane behavior by claiming that he is rebelling against authority, the novel provides no convincing evidence for this. Tommy kills police officers even though he has no deep resentment toward either his father or his father's colleagues. He murders a

Catholic priest even though he has no strong feelings against religion in general or Catholicism in particular. And he shoots a nineteen-year-old girl for no better reason than the fact that she happens to be present in a secluded area when he is holding a gun that he could easily conceal. Tommy's terrible violence makes about as much sense as the violence in Poe's "The Black Cat," which explains such action as the eruption of completely irrational impulses, what Poe described as "perverseness" (*Selected Writings* 226) rather than any behavior that can be logically analyzed and understood.[4]

Another way to understand how radically different *A Father's Law* is from *Native Son* is to contrast the way these two novels begin and end. *A Father's Law* opens with Ruddy dreaming of something that is orderly in a most reassuring way, a police officer calmly directing traffic in perfect compliance with the way he has been instructed to do in the *Metropolitan Handbook for Traffic Policemen*. This dream squares exactly with the way Ruddy imagines his life as a reasonable sequence of events resulting in his steady "rise" on the ladder of American success. The novel concludes, however, in precisely the opposite way, with Ruddy realizing that his identity has been constructed around a false veneer of order symbolized by his uniform and police revolver. He finally realizes that the events of the novel are the opposite of his dream and have in fact been an extended nightmare of perverse crimes. As he discovers the full truth about Tommy, he feels helplessly drawn into "darkness" (*FL* 242), and his shocked eyes are described as "sightless" (268). A novel that began with a bright dream of order concludes with its central character blinded, stunned into a terrified vision of chaos and madness.

This is a complete reversal of the way in which *Native Son* opens and concludes. The novel begins with Bigger wakened from sleep into a stunned awareness of a world characterized by physical chaos and emotional confusion when a rat enters his family's run-down kitchenette and reduces them to blinding terror. Bigger kills the rat in a spasm of revulsion and instinctive self-defense but then prolongs his family's fears by dangling the rat's corpse in his sister's face, perversely laughing as he does so. Mrs. Thomas, furious at Bigger and also shrieking in horror at the rat, questions her son's sanity, characterizing him as "just crazy . . . just plain dumb black crazy" (1998 *NS* 8).

The novel concludes, however, with a dramatic reversal of this scene of physical chaos and blindly instinctive behavior. Throughout the novel Bigger gradually comes to a lucid understanding of how his behavior has been shaped by a racist environment that has treated him and other black people as rats, pushing them into a corner and then killing them when they lash back at such a world with the self-defensive "defiance" (6) that the rat exhibits in the opening scene. By the end of the novel he has developed a "thin hard core of consciousness" (360) that enables him to see his world in clear, rational terms as a social environment shaping human behavior. Although his eyes were blurred with fear and out of focus from the glare of the lightbulb that "flooded the room" (3) at the beginning of the novel, in the novel's final paragraph, his eyes are wide open and sharply focused as he glares ironically at Max, smiling "a faint, wry bitter smile" (430). Unlike Ruddy Turner, who has been reduced to blind terror by his experience of a world that is essentially irrational, Bigger achieves a lucid vision of what his life means and how his environment works. *Native Son* ends with the hope that the same environment that crushes Bigger can be reshaped if people "wake up" and reengineer the environment to make it a more just and reasonable society centered on Marxist and Socialist ideals. But in *A Father's Law*, written late in his life when he had lost faith in those affirmations, Wright deliberately inverted the structure of *Native Son*. While *A Father's Law* opens with Ruddy Turner's dreams of order as he confidently directs traffic, it concludes with his "waking up" to a living nightmare as he becomes aware of his son's brutal crimes that defy rational explanation. The confident, powerful police officer described in the novel's opening pages is replaced by the terrified, powerless father whose "sightless eyes" (268) try to come to terms with a dark universe that forces him to relinquish "moral leadership" (268) over his world.

Biographical Parallels

Henry Louis Gates Jr. in *Figures in Black* has argued that "signifying" is a mode of discourse at the heart of African American literary and musical traditions that creatively engages previous discourse, thus creating a kind of conversation between current and previously existing texts. As such, it can take either of two forms: (1) honorific signifying, which deepens the meaning of a text by echoing motifs from another work in a positive way, or (2) ironic signifying, in which the meaning of an earlier text is reversed or undercut, thus creating what Gates has called a distinctive "black difference" (xxviii). For example, Alice Walker's *The Color Purple* echoes themes, images, and characters from Zora Neale Hurston's *Their Eyes Were Watching God* in a very positive way as a means of honoring a literary ancestor as well as enriching the meaning of her own work. But Ralph Ellison's *Invisible Man* signifies ironically on Horatio Alger's rags-to-riches novels to challenge and discredit Alger's vision of American life, artfully redefining "success" in black terms, thus inverting the meaning of the earlier texts.

Wright consciously employed both kinds of signifying in *A Father's Law*, establishing a very rich and complex conversation with his masterpiece, *Native Son*. He makes many revealing, positive thematic connections between these two novels to universalize these themes, stressing that characters like Bigger Thomas, who come from environments of extreme racism and poverty, experience many of the same problems faced by characters like Tommy Turner who were raised with social backgrounds characterized by economic success and social privilege. This kind of signifying enabled Wright to highlight an idea that runs through most of his work, that his vision of life transcended race and economics. When Wright proclaimed in *White Man, Listen!* that "the Negro is the metaphor of America" (1957 *WML!* 72), he meant that the problems faced by poverty-stricken blacks are also faced in other ways by people from all social backgrounds. But *A Father's Law* also signifies ironically on *Native Son* as a way of underlining the fact that Wright's vision at the end of his career was significantly different from that which he embraced as a young writer. As this paper has argued, his final work was much more pessimistic than his earlier writing because it challenges and discredits the rational assumptions that Wright could commit himself to as a young Communist who still had faith in Marxist ideology.

It is tempting to explain these important changes in Wright's outlook with a study of his personal life. As Wright himself once observed, "All writing is a secret form of autobiography" (Rowley 410). There are certainly strong connections between important aspects of the novel and specific parts of Wright's life. The most obvious biographical connection is the fact that both Wright and Tommy Turner were engaged to women who failed the Wasserman test required by New York state law, thus preventing them from becoming married. In May 1938 Wright proposed to Marian Sawyer, the daughter of his landlady in Brooklyn, and they sent out wedding invitations. But when they tried to secure a marriage license, the Wasserman test revealed that Marian suffered from a severe case of congenital syphilis. Wright immediately broke off his relationship with his fiancée and had little to do with her afterward. According to Hazel Rowley, he was for many years "haunted by his cruelty toward Marian Sawyer" (148). Tommy Turner undergoes a similar shocking experience when the woman he plans to marry is diagnosed with congenital syphilis and he is overcome both by feelings of revulsion toward her and intense feelings of guilt for coldly abandoning her, even though he, like Wright, knew that his fiancée might be cured by modern drugs. He feels "poisoned" (*FL* 89) by her disease, although a series of tests reveals that he has not literally contracted her disease. Like Wright, he is sickened with guilt by his simply "dropping" (175) Marie and confides to his father that in so doing he has "killed her" (175). Tommy's failed relationship with Marie causes him to lose faith in a just and reasonable universe, and he begins a rapid descent into a dark nihilism that results in his becoming a serial killer.

Even stronger biographical parallels can be found between Wright and Ruddy Turner. Both grew up in the South, where they were victimized by racism and poverty. Like Wright, Ruddy rebelled against Southern injustice as he "curse[d] the look of a world that excluded him" (34) and entertained "wild dreams" (34) of someday overthrowing the system of segregation to create a reformed society whose "sole aim was racial equality" (34). At other times, however, "the sheer void of his existence" (34) tempts him to become a criminal who could express his hatred of authority by wantonly breaking laws. (Wright, who, as a young man, developed a lifelong fascination with criminals, also expressed his contempt for Southern injustice by engaging in petty crimes.)

The pivotal moment in the lives of both Wright and Ruddy was leaving Memphis as young men and moving to Chicago, where they were able to construct positive new lives. Ruddy, who is accurately described by his wife as a "self-made" (80) man, was able, like Wright, to avoid the extremes of either criminal rebellion against the law or passive acceptance of the dehumanizing roles that Southern law guaranteed. Just as Wright's vocation as a writer empowered him to construct a self that could help him to free himself from the prison of racial injustice in both the South and the North, Ruddy's profession as a police officer enabled him to find a way to "master" himself (36) and then lead a life that is both meaningful and productive. Ruddy sees police work precisely as Wright saw art—as a means of imposing order on experience that alternated between the equally meaningless extremes of chaos and emptiness.

Late in his life, Wright seriously considered retiring from his life as a creative writer. Beset by serious health problems, the deaths of close friends and family members, and the negative critical response to his recent books, he revealed in a March 2, 1959, letter to his agent Paul Reynolds Jr. that he was thinking of "dropping writing about the Negro entirely," feeling that "nobody, not even Negroes, wants to listen anymore" (Fabre, 1973 *UQ* 485). Michel Fabre has pointed out that Wright was so disappointed by the reviews of *The Long Dream* "that he thought he might stop writing for a time and look for another profession" (491), working in Ghana as a teacher or "getting a job in some English-speaking country, which would support his family" (491). At the beginning of *A Father's Law*, Ruddy is also about to retire from police work because he is tired out by the pressures of his job and is eager to find less demanding employment. Both men, however, are drawn back into their chosen professions by exciting new challenges that renew their energy. In an August 2, 1960, letter to Margrit de Sablonière, Wright revealed that he "was writing *A Father's Law* in a state of great excitement and felt that the book's theme . . . has me by the throat" (Rowley 516). In a dramatically similar way, Ruddy is powerfully engaged by the challenge of investigating the serial killings that have erupted in Brentwood, and instead of retiring he accepts the job of police chief in charge of the investigation. He works compulsively on the case, depriving himself of food and sleep. As his wife observes, "The job has got you by the throat" (*FL* 112), using nearly identical words that Wright employed to suggest the excitement and intensity he felt while working on his novel.

Wright also observed in his letter to Sablonière that his writing of *A Father's Law* was deeply therapeutic. He compared the process of writing the novel to "being psychoanalyzed" and felt "all the poison being drained out" of his system (Julia Wright, "Introduction," *FL* v). As Hazel Rowley has speculated, Wright at this time could have been literally poisoned by the excessive amounts of bismuth that his doctor had prescribed as a cure for his stomach problems, but in a broader sense Wright felt he was "poisoned" by the depression and anxiety brought about by personal problems and his feelings that he was being hounded by the FBI and CIA (Rowley 522). But if Wright's conscious intent in writing *A Father's Law* was to somehow snap himself out of the depression and despair that haunted him late in life, it is unlikely that the unfinished novel that he produced could have done much to shed light on or relieve his psychological burdens. Like Ruddy Turner, who is finally poisoned by a vision of motiveless evil that he can neither understand nor control, Wright created a novel that got progressively darker as he wrote it, deconstructing all of the affirmations of his early work such as *Native Son*.

At the end of "How 'Bigger' Was Born," Wright observed that "if Poe were alive, he would not have to invent horror; horror would invent him" (1998 *NS* 462). But the nightmarish world evoked in *Native Son* is presented with the Marxist, rationalist confidence that it can be dispelled if people finally respond to the alarms that the novel sounds and "wake up" to rationally construct a new and better world through political action and personal commitment. By 1960, Wright had lost this faith. One could not awaken from the nightmare world depicted in *A Father's Law*. On the contrary, the "waking up" portrayed in this novel forces the reader to give up dreams of human rationality and order, and plunges him into a universe of motiveless evil and absurdity that Poe would surely have understood.

Notes

This essay first appeared in *CLA Journal* 52, no. 1 (September 2008): 55–73.

1. Weimer uses this term to describe the urban setting employed in Stephen Crane's *Maggie: A Girl of the Streets*, a novel that Wright first read in 1929 when he was beginning to adjust to the harsh realities of living in Chicago. In a 1940 interview, he listed Crane as an important influence on his fiction (Kinnamon and Fabre 32).

2. Wright's fiction contains many examples of a character's life being forever changed for the worse by a single dramatic turn of events. Bobo in "Big Boy Leaves Home" finds his life completely turned upside down when a white woman accidentally discovers him swimming naked with his friends in a white man's pond. Saul, in "The Man Who Killed a Shadow," also is plunged into self-destructive violence when he murders a white woman to stop her from screaming. The lives of the central characters in *The Man Who Lived Underground*, *The Outsider*, and *Savage Holiday* are also turned around suddenly by surprising chance events that trigger terrible sets of deadly violence.

3. See my article "The Loeb and Leopold Case: A Neglected Source for *Native Son*." *African American Review* 39, no. 4 (Winter 2005): 555–67. Wright carefully studied the Loeb/Leopold case and had a copy of Clarence Darrow's *Pleas in Defense of Loeb and Leopold* on his writing desk when he composed *Native Son*. He also carefully examined the court records of the trial as he wrote *Native Son*. Loeb and Leopold were able to avoid the death penalty even though they were cold-blooded murderers who showed little remorse for their crimes because their parents were wealthy people who could afford to hire Clarence Darrow and his team of experts. Bigger, in contrast, is poor and is sent to the electric chair, despite the fact that he did not murder Mary Dalton, he shows genuine remorse in court, and his lawyer's defense of him is remarkably similar to the one used by Darrow to save his clients from the death penalty.

4. Poe's strong influence on Wright has been carefully studied. See Michel Fabre's "Black Cat and White Cat: Wright's Gothic and the Influence of Poe" in his *World of Richard Wright* and Dan McCall's *The Example of Richard Wright* (New York: Harcourt, 1969). Both studies argue convincingly that Wright used Gothic techniques. In *A Father's Law*, Wright seems to be particularly influenced by Poe's concept of "perverseness," his belief that human beings are driven by fundamentally irrational impulses that are self-destructive. In "The Imp of the Perverse," Poe argues that such mad impulses comprise the "*primum mobile*" of the human soul (*Selected Writings* 225).

Richard Wright and the American South

—SACHI NAKACHI—

In his essay "Imaginary Homeland," Salman Rushdie writes about literature that was produced out of phenomena of cultural transplantation. He speculates on writing about India in England, saying: "Can they do more than describe, from a distance, the world that they have left? Or does the distance open any other doors?" (13). To these questions, Rushdie answers, " If literature is in part the business of finding new angles at which to enter reality, then once again our distance, our long geographical perspective, may provide us with such angles" (15). In this essay Rushdie mentions Richard Wright twice but does not say that Richard Wright himself was in exile in Paris in his later years and wrote about the United States from a distance. But if we consider Richard Wright as one of the pioneers of transnational/postcolonial literature after World War II, Rushdie's idea of the meaning of writing from a distance can be applied to Wright's works, too. By displacing himself from the United States, Wright tried to acquire new angles to enter the American reality.

In his later years, Wright came to be keenly aware of his new role as a transnational writer. In February 1947, six months before he moved to Paris, Wright said in an interview: "The voice of the American Negro is no longer a lone voice. You hear echoing voices in the people of Burma, China, South Africa. Three-quarters of the world's population is colored. The attitude toward the Negro problem is entering a new phase" 124). After he traveled in Europe and developed a friendship with European and African intellectuals, Wright came to regard the American Negro as "a colonial subject" and that race problems of America should be examined from a global context of colonialism. His international concerns, especially about the Third World, were intensified in the 1950s. From June to August 1953, Wright traveled in the Gold Coast. A year later, he published a nonfiction book about his trip to Africa with the title *Black Power: A Record of Reactions in a Land of Pathos*. Then, in February 1955, Wright went to Bandung, Indonesia, to attend the first Afro-Asian conference in the world. He came to Bandung from Madrid, via Rome, Cairo, Baghdad, Calcutta, and Bangkok. His journey itself proves that he was eager to broaden his international knowledge and establish human connections beyond nations.

His experiences at the Bandung conference appeared in *The Color Curtain: A Report on the Bandung Conference* published in 1955 (see Wright, *Three Books from Exile* 659–812). In 1957, Wright published *White Man, Listen!*, a nonfiction collection of essays in which he examined colonialism and its effects on people throughout the world. These various speeches and books prove that Wright was interested in Afro-Asian affairs and politics many years before his death.

Wright, however, did not become a black nationalist in spite of his close contact with pan-Africanists like George Padmore, President Kwame Nkrumah of Ghana, Frantz Fanon, Léopold Sédar Senghor, Aimé Césaire, and Alioune Diop. He had never been comfortable with "the Negritude movement and its racial mysticism" (Rowley 478). There was "not an ounce of romanticism left or cultural sentimentalism in Wright" (West ix). He was attracted to the idea of black nationalism, but he could not believe in it. In 1956, Wright publicly repudiated his statement on black nationalism that he made in his 1938 essay "Blueprint for Negro Writing" during his presentation at the First Congress of Negro Artists and Writers. In the article, Wright talks about the political role that "Negro writers" should play in ensuring cultural survival. He says: "Negro writers must accept the nationalistic implications of their lives, not in order to encourage them, but in order to change and transcend them. They must accept the concept of nationalism because, in order to transcend it, they must *possess* and *understand* it" (Wright, "Blueprint," *RWR* 42; emphasis mine). Here, Wright uses the infinitive *to transcend* twice. He asserts that African American writers should convey political messages that appeal to the African American collective consciousness. Their statements should be politically oriented in order for them to surpass the limitations of black nationalistic ideas so as to embrace broader issues concerning the universal human condition. In "Blueprint," Wright also states that a black writer must "create values by which his race is to struggle, live and die" (43), but he adds: "This does not mean that a Negro writer's sole concern must be with rendering the social scene" as the major concern (46). In other words, black writers should broaden their nationalistic concerns so that additionally they will foster global humanism.

Wright's ambivalent position sometimes aroused controversy among black scholars and writers. His paper "Tradition and Industrialization," which he presented in 1956 at the Negro Artists and Writers Congress in Paris, angered some participants because Wright boldly claimed, according to James Baldwin, that "Europe had brought the Enlightenment to Africa" (1992 *Nobody Knows* 46). He began his speech by stating that his position as a black Westerner was "a split one" (Walker, 1988 Amistad ed. *DG* 282). And he argued that the European colonial conquest of Africa "in part saved the African from an irrational religion" (Fabre, 1993 *UQ* 437). Wright was against colonialism, but he was more critical about the superstitious religious customs in Africa. In an interview in 1960, he said:

> Most Asian and African writers I have been in contact with are steeped in religious feelings, and their works and political struggles are suffused with their religious conceptions. This seems somewhat strange to an American Negro like me: in the United States, we fight for a real application of the Constitution, which is not the case in African nations. We fight to become a part of civilization which we accept. We do not oppose the West; we want the effective application of Western principles of freedom. (Kinnamon and Fabre 201–2)

Consistently in his speeches, Wright would condemn religion being mixed with politics because religion, according to him, inspires irrational thinking.

When we examine Wright's works in his later years, it is especially important to pay attention to his double and split perspectives. In his later years, he came to feel himself as being "a man between two worlds." According to one critic, "he had begun to see himself as an independent radical thinker, a kind of H. L. Mencken on the world stage, fighting 'the battle of the Negro in the nation's thought' and challenging the West to live its highest ideals in dealing with its colonies and former colonies in Asia and Africa" (Singh, "Afterword" 612). Wright recognized the complex and even contradictory natures of his shifting, dualistic positions as a marginalized insider within a unit. In an interview in October 1960, he said: "A man between two worlds would be a complicated thing. He is not *between* two worlds, but really *of* two worlds. He is not apart from the white world and outside of the Negro world but in both of them" (Kinnamon and Fabre 220). By placing himself in a mediate position of admixture within nations or cultures, Wright had succeeded in achieving his intellectual freedom by becoming a bifurcated insider-outsider spanning two worlds, two nations, two cultures. This latter dualistic state allowed Wright to examine the systems of American racism from a domestic or distant, international perspective. As an expatriate living in Paris, he managed to achieve that outsider-within point of view. We also find that Wright's feelings of loneliness or isolation were strengthened by his living in two worlds, as his later works illustrate.

◆ ◆ ◆

Wright composed haiku poems during the later stages of his life from 1959 to 1960. His haiku are a product of his colonial ambivalence, just as the travelogues *Black Power* and *The Color Curtain* reveal Wright's ambivalent attitude toward the Third World (Wright, *Three Books from Exile*). On the one hand, his interest in haiku, a non-Western form of poetry, is the reflection of his interest in Asia. According to Margaret Walker, Wright began to think he would like to visit Japan in the 1950s because it was "one of the places he had never been" (1988 Amistad ed. *DG* 314). Before starting to compose haiku, Wright was already interested in Japan. In an interview in 1955, his being asked about what would be the date most notable to him for its historical significance, Wright answers: "The 1905 victory of the Japanese over Russia. That date marked the beginning of the termination of the Godlike role which the Western white man had been playing to mankind. That date marked the beginning of the de-Occidentalization of the world" (Kinnamon and Fabre 165). Wright's words also remind us of those spoken by W. E. B. Du Bois, who was delighted with the Japanese victory over Russia. He stated: "The magic of the word 'white' is already broken, and the Color Line in civilization has been crossed in modern times as it was in the great past."[1] Wright considered Japan to be a colored nation that had broken a myth of white supremacy and had initiated a new stage in the history of the world. Although Du Bois stopped admiring Japan when Japan had adopted their imperialist policy of expansion in the 1930s, Wright seems to have continued to consider Japan favorably. His interest in haiku, in this sense, can be considered as a continuation of his interest in Asian African affairs.

But it is also true that Wright's motivation for haiku was "Western" driven. Just like the Imagist poets in the 1920s who had become interested in haiku's minimalist form, Wright, too, became interested in adopting the simplistic form of haiku. Although some critics say that Wright was more interested in Zen philosophy, it is unlikely that Wright was absorbed in Zen Buddhism when we think of his phobia over religion. It is more reasonable to assume that Wright was fascinated with the form of haiku. Actually, there is nothing exotic or Japanese in Wright's haiku. He was a modernist experimental poet and a follower of Ezra Pound. Wright's adoption of haiku poetry was, after all, a Western application of an Asian literary form.

Many critics do not pose questions about the ideological and political meanings accompanying the translations of haiku. Charles Trumbull says that the works of haiku scholarship in the mid-twentieth century enabled Western poets "to reach toward a deeper and truer understanding of the nature of haiku, even though they were unable to read or study Japanese haiku in the original language."[2] However, we should note that translations of non-Western texts that include Japanese haiku were products of European colonialism. These productions functioned as a cultural force that additionally promoted their translations and points of view of non-Western texts. The haiku boom in the 1960s is often distinguished from that of the 1920s because of its better understanding of Japanese Zen Buddhism. But recent scholars in Buddhism studies claim that Zen was not a traditional Japanese religion and that it was just used in order to make Buddhism popular among Westerners. The writers became labeled as Buddhist modernists.[3] We cannot say that translations of haiku in the mid-twentieth century were completely free from politics.

In fact, Harold G. Henderson and Reginald Horace Blythe, two towers of the postwar American haiku world, were closely connected with the American military leaders in the years of the American occupation of Japan. Henderson, who was regarded as a haiku expert by his publication of *The Bamboo Broom* in 1934, was a special adviser for the Civil Information and Education Staff Section under General Douglas MacArthur. Blythe, who was born in England, had been in a teaching position at a Japanese university in those days. Blythe was interested in Japanese literature and became a good friend of Henderson in Japan. Because of his introduction to Henderson, Blythe started to work as a special tutor of a Japanese crown prince. Later, Henderson and Blythe worked together to make a draft of *Ningen Sengen*, through which Emperor Hirohito declared himself to be a human being. Neither Henderson nor Blythe translated haiku for the American government, but the roles they played in the war period were almost the same as that of Ruth Benedict. She wrote *Sword and Chrysanthemum*, a book on Japanese culture, which provided the information on Japanese culture and psychology to American military leaders during the war.

It is also important to recognize that haiku translators in this period had become interested in exploring the possibilities of publishing haiku poems in English. Lawrence M. Venui observes that one of the two tendencies of translators in the early twentieth century was to adhere to the formalist technique. It was still the dominant literary technique that writers and poets used in their translations and publications of haiku during the mid-twentieth century.[4] Henderson was a formalist who was interested in how to compose haiku in English. In *The Bamboo Broom: An Introduction to Japanese Haiku* published in 1934, Henderson raised the following question: "What the final English haiku-form will be, I do not know. It may be two lines or three or four; it may be rimed or unrimed. But I am sure that whatever it is, it will be a definite form, for a haiku is a poem and not a dribble of prose" (124). Henderson' s *Haiku in English,* published in 1965, is said to be the first how-to book on Western haiku. In short, Henderson was very interested in exploiting and domesticating Japanese haiku into the English context.

An attempt to domesticate haiku into the English context was also seen in Blythe's translations. Blythe's translations are often characterized by his emphasis on Zen philosophy, but they are also characterized by Blythe's admiration for English Romantic poets. In his books, Japanese haiku in the seventeenth and eighteenth centuries are translated, but they are often compared to the poetry written by English Romantic poets. Blythe, who was born in a poor working-class family and moved from England because of economic necessity, inscribed his English identity in his translation of Japanese haiku. When Blythe talks about how the Japanese admire nature in their art and literature, he correlates it to the concept of nature occurring in the works of Romantic poets. For example, the image of a Japanese peasant is often compared to the image of an English peasant as depicted by William Wordsworth.

Blythe's translations of haiku appealed to many Westerners because it made Japanese poetry understandable. His introducing a new knowledge of Zen philosophy by placing the haiku in the context of English literature gave the poems a sense of their Asianness. Interestingly, his English translation of haiku was also welcomed in Japan, which, after its defeat in World War II, had begun to forge a new national identity that included its quest for international recognition. For the Japanese, Blythe was a good agent who served as a bridge between Japanese culture and Euro-American cultures.

It is difficult to find out which of Blythe's works most appealed to Wright, but Wright seems to have been interested in the idea of exploring a new literary expression by mixing the poetry of the East with the poetry of the West. His tendency to mix cultures or literary forms correlates to his own third position of admixture, not between, but of two worlds. It is true that Wright was interested in Japan, but Wright's motivation for adopting haiku was almost the same as that of other Western modernists who had been searching for a new form of literature. But Wright's attempt is worth noting because he tried to explore African American themes in his haiku and to develop original literary expressions. Wright's haiku are significant as an example of African American modernist poetry, which he had based on the soil of the American South.

◆ ◆ ◆

Wright had begun the second chapter of his 1941 photographic text *12 Million Black Voices: A Folk History of the Negro in the United States* (1985 *12MBV*) by describing how the American South remains beautiful every season of the year. He writes: "Our southern springs are filled with quiet noises and scenes of growth. Apples laugh into blossom. Honeysuckles creep up the sides of houses. Sunflowers nod in the hot fields" (32). Wright's description of four seasons reminds us of Blythe's four volumes of *Haiku,* which, in format, are ordered by seasons. On the first page of each book, Blythe explains what kind of natural scenery exists that connects animals, birds, and flowers to each season. Wright's *12 Million Black Voices*, however, does not maintain a serene tone, which Blythe's *Haiku* books maintain. Instead, Wright describes the lives of African Americans in autumn as becoming turbulent periods of torture and death:

> Most of the flogging and lynching occur at harvest time, when fruit hangs heavy and ripe, when the leaves are red and gold, when nuts fall from the trees, when the earth offers its best. The thought of harvest steals upon us with a sense of an inescapable judgment. It is time now to settle accounts with the Lords of the Land, to divide the crops and pay old debts, and we are afraid. (41–42)

From his description of nature in *Black Boy*, we know that Wright had cultivated a loving sense of nature during his childhood. However, as a son of an African American sharecropper, Wright also recognized that African Americans have been deprived of their rights to enjoy the bounty of the natural world that they had cultivated and brought to life. The text tells us that African Americans, themselves living and working in the agrarian South, could not enjoy the beautiful harvest season or its fruits because they faced the landlord's harsh "judgment" at harvest time to determine whether they lived or died.

It is ironic that Wright uses the term "the Lords" in the phrase "the Lords of the Land." But he is referring to the typical behavior of white plantation owners and their callous ways by depicting them as two-dimensional objects. They would set themselves up in a godlike position of authority as proud owners of slaves or landlords of African American sharecroppers because, similar to the conditions of slavery, the plantation owners required absolute obedience from their neoslave sharecroppers. Wright exposes them in *12 Million Black Voices* by conveying how the Lords of the Land would routinely incite reigns of terror throughout the South:

> The Lords of the Land will preach the doctrine of "white supremacy" to the poor whites who are eager to form mobs. In the midst of general hysteria they will seize one of us—it does not matter who—the innocent or guilty—and, as a token, a naked and bleeding body will be dragged through the dusty streets. . . . Our bodies will be swung by ropes from the limbs of trees, will be shot at and mutilated. And we cannot fight back; we have no arms, we cannot vote; and the law is white. (43)

Chapter 2 of *12 Million Black Voices* begins with Wright's description of a beautiful landscape in the South, but the image is oxymoronic. The panoramic scene belies the truth of its hidden meaning as the site of terrible acts of violence. Its beautiful setting has been the location of ugly deeds during which white mobs have carried out their lynching bees of African Americans.

From the start of his career, Wright has exposed how racism has entered every facet of the lives of African Americans in the American South. American racism has prevented African Americans from reaping the benefits of the natural world. His short story "Big Boy Leaves Home" in *Uncle Tom's Children* (1938) can be labeled as a representative work in which Wright, in fictional form, protests against white society and its violent methods of denying African American adolescent males their enjoyment of nature. On a hot summer day, Big Boy and his three boyhood friends decide to swim in a creek on someone's property. Their moments of enjoyment in nature reverse and turn into a nightmare from humans when a white woman discovers the naked boys and screams. Violence from a white lynch mob immediately ensues. Big Boy, the eyewitness to everything, just barely escapes death that night by hiding in a wagon heading north. In Wright's works, the natural world is not always benevolent, either. In a companion short story, "Down by the Riverside," Wright considers a flood as a natural phenomenon, but it causes havoc for the African American protagonist as he attempts to rush his pregnant wife to a hospital. In this piece, the flood alters the peaceable life of Mann and leads to his and his family's tragic demises (*Uncle Tom's Children, Early Works* 278).

Wright's concept of nature, in this sense, should be examined carefully. Referring to Wright's love of nature, Michel Fabre says, "At the final stage of his evolution, at a moment when nature and the individual played an increasingly important part in his thinking, the poet developed a taste for these intimate tercets in which he could condense the quintessence of his art" ("Poetry" 270). Fabre's words, however, sound naive because it is almost impossible for anyone to experience the beauty of nature in a pure primordial space. As Fabre claims, Wright's appreciation for natural beauty grew out of those peaceable moments from turmoil with his childhood relations, for we should note that Wright, the descendent of African American slaves, had a complicated relationship with a sometimes uncompromising natural world as well.[5]

It is not surprising that Wright's attitude toward nature is different from that of the Romantic poets whom Blythe introduces in his books. In Wright's haiku, the Romantic outlook of the sublime in nature is hardly seen. He rarely embodies or extols the wonders of the natural world as do the Romantics in their representations of huge mountains, roaring seas, or vast prairies. Nature, to the Romantics, is beyond human power, but there is nothing religious or mystical in Wright's descriptions of nature. Robert Tener says that Wright created "his own Wordsworthian 'spots of time,' seeing into the life of a thing" (296). But it is better not to have a Romantic analogy in mind when we examine Wright's haiku, for Wright's haiku do not convey a bit of Romanticism. Wright links the natural life to small animals, birds, and insects to which people usually do not pay attention. But his view on those creatures is basically different from that of Romantic poets because Wright, an atheist, never considers them to be God's creatures.

Wright's appreciation for natural life is different from the Japanese's love of it, although Japanese poets do love to depict small animals, birds, and insects without any religious feelings. Generally speaking, Japanese traditional arts have formalist characteristics and they follow strict rules. In traditional Japanese haiku, the description of *Kachofugetsu* (flowers, birds, winds, moon) is a dominant principle and anything grotesque in the natural world is not allowed to be depicted. As Yoshinobu Hakutani writes in the afterword of *This Other World*, "[Japanese] haiku traditionally avoided such subjects as earthquakes, floods, illnesses, and eroticism—ugly aspects of nature" (Hakutani and Tener 245). This is partly because traditional Japanese art and culture were created by aristocrats in the court. Elegance and delicacy were considered to be important by traditional Japanese artists. Wright, however, often chooses ugly things in the world. Vermin such as rats, mice, flies, cockroaches, lice, and disgusting small animals and insects such as serpents, snakes, crows, snails, spiders, and moths are often depicted in his haiku. What Julia Kristeva calls the symptom of "abjection"—sweating, urinating, or vomiting—is also often represented in Wright's haiku (1). Death, sickness, poverty, and loneliness are also Wright's major themes in his haiku because they resonate on the horrors of the natural world experienced by African Americans in their daily sufferings (1). Nature is not kind and more like the abominable, awful, and aggressive nature depicted by nineteenth-century Victorian poets. Wright's haiku, thus, are essentially different from traditional Japanese haiku.

As Robert Tener points out, humor is also certainly one of the characteristics of Wright's haiku, but we should be cautious about linking Wright's humor with that in Zen, for Wright, who always distrusted religion and had a negative view of anything mystical, was unlikely to seek for enlightenment through Zen. Rather, it is important to understand that many of Wright's humorous haiku poems deal with the relationships of humans with small, annoying insects and animals as we find in the following selections:

> Shut up, you crickets!
> How can I hear what my wife
> Is saying to me? (10)
>
> You moths must leave now;
> I am turning out the light
> And going to sleep. (11)

These poems are humorous, but it is clear that Wright feels annoyance rather than pity for these small insects. Wright's humor does not stem from the Buddhist sense of nature that is merciful; every living creature is important.

In my opinion, one of the most important characteristics of Wright's haiku is his development of the theme of the grotesque, which cannot be found either in Blythe's Romantic haiku or Japanese haiku. Seen from the fact that Wright revised the episode of the murder scene in *Native Son* and then wrote a similar reenactment in his later short story "The Man Who Killed a Shadow" in *Eight Men* (1996 edition), the grotesque was a theme that obsessed Wright throughout his life. And, because of his having grown up in the South where whites performed gruesome atrocities against African Americans on a daily basis, Wright seems to have regarded the grotesque as a unique African American experience, especially because of the high numbers of lynching rituals. In fact, Wright's haiku are not full of peaceful, beautiful scenes that we would expect from the poetry. Rather, Wright's landscapes in his haiku poems convey a psychological reaction, for they are full of images of violence and cruelty occurring daily in the American South.

◆ ◆ ◆

Wright's haiku often deal with the death of small insects and animals such as flies, snakes, and mice. The dead bodies of animals are often the focus of his poems. When we remember Wright's powerful representation of a white woman's dead body in *Native Son,* Wright's obsession with the dead bodies of animals in his haiku is worth noting. It shows that Wright's haiku poems are closely related to his earlier works because of common themes. Haiku 70, 408, 711, and 801 are poems about dead animals:

At the water's edge,
Amid drifting brown leaves,
A dead bloated fish. (70)

A dead mouse floating
Atop a bucket of cream
In the dawn spring light. (408)

With solemnity
The magpies are dissecting
A cat's dead body. (711)

In a full zinc tub,
Winter rain pelting a rat,
Floating and bloated. (801)

In these poems, the grotesque bloated, inactive, or rigid bodies of dead animals are under Wright's objective gaze. He seems to regard their death as something ordinary, unsurprising, or inevitable. A sense of unity with Mother Nature is not visualized or glorified in these poems. It is partly because these small animals do not seem to have died from natural causes of age-related conditions. Mother Nature has not been kind to them. The natural world that Wright describes is full of cruel and merciless forces.

Although Wright does not write about racial problems in his haiku explicitly, critics agree that some of his poems may be interpreted from a racial point of view. Haiku 474 is one of the representatives of Wright's grotesque haiku poems that may have racial overtones. We cannot say definitively that Wright tried to embody racial imageries here, but this poem evokes vivid images of a white man's violence against a black man, whatever his intentions may be:

> A white butterfly
> Sits with slowly moving wings
> On a dead black snake. (474)

A white butterfly that sits on a dead snake reminds us of an ominous image of the Ku Klux Klan, whose white clothes often flutter like the wings of a butterfly. A dead black snake reminds us of a lynched black body, which has become too grotesquely battered to appear to be a human being. Orlando Patterson estimates the number of lynchings of African Americans in America to be more than five thousand between the 1865 ending of the Civil War and 1968 (173). The states of Mississippi, Louisiana, Alabama, Georgia, and Texas had the highest numbers. Actions of whites staging lynching rituals and murders of blacks in the South drew national attention during the 1950s because of the infamous cases of Willie Magee, Emmett Till, and Charles Parker. It has been noted that "Wright had joined protest groups in an outcry against the injustice" (Walker, 1988 Amistad ed. *DG* 303). Although Wright's protest against racism is not explicit in his haiku, it might be argued that Wright used the dead bodies of animals as metaphors for the lynched bodies of African Americans. As Abdul JanMohamed says in *The Death-Bound Subject: Richard Wright's Archaeology of Death*, we can say with certainty that "Wright was clearly obsessed with death and violence" throughout his life (1).

For Wright, who was born in 1908 into a racially and class-defined world in Mississippi, the American South was not a place where he could experience a feeling of nostalgia. Speaking about Mississippi, he said in an interview with *L'Express* in August 1960: "Mississippi is only an immense black ghetto, a vast prison where the whites are the jailers and the Negroes are the prisoners" ("Entretien" 449). Mississippi, his native state, was marked in his memory because of its racial violence. Haiku 191 is also a poem about violence, although at a first glance it looks like a poem describing a peaceful pastoral landscape in winter:

Little boys tossing
Stones at a guilty scarecrow
In a snowy field.

Although there is no racial signification in the reference to boys tossing stones at a scarecrow, we can say that the image of a snowy field represents white people. There is no explanation why a lifeless scarecrow is portrayed to be guilty. However, just as African Americans were discriminated against without any reason other than the color of their skin, Wright's scarecrow is labeled as a guilty object without any rationale. It becomes an object of abuse similar to the irrational acts of violence that whites have waged against African Americans.

In Wright's haiku, a scarecrow is often used to develop his notion of the grotesque. Many critics say that Wright mimicked Japanese haiku very skillfully and used seasonal words properly. But we also discover that Wright is as contradictory in his poetry as in his prose works. He does not always follow the haiku rules. In Japanese haiku, a scarecrow is always a seasonal word associated with autumn. If a seasonal word is used, other words signifying a season should not be used in order to avoid redundancy in a poem. However, Wright's poems on scarecrows are often set in winter. Scarecrows are often funny and comical in Japanese haiku, but Wright's scarecrows are always miserable and tragic. They are often "skinny," "lonely," "frozen," and "starved." Wright's scarecrows are the embodiments of the resentment felt by African Americans toward white people for forcing them to live in a Jim Crow society. Haiku 577 is another example of deprivation:

Scarecrow, who starved you,
Set you in that icy wind,
And then forgot you?

A scarecrow is used to represent a human experience, and specifically one or more African American victims of America's racist world. It is starved and left out in a cold wind, but does not gain attention or sympathy from anyone. Haiku 150 also develops the same theme of social ostracism when a scarecrow turns into a more grotesque figure because of hunger:

Late one winter night
I saw a skinny scarecrow
Gobbling slabs of meat.

Here, Wright presents a nightmarish image of a scarecrow feeding hungrily upon "slabs of meat." Just like a zombie coming back from the grave to prey on human flesh, a hungry scarecrow wakes up late in the night and devours whatever parcels of meat it can scavenge. It should be remembered that *hunger* is a key word that Wright used frequently in *Black Boy*, his autobiography, to speak about his impoverished childhood and adolescence. Wright also states in *12 Million Black Voices* that African Americans led miserable lives and suffered from poverty and hunger during the 1930s Great Depression. A skinny, hungry scarecrow, in this sense, can represent any poor African American who has felt the pangs of starvation while living in the rural areas of the American South.

Notably, a scarecrow is also identified with Wright himself in his haiku. In the following poems, a scarecrow even becomes Wright's shadow self, an alternative ego:

> When I turn about,
> My shadow lies alongside
> That of a scarecrow. (492)

> A skinny scarecrow
> And its skinnier shadows
> Fleeing a cold moon. (611)

The reason for his identification with a scarecrow is not clear. But Wright alludes to his thin appearance as a child and youth, and then his being substantially underweight to qualify for a job with the United States post office during the 1930s while he was living in Chicago. In the latter haiku, he also seems to consider himself to be a man who is lonely and dispossessed. In fact, haiku 1 manifests Wright's position as one of the dispossessed when he announces that he is "nobody":

> I am nobody:
> A red sinking autumn sun
> Took my name away. (1)

This poem can be read as Wright's reflection upon the nihilistic effects of the European American slave trade. The African ancestors of the generationally transformed American Negro had been abducted from Africa, stripped of their identities, and recodified as "nobody" slaves. They were then made to work relentlessly as captives in the American South. Even when they acquired property after emancipation, whites stole that as well, which then made them a homeless "nobody" again. In the 1950s, Wright was already famous as an internationally recognized American intellectual, and he was no longer a "nobody." But by representing himself as "nobody," he seems to have identified himself with the thousands of nameless Africans who sank in the bottom of the Middle

Passage while a red autumn sun beamed overhead, or those slaves who had to work relentlessly while a "red autumn sun" sank into the West.

◆ ◆ ◆

Wright, however, did not display any concern about the amount of violence appearing in his haiku. He certainly encoded some racial themes, but they do not explicitly express it as an issue in most of them. Generally speaking, Wright's tone in his haiku is melancholic. In his famous essay "Mourning and Melancholy" published in 1917, Sigmund Freud challenged the notion of melancholy. According to Freud, both mourning and melancholy are related to loss, but they are different levels of feelings. Contrary to the act of mourning, what is lost is not clear in the state of melancholia. Freud's theory is useful to understand Wright's haiku poems because we find that a sense of loss is found in many of Wright's haiku. Most of them are ambiguous about what is lost, and they are also dominated by gloomy feelings evoked by the natural scenery. Natural objects such as autumn rain, mist, fog, snowflakes, a cold moon, moonlight, a setting sun, frozen stars, and a winter wind are often the themes that make him melancholy. For example, Wright feels gloomy when he hears birds cry:

> Crying and crying,
> Melodious strings of geese
> Passing a graveyard. (120)

Geese seem to be crying because they grieve over someone's death. Wright also feels melancholic when he smells magnolia, a flower typically seen in the American South:

> How melancholy
> That these sweet magnolias
> Cannot smell themselves. (312)

Why the sweet scent of magnolia makes Wright melancholy is not clear, but it is a pungent smell. A magnolia, in this case, could be a metaphor for a fair-skinned Southern black woman who consumes her youth and beauty in vain, and cannot smell danger. Haiku 140 depicts the death of a young woman, but it is not an elegy, a mourning song. The overall tone of this haiku is melancholic:

> A spring pond as calm
> As the lips of the dead girl
> Under its water.

The calmness of a spring pond clashes with the silent lips of the dead girl seen just below the surface of the water. Her stillness and calmness symbolize death—the death of a young girl who cannot speak any more.

We never know where Wright's moods of melancholy come from. However, his short story "The Man Who Killed His Shadow" shows that Wright was deeply interested in the symptoms of melancholia and defined it as a general psychological trait of African Americans who were forced to live in two worlds as bicultural people. The protagonist of "The Man Who Killed His Shadow" is haunted by shadows of white Americans, and consequently becomes driven to commit a crime of murder. Wright's interest in melancholy is also found in his haiku, but it seems that he has decided to use it differently.

Wright revived his interest in the blues during the 1950s. Although Wright is famous as a writer of fiction, he actually started his literary career as a poet and published his early poetry in Communist magazines. In the 1930s, he wrote several blues poems, and also devoted much time to writing blues pieces into the early 1940s.[6] In the late period of the 1950s, Wright became interested in the blues again because he found that the blues had not only become an artistic heritage borne out of American colonialism and enslavement of African Americans, but it also had universal appeal to people beyond national boundaries. In 1959, Wright was asked to write the foreword to Paul Oliver's *Blues Fell This Morning*. He states:

> Not only did those Blacks, torn from their tribal moorings in Africa, transported across the Atlantic, survive under hostile conditions of life, but they left a vivid record of their sufferings and longings in those astounding religious songs known as the spirituals, and their descendants, freed and cast upon their own in an alien culture, created the blues, a form of exuberantly melancholy folk songs that has circulated the globe. ("Foreword" xiii)

It might be argued that Wright applied an aspect of the blues to his haiku to make it an African American expression. Although many Wright scholars say that Wright achieved what Joan Giroux calls the "the haiku moment," a moment "in which man becomes united to an object, . . . becomes the object and realizes the eternal, universal truth contained in being" (46) in his haiku, we should rather call Wright's poetic moment as his "haiku-blues" moment. What dominates Wright's haiku is not his sense of harmony with Mother Nature, but rather his melancholic lament for the world, which is expressed in the blues.

Just as Ralph Ellison discovered aspects of the blues in Wright's autobiography *Black Boy*, blues is a key to understanding Wright's literary works. In terms of the linkage between the blues and lynching, Wright's works are notable. Billie Holiday's recording of "Strange Fruit" in 1939 is often considered to be the first work equating lynching with the blues. Adam Gussow argues that many African American blues singers and poets produced blues songs on lynching before Billie Holiday released her version; he also argues that Wright's poem "Between the World and Me," which appeared in the July–August issue of *Partisan Review* in 1935, is one of the early blues poems on lynching.[7] What is interesting is that "Between the World and Me" shares a common theme with Wright's haiku: it is an odd combination of violence and the beauty of nature. "Between the World and Me" has a stylistic connection to Robert Frost's style of starting out in pastoral prose. Wright's lines, modified herewith, say: "And one morning while in the woods I . . . / Stumbled upon it in a grassy clearing . . ." and continues:

> And the sooty details of the scene rose, thrusting
> Themselves between the world and me. . . . ("Between the World" 246)

The poem quickly moves from a pastoral scene to a grotesque scene in the next line, for what the author finds there is a lynched and burned body of an African American man. Already in the 1930s Wright had begun to mix natural beauty with the grotesque in order to describe the poignant reality of African American rural life. The poem ends in a melancholic tone with the author himself identifying with and dissolving into the body of the dead man: "Now I am dry bones and my face a stony skull" (247). Wright has shifted his outsider's perspective into an insider's gaze.

In "Between the World and Me," the poem registers no word of protest, but it expresses the anger and grief that African Americans in the South have felt but could not articulate clearly in those lynching days. To write about lynching, a traumatic experience, Wright chose the form of the blues that conveys pain and suffering because he believed that the blues also had a cathartic effect. In the foreword to Paul Oliver's *Blues Fell This Morning*, Wright defines the essence of the blues:

> Yet the most astonishing aspect of the blues is that, though replete with a sense of defeat and down-heartedness, they are not intrinsically pessimistic; their burden of woe and melancholy is dialectically redeemed through sheer force of sensuality, into an almost exultant affirmation of life, of sex, of movement, of hope. No matter how repressive was the American environment, the Negro never lost faith in or doubted his deeply endemic capacity to live. ("Foreword" xv)

From the beginning of his career as a writer, Wright was a bluesman who believed in the capacity of African Americans to overcome grief and woe in their lives. Haiku 721 is significant to note as a poem expressing his idea of the blues in the form of haiku:

As my anger ebbs,
The spring stars grow bright again
And the wind returns. (Wright and Fabre, *RWR* 299)

In the blues, Wright tried to find a cathartic moment in which "the spring stars grow bright again / And the wind returns." In his later years, he used the haiku form to express the African American blues experience.[8]

Since the summer of 1959, Wright had been very sick and figuratively chained to a bed. He wanted to return to Africa again, but he was physically unable to travel.[9] When Wright died in December 1960, he left about 4,000 unpublished haiku poems.[10] His extraordinary production of haiku poems shows that haiku was not just an amusement for Wright. It was therapeutic, but his personal motive must yield to his professional drive. By his adopting the style of haiku, Wright seems to have created a new transnational African American literary expression in the postcolonial era.

Notes

A version of this paper titled "From *Japonisme* to Modernism: Richard Wright's African American Haiku" was published in *The Other World of Richard Wright: Perspectives on His Haiku*. Ed. John Zheng. Jackson: University Press of Mississippi, 2011.

1. W. E. B. Du Bois, "Color Line Belts the World," *Collier's Weekly*, October 20, 960–20.

2. See Charles Trumbull, "The American Haiku Movement Part 1: Haiku in English," *Modern Haiku* 36 (2005). Web.

3. See Sharf, "Zen of Japanese Nationalism," and David L. McMahan, *The Making of Buddhist Modernism* (New York: Oxford University Press, 2008).

4. Venui, *Translation Studies Reader*, 72.

5. For the African American experience of nature and black environmental thoughts, see Smith, *African American Environmental Thought*, and Glave, *Rooted in the Earth*.

6. Wright and Fabre, *Richard Wright Reader*, 242.

7. See the first chapter of Gussow, *Seems Like Murder Here*.

8. In 1960, Wright wrote a few blues, too, and all of them are "filled with melancholy." Fabre, 1993 *Unfinished Quest*, 516. The similarity between his later blues and haiku should be noted.

9. Walker, 1988 Amistad ed. 329.

10. Fabre, 1993 *Unfinished Quest*, 505.

Richard Wright's Poetic Spirit through the Influence of Zen

—JOHN ZHENG—

According to Ollie Harrington, the last two years of Richard Wright's life in Paris, France, "were periods of prolific output" (11). Among his writings during this late 1950s time period, the most prominent ones were a novel, *A Father's Law,* published posthumously in 2008, and some 4,000 haiku, of which 817 appeared in a collection that was published posthumously under the title of *Haiku: This Other World* in 1998. In fact, the collection contains only 816 of Wright's haiku because haiku 349 and 439 are exactly the same. Haiku writing became Wright's new interest between 1959 and 1960 (the year of his death) because the exquisite Japanese form enabled him to convey his true self. His oldest daughter, Julia Wright, recalls in her introduction to *This Other World* that her father's routine during that last year revolved around his applying and adapting the rules of haiku writing (viii). Wright wrote haiku "at all hours: in bed as he slowly recovered from a year-long, grueling battle against amoebic dysentery; in cafés and restaurants where he counted syllables on napkins; in the country in a writing community owned by French friends, *Le Moulin d'Andé,* . . . he would hang pages and pages of them up, as if to dry, on long metal rods strung across the narrow office area of his tiny sunless studio in Paris" (vii–viii). For Wright, as soon as he discovered haiku, he could not stop delving into it. He states that he could not give up "those damned haikus" (Fabre, *World* 54). Quite different from his novels, his haiku collection presents to readers a totally different image of himself: a poet of nature, a human being with tender feelings, and a person seeking to find his true being in and with nature. Ironically, contrary to the broad criticism of his works such as *Native Son* and *Black Boy,* his haiku collection has received little critical attention since its debut in 1998. It has remained largely unknown to readers or has been intentionally ignored by critics, even in the twenty-first century. Two reasons for this could be the weaknesses of Wright's using the haiku techniques correctly or because haiku writing has been deemed to be unimportant to the mainstream critics and writers of American literature.

At a glance, it appears that most of Richard Wright's haiku are complete sentences or prose statements or phrases without much use of haiku techniques such as internal comparison. Yet most of the 4,000 haiku show the significance of historical records to this most internationally known African American writer who experienced a change of his aesthetic attitude toward the world and himself in the last two years of his life in Paris, France. Such a change, as pointed out by Sanehide Kodama, "is so remarkable as to seem almost a religious awakening" (68). This awakening starts with Wright's interest in reading the four volumes of Japanese haiku translated by R. H. Blythe[1] and then learning about Zen philosophy, in which he found echoes of his dormant feelings of humans achieving harmony with nature. There is little doubt that Wright's readings of haiku and Zen Buddhism challenged him to turn his attention to East Asian culture and literature and to reflect upon the interrelations between nature and human nature. Furthermore, Wright's enthusiasm for haiku writing shows that he became receptive to the influence of Japanese aesthetics and Zen philosophy. For him, the latter two as well as haiku writing became a stepping stone for him to learn more about himself and to rediscover his poetic spirit. What is Wright's poetic spirit? It is his realization of his real being with nature, his spirit in finding beauty in nature, and his aesthetic attitude toward his present life and afterlife.

It is important to see how Wright presents his poetic spirit through his haiku and how they reflect the influences of Japanese aesthetics and Zen philosophy. In his essay "Japanese Aesthetics," Donald Keene states that "most Japanese critics would agree that the prevailing preference in Japanese aesthetics has been for the monochrome" (296). He uses the famous crow haiku ("On the withered bough / A crow has alighted: / Nightfall in autumn") by the Japanese haiku master Matsuo Bashō to demonstrate his belief: "The *haiku* on the alighting crow exemplifies a related aspect of Japanese aesthetics, the preference for monochromes to bright colors. . . . The black crow alighting on a withered branch at a time of day and season when all color has vanished suggests the lonely beauty admired by countless Japanese poets" (296). Haiku 548 by Wright exemplifies the influence of Japanese aesthetics:

> One caw of a crow
> Tints all of the fallen leaves
> A deeper yellow.

One of the Japanese aesthetic elements reflected in this haiku is juxtaposition, which is a primary haiku technique that functions to reveal an internal comparison for understanding the significance of a haiku and to arouse the feelings of the reader. Wright's haiku 548 uses the external phenomenon of nature to show the hidden feeling of the observer; that is, in the emphatic and synesthetic caw of the lonely black crow, the beauty of autumn can be seen in the deeper yellow color of the fallen leaves. Moreover, when the caw is juxtaposed with the color of yellow, loneliness becomes a tangible part of nature, thus revealing the interactions of nature and human nature.

Another example that shows different spectrums of the influence of Japanese or Eastern aesthetics is haiku 1, which I would like to discuss in greater detail:

I am nobody:
A red sinking autumn sun
Took my name away. (1)

Obviously, this haiku is again an example of juxtaposition. Wright juxtaposes the speaker's state of mind upon the red autumn sunset to reveal his poetic spirit of his fusion with nature. Another aesthetic element reflected in this haiku is perishability, which is "perhaps the most distinctively Japanese aesthetic ideal" (Keene 304). According to Donald Keene, there exists a striking difference between the Western aesthetic ideal and Japanese perishability:

> The desire in the West has generally been to achieve artistic immortality, and this has led men to erect monuments in deathless marble. The realization that even such monuments crumble and disappear has brought tears to the eyes of the poets. The Japanese have built for impermanence, though paradoxically some of the oldest buildings in the world exist in Japan. The Japanese belief that perishability is a necessary element in beauty does not . . . mean that they have been insensitive to the poignance of the passage of time. Far from it. Whatever the subject matter of the old poems, the underlying meaning was often an expression of grief over the fragility of beauty and love. Yet the Japanese were keenly aware that without this mortality there could be no beauty. . . . The frailty of human existence . . . has rarely been recognized as the necessary condition of beauty. The Japanese not only knew this, but expressed their preference for varieties of beauty which most conspicuously betrayed their impermanence. (304–5)

Based upon Keene's elaboration, this Japanese aesthetic element stresses that beauty of life lies in its perishability or impermanence. Without doubt, the feeling of mortality is always a common theme in all world literatures. Wright, a Western writer who read extensively, should have known the different modes of expression of this feeling and understood the philosophical view of mortality or the impermanence of human existence in this world. But his aesthetic ideal in "I am nobody" is to catch the beauty of mortality and transcend perishability for spiritual fulfillment through his harmony with nature. This transcendence, revealed in lines 2 and 3 of haiku 1, shows the influence of Japanese aesthetics and the culmination of Wright's poetic spirit.

This spirit of harmonious fulfillment with nature also echoes the Taoist doctrine since Zen itself is a mixture of Buddhism, Taoism, and Confucianism. Fritjof Capra asserts in *The Tao of Physics* that Zen is "a way of life which is typically Japanese, and yet it reflects the mysticism of India, the Taoist love of naturalness and spontaneity and the thorough pragmatism of the Confucian mind" (121). When Buddhism, which originated in India, appeared in China, its emphasis on *dhyana* (the Sanskrit word for meditation) resulted in the formation of a sect of Ch'an Buddhism, which is called Zen Buddhism in Japan. Both *Ch'an* and *Zen* mean *meditation.* According to Hui Neng, the sixth patriarch of Chinese Ch'an Buddhism, in order to relieve oneself from bias or selfish vision of reality or nature, one must attain the state of "no-thought" or "mindlessness" so that one can reflect the wisdom inherent in reality and elevate one's spirit. In Hui Neng's words, "To deepen one's spirit is to live in harmony with the true or 'self-nature' of all things" (Moore and Bruder 556). Hui Neng's thought surely reflects the Taoist doctrines that a wise man is free of selfish desires and knows how to cultivate tranquility for peace of mind and do nothing to recognize the Tao. In other words, to have peace of mind, one has to know oneself and become empty; that is, nobody. Therefore, to be nobody is a realization of oneness with nature and an abandonment of personal nameness for impersonal namelessness. Lao Tzu, the patriarch of Taoism, says about Tao and name or mortality in *Tao Te Ching*:

> The tao that can be told
> is not the eternal tao.
> The name that can be named
> is not the eternal Name.
> The unnameable is the eternally real.
> Naming is the origin
> of all particular things.
> Free from desire, you realize the mystery.
> Caught in desire, you see only the manifestations. (Novak 146–47)

Wright's "I am nobody" haiku certainly is an echo of Lao Tzu's saying. What he reflects, probably indirectly, in this haiku is Lao Tzu's dialectic idea about naturalness and nameness. Moreover, Wright understands more clearly the interrelationship between the temporality of a human being and the infinity of nature through attaining *satori*, which means *enlightenment* in Zen. This haiku also corresponds to Confucius's saying: "The gentleman is calm and peaceful; the small man is always emotional" (Confucius 27). The speaker in the haiku states that he is nobody since he realizes that his real being with reality and nature comes after he attains peace of mind.

Sabi is another Japanese aesthetic element reflected in Wright's haiku 1. Haruo Shirane defines *sabi* as "a sense of beauty and spiritual depth in loneliness and tranquility, especially in natural images, generating a subtle sentiment that emerges quietly in the overtones of the poem" (297). This is typically the Japanese poetic ideal that relates the self-content of loneliness with nature. Therefore, in Wright's haiku 1 the loneliness of the speaker ideally incorporated into the autumn sun suggests peace of mind. Moreover, the beauty of this haiku relies also on the power of suggestion, which is another Japanese aesthetic element discussed by Keene. *Suggestion* means to say something implicitly rather than explicitly or to convey more meanings than words can express so as to challenge the imagination of a reader. In haiku 1, a feeling of loneliness or a loss of nameness suggests lonelinessness, and this is Wright's metamorphosis that shows his realization of being in the state of nothingness, which is a process of *metanoia*—a real knowing of spiritual or transformational change in one's being. The sense of lonelinessness shows again a clue that Wright is receptive to the influence of East Asian philosophy. In the first volume of R. H. Blythe's four *Haiku* volumes that Wright read, there are "six pages for Buddhism, eleven pages for Taoism, and sixteen pages for Confucianism" (Kiuchi 23). Other books on Zen Buddhism collected by Wright also show a trace of his interest in Zen philosophy.[2]

Poetry is open to different interpretations. Some scholars have a different opinion on haiku 1. Hazel Rowley, in her biography of Richard Wright, which contains a chapter titled "I Am Nobody," believes that Wright's haiku 1 seems to say that "he had failed in life, that the bright promises of his early adulthood were mocking him" (506). Michel Fabre, a prominent Richard Wright scholar, interprets haiku 1 as "a real cry of despair, the recognition that the individual can no longer define his being when the star of light and meaning disappears with his name" (*World* 52). Fabre's interpretation relates the allusion of haiku 1 to a reader. However, even though the first line suggests a cry of despair, Wright should reach the spiritual height of *sabi* by purging his personal emotion in the second part of the haiku. Kodama points out that Blythe uses about one hundred pages on the Buddhist influence on haiku in the section of "Zen, the State of Mind for Haiku," and this section may have had a direct effect on Wright when he read it carefully (67). So, in considering the influence of Zen philosophy on Wright, we can assume that what Wright wants to express in haiku 1 is an aesthetic sensibility of naturalness or permanence imbued with perishability or impermanence rather than a personal cry of despair or failure. In their afterword to Wright's haiku collection, Hakutani and Tener provide an explanation of what Wright looked for through his reading of Zen:

> Unlike the other sects of Buddhism, Zen teaches that every individual possesses Buddhahood and all he or she must do is to realize it. One must purge one's mind and heart of any materialistic thoughts or feelings, and appreciate the wonder of the world here and now. Zen is a way of self-discipline and self-reliance. Its emphasis on self is derived from the prophetic admonishment Gautama Buddha is said to have given to his disciples: "Seek within, you are the Buddha." Satori . . . is an enlightenment that transcends time and place, and even the consciousness of self. In the African primal outlook upon existence, a person's consciousness of self, as Wright explains, corresponds to the spirit of nature. (296)

This passage should serve as a supplementary note to haiku 1. Zen Buddhism believes that there is oneness of all things. To see the truth of oneness and achieve peace of mind and enlightenment, one must be free of desires.

A story exists about a poetry competition on oneness to determine the successor of Master Hong Ren, the fifth patriarch of Chinese Ch'an Buddhism. Hong Ren asks the monks to write a poem that shows their insight into the truth of fundamental oneness, which is latent in human beings. Shen Xiu, who is the senior monk at the temple, presents his four-line poem:

> The body is a Bodhi tree,
> The mind a mirror bright;
> Take care to clean it carefully
> And let no dust alight. (Novak 97–98)

When the fifth patriarch hears the poem, he says to Shen Xiu that it shows no depth of insight into the fundamental truth of oneness because it still does not surpass the normal thought of purging the mind intentionally ("clean it carefully") in order to become the Buddha. Zen says, "Seek within, you are the Buddha." Shen Xiu's poem, however, ends in seeking outside. To clean something outside, dust should have already alighted on the mind. Thus, Hui Neng, who is an illiterate kitchen helper at the temple, composes a reply upon hearing Shen Xiu's poem recited by another monk:

> The Bodhi tree does not exist
> Nor does the mirror bright.
> Since everything is empty
> Where can dust alight? (Novak 98)

Hui Neng's poem is different from Shen Xiu's in that it reflects the principle of emptiness of Buddhism. If the body and mind are empty, the bodhi tree and mirror are empty too; therefore, there is a fundamental nature of oneness of all things. When all things are empty, where can dust alight? This poem shows that Hui Neng, with his enlightened mind, can escape the normal thought of reality by seeing the ultimate truth of oneness in reality and nature.

As for haiku 1, I believe that Wright frees himself of all kinds of desires by seeking within himself the true nature of human existence in nature and the "no-thought" or "selflessness" of his individual entity. In other words, since being selfless is the intrinsic meaning of nature that Wright seeks within, haiku 1 shows that he reaches the sphere of realization of the Buddhist spirit through his oneness with nature. The loss of his personal name or ego has turned into a gain of selflessness or egolessness so that he can gain his spiritual harmony with the natural world. Blythe says that "selflessness is of the essence of Buddhism" ("Buddhism and Haiku" 313). Evidently, a feeling of selflessness or egolessness prevails in many of Wright's haiku. Particularly in haiku 1, Wright forbids his old self to enter as if he is going through a catharsis to gain freedom of sentimentality so that he can become part of the sun with a feeling of selfless fulfillment with nature. This is true beauty that surfaces with vitality from haiku 1. Wright must think that this haiku can be "an expression of his realization of the importance of a 'selflessness' attitude to life, suggesting also the rejection of his previous way of life" (Kodama 69). And this rejection indicates as well the poetic significance of Wright's spiritual oneness with nature.

Nature, the essence of the Japanese poetic spirit in haiku, has become the central theme of Wright's haiku. With this poetic spirit, as illuminated by Bashō, "man follows the creative energy of nature and makes communion with the things of the four seasons. For those who understand the spirit, everything they see becomes a lovely flower, and everything they imagine becomes a beautiful moon" (Ueda 423). Bashō's proposition of making communion with nature calls for an aesthetic appreciation of spiritual life and an aesthetic idea about nature. It finds an echo in Wright's haiku. Here, for comparison, are two haiku about rain written, respectively, by Bashō and Wright. A haiku by Bashō states:

Spring rain—
under trees
a crystal stream. (26)

Bashō says, "When we observe calmly, we discover that all things have their fulfillment" (Ueda 424). When spring comes, the rainfall in the woods becomes a crystal stream that brings the color of green back to trees. This is how Bashō imagines the spring rain through his poetic sensibility to nature. He extols rain while welcoming spring. The juxtaposition of the two visual images, rain and stream, illustrates Bashō's keen perception of harmony and fulfillment of all things in nature. Similarly, a haiku by Wright states:

The valley is full
Of the scent of violets
Scattered by spring rain. (274)

Like Bashō, Wright, whose latent poetic sensibility to nature has been awakened by his outburst of enthusiasm for haiku, uses the image of rain to present his perception of things in nature interacting with each other by presenting the harmonious beauty of spring. The rain (a visual and auditory image) scattering the scent of violets (an olfactory image) reflects Wright's feeling of sensibility. In a sense, the human appreciation of natural beauty becomes suggestive in the action of an invisible speaker smelling the scent of violets.

It is evident that human involvement is everywhere in Wright's haiku. Haiku 163 is another example that shows a harmonious connection of human beings with nature:

As the music stops,
Flooding strongly to the ear,
The sound of spring rain.

The music and the rain complement each other. As soon as the music, which is a human creation, stops, the spring rain, which is a natural creation, begins to sound. The light humor in this haiku is that the human musical sounds seem like a prelude to the natural music, and the two kinds of music become an inseparable piece.

Thus far we have read two of Wright's haiku that involve the participation of humans in either a suggestive or apparent way. The following haiku shows Wright's eyescape of harmony existing between human beings and nature even though the environment is less harmonious:

Seen from a hilltop,
Shadowy in winter rain,
A man and his mule. (42)

The invisible observer on a hilltop, the shadowy man and mule in the field, and the rain are arranged to present an organic eyescape that reveals Wright's mindscape, the metaphysical union of human beings with nature—even in this rainy winter season that implies an environment less harmonious. This power of transference from images to ideas, from human sensibility to wit, from visibility to invisibility is inherent in many of Wright's haiku.

Besides the theme of human spiritual union with nature, Wright also presents his imagination of interaction between human beings and nature. The following two haiku (103 and 106) use the umbrella image to show both the poet's eyescape and mindscape by his effective use of synesthesia. Read first, haiku 103 says:

Just enough of rain
To bring the smell of silk
From umbrellas.

This haiku juxtaposes two different senses by illustrating the correspondence between the sound of rain and the smell of silk. The umbrellas, all manmade objects, rely on rain, a natural object, to bring out the smell of silk, that, in turn, suggests a fleeting moment of joy that is both beautiful and natural. To Wright, his haiku moment is finding new meanings from a momentary period of enlightenment, as shown also in haiku 106:

Beads of quicksilver
On a black umbrella:
Moonlit April rain.

This haiku implies a blending of sound and color. Rain needs both a black-and-white backdrop, from both nature (moonlight) and a human object (a black umbrella), in order to create a visual effect of its beauty (beads of quicksilver). Although natural beauty exists in its own grandeur, the human involvement can always enrich it by illuminating even the smallest act of wonderment. In other words, beauty in nature depends upon human perception. Many of Wright's haiku obviously show that "one of his chief aims as a haiku poet is to create beauty in his perception of nature" (Hakutani and Tener 285). There is no doubt that Wright is good at portraying various effects upon the senses to present his different views of nature. For instance:

In the autumn dusk:
A faintly lighted window
And the smell of rain. (441)

This haiku shows Wright's poetic imagination in a vivid way: the beauty of autumn dusk is transformed as it visually filters through a lighted window to affect the olfactory nerves ingesting the smell of rain. Rain nurtures not only life in nature but also the human desire for connection with nature.

In addition to expressing his sensibility to the inseparable oneness of human beings with nature, Wright also uses nature as a bond to connect human beings themselves. Such a bond is more interesting when the union is presented as occurring between a person who can see and another who cannot. In haiku 127:

Why does the blindman
Stop so still for a second
In the drizzling dusk?

The drizzling rain at dusk, which is a visual experience for the person who can see it happening, becomes an auditory and tactile experience for the blind man who cannot see. This haiku presents a heart-wrenching picture during which a blind man stands still only for a second in order to listen to or feel the drizzle at dusk. The person's eagerness also to be touched by the drizzle reveals his spontaneous moment of bonding with nature because of another person's reaction. Similarly, in haiku 128:

This autumn drizzle
Is our bond with other eyes
That can see no more.

While haiku 127 presents the human experience of bonding with nature by raising a rhetorical question, Wright's haiku 128 states an answer that nature is a bridge that connects people. For those persons who can see and those persons who cannot, they still maintain a connection when they carry nature within themselves. This haiku shows that when seeking within, a person can find his true self, his inner sense of beauty by means of nature and human nature. The next haiku again reveals a sensory reaction to beauty:

O if I could live
In that house where a peach tree
Blooms in the rain! (520)

The house that has a peach tree blooming in the spring rain looks so beautiful and integrated with nature that the poet has to utter an exclamation of his wish to live there.

Wright is also good at using the technique of internal comparison to present his sensibility to nature. "Most of Wright's better haiku," as Lee Gurga has noted, "make use of the technique of internal comparison through the juxtaposition of images" (38). Haiku 583 is a good example:

A long winter rain:
A whistling old man whittles
A dream on a stick.

Wright uses juxtaposition to create an internal comparison of a winter rainy day to an old man's act of whittling on wood. A long winter rain may suggest an uncomfortable environment, but the man's whistling while he whittles indicates that the weather has not circumvented his carving out his dream on a stick. His aloofness to his cold environment simply indicates that he can handle any kind of adverse situation. Haiku 722 is another good example of Wright's juxtaposition of images:

> Lines of winter rain
> Gleam only as they flash past
> My lighted window.

Again, winter rain, an image of nature, by juxtaposition is compared to a lighted window, an image of the human world. Natural beauty is reflected and the sheets of rain fully appreciated when the poet's inside lights capture the glistening lines of rain moving quickly in a flash past his window. The moment of brightness suggests how human beings react to nature during everyday life.

All of the haiku discussed so far show that writing haiku opens a space for Wright to respond directly to nature. In turn, this direct response expands his poetic vision toward the world that he lives in and toward nature where he finds his poetic spirit. More importantly, what interests Wright so much is not the haiku form but the poetic spirit and the Zen attitude toward human existence in nature. According to Hakutani and Tener, "Only when [Wright] attains a state of nothingness and a total attitude towards life can he perceive nature with his enlightened senses" (300). Here is a famous Zen saying that best describes Wright after he gets in touch with Zen through his haiku journey:

> Before you study Zen, mountains are mountains and rivers are rivers; while you are studying Zen, mountains are no longer mountains and rivers are no longer rivers; but once you have had enlightenment, mountains are once again mountains and rivers again rivers. (Capra 124)

To be enlightened, Wright undergoes a spiritual change of attitude, not only toward the world but toward himself as well. His haiku, the consequences of this change, function as a vehicle that transforms him from the human world to the natural world, and they also lead us with certainty into a world we human beings have long overlooked—the world of nature within ourselves.

Significantly, Wright's haiku echo the Zen saying of "seek within, you are the Buddha." They show that what he has been searching for is enlightenment. Only when he is enlightened can Wright see nature with a new vision. For example, in haiku 425, he writes:

An empty sickbed:
An indented white pillow
In weak winter sun.

This haiku creates a world where sickness or death is associated with nature; it is a world where Wright achieves *satori*—enlightenment that is "defined as the state of *mu*, nothingness, which is absolutely free of any thought or emotion" (Hakutani and Tener 250). The association of the empty sickbed with the weak winter sun reveals the *mu* of the poet's personal emotion, since death itself is *mu*. On the other hand, it is interesting to note that some of Wright's haiku record his feelings about his illness, as in haiku 224:

While convalescing,
The red roses have no smell,
Gently mocking me.

This haiku reveals the speaker's momentary confrontation with his illness. He tries to be light-hearted by saying that the roses mock him. In haiku 361, Wright also pretends to be light-hearted and mocks himself in a humorous, but bitter, tone:

At slow intervals
The hospital's lights wink out
In the summer rain.

Margaret Walker elaborates upon Wright's illness in *Daemonic Genius*. She remarks:

> [Wright] had been ill since the summer of 1959. . . . He was chained to a bed of sickness. He had never before had a long, confining illness in his life . . . and he had always been susceptible to colds and upper-respiratory infections, like grippe and flu . . . but nothing like his present illness. He complained of an enervating weakness, of sudden changes in his body temperature, and of breaking out in cold sweats. . . . Amoebic dysentery was very debilitating, and the medicine made him feel even worse." (1988 Amistad ed. *DG* 329)

Sometimes his illness would make him feel lonely, and this feeling of loneliness becomes stronger when it is juxtaposed with the season of autumn, as in haiku 243:

Leaving the doctor,
The whole world looks different
This autumn morning.

Sometimes his illness exhausts him, as he suggests in haiku 250:

Even toy soldiers
Perspire with weariness
In the autumn mist.

The seasonal reference and the hyperbolic citation of inanimate objects—toy soldiers—make the weariness more unbearable. The next haiku also shows Wright's reliance on the use of his senses to express his feelings about illness:

The sound of the rain,
Blotted out now and then
By a sticky cough. (34)

The auditory reference to rain becomes overshadowed by the loudness of his sticky cough. On November 28, 1960, Wright died unexpectedly. He had devoted his life to haiku writing in the final stage of his writing career because haiku, as an exotic art, can be "such a ruthless taskmaster that when the artist stumbles perhaps he pays with his life" (Harrington 20). His interest in haiku, as Margaret Walker says, "may have been the beginning of an interest in Eastern philosophy and religion" (1988 Amistad ed. *DG* 314).

In sum, Wright's writing of 4,000 haiku during his illness may show that his human nature had gradually grown into a tender sensibility to nature, and this sensibility emanates from within him for both his discovery and for ours. What survives best in Wright's haiku is his presentation of his poetic spirit, his rebirth as a poet, and his willingness to be in harmony with nature. If Wright presents his physical hunger and hunger for knowledge in *Black Boy*, he strives to present a new form of hunger as a new vision of nature or insight into the real being of human nature as part of nature. Given his spirituality and the wholeness that Wright tries to keep, it is more likely that Wright beats his rhythm with the unbreakable cycle of nature. Chester Himes says in an interview that Wright's work belongs to "a literature for the world" (Fabre and Skinner 7), and I think this should include his haiku.

Notes

1. These volumes were "bought by Ellen Wright in London in 1959 at the request of Wright, who was using a set borrowed from Sinclair Beiles," a South African poet who was born in Uganda. Fabre, *Books and Writers*, 14.

2. In Fabre, *Books and Writers*, one can find titles of books that show Wright's interest in Zen Buddhism: Christmas Humphreys, *Zen Buddhism* (75), and Daisetz T. Suzuki, *An Introduction to Zen Buddhism*; *Essays in Zen Buddhism*; and *The Complete Works of D. T. Suzuki* (156).

The Triangular Vision of Richard Wright: The African American Poet's Achievement of Solace by Means of Eastern Poetics and African Philosophy

—YOSHINOBU HAKUTANI—

Richard Wright is renowned for his powerful prose in such books as his novel *Native Son* (1940) and his autobiography *Black Boy* (1945), which he had written earlier in his career. These two works encapsulated his vision about the injustices continuously experienced by African Americans living in America. Wright never cast his gaze away from America for too long. He would consistently stress in his writings his native birth as an African American. But Wright refused to be confined to narrowed thinking or to be restricted in his movements. He developed a broader perspective of the world after moving to Paris, France, in 1947. In the late 1950s, he once again became interested in poetry, which earlier in the 1930s had inaugurated his career as a professional writer. Traveling the globe introduced him to Eastern poetics and the philosophy inspiring the African way of life. In 1953, he traveled to Africa and published his nonfiction book *Black Power: A Record of Reactions in a Land of Pathos* in 1954. In 1955, he attended the Bandung Conference of the Third World in Jakarta, Indonesia, and published his second nonfiction book *The Color Curtain: A Report of the Bandung Conference* that same year. And in the following year, he served as a member of the First Congress of Negro Artists and Writers, which convened in Paris in September 1956. During this same active period of traveling, lecturing, conferencing, and writing, Wright found relaxation by working in his garden at his farm in Neuilly, France. The agrarian, pastoral setting, far from the rush and noise of urban Paris, supplied many themes for the haiku poetry that he produced in the last eighteen months of his life (Fabre, 1973 *UQ* 375, 447). In fact, he composed over 4,000 separate haiku in France during this period.

Of his many foreign experiences during the early 1950s, it appears that Wright's travel to the newly independent nation-state of Ghana in West Africa had a great impact upon his writing of haiku. As a native-born African American, he illustrates how his triangular, global vision works when he appropriates and adapts a Japanese art form by further reflecting its affinity to the African philosophy of life in terms of human and nonhuman relations to the natural world. Ultimately, Wright creates his own brand of haiku by meshing his concepts of nature intrinsic to African American, African, and Eastern cultures. Africa and Asia especially intrigued him by their similar perspectives on life and death. He, the travel writer and poet, had witnessed firsthand "the African primal outlook upon life," as Wright called it, and never forgot how the Ashanti people of West Africa practiced its spiritual precepts in their daily lives. Their cultural beliefs served as an inspiration for his aesthetic expression and poetic sensibility, and resonate in many of his haiku and reflect the triangular cultures and philosophies that he imparts.

In Search of Aesthetic Spirituality

The decade of the 1950s was rich in possibilities for Wright. The Third World was coming into its own artistically, socially, and politically. But set against this positive cultural climate were the aggravating preponderance of negative events caused by his financial woes and personal problems. Financial earnings from his earlier publications were weak, nor had he written anything in the past few years that was a literary or financial success. Complicating matters, Wright was sick from bouts of amoebic dysentery at the beginning of 1959, which took its toll and often confined him to his bed. He was approaching the end of the decade in an ambivalent mood and ready for union with that state of intangibility that lies beyond the physical being of the artist—a sense of nothingness thematically appropriate for haiku. Overall, the combination of financial woes and protracted sickness proved to be a polemical drain on his rational powers. He was mentally and emotionally receptive to the ideas, beauty, and form of haiku shown by R. H. Blythe[1] after reading how Blythe incorporated concepts of Zen. Zen seemed to correspond with certain cultural beliefs that daily influenced the philosophy of life practiced by West Africans as witnessed by Wright. Both aesthetic influences seemed to provide him with a form of liberation from his self-imposed adherence to rational principles. Now, without guilt, he was able to abandon intellectual restrictions and enjoy the free reign of his intuitive responses to other powers and images residing latently within himself.

Sometime during the summer of 1959, Wright had been introduced to haiku by Sinclair Beiles, a South African Beat poet living in Paris and associating with Wright and other artists interested in Zen. Wright borrowed Blythe's four volumes on the art of haiku and its relationship to Zen, and then settled down to rediscover and to explore his old dream of achieving oneness with all life. It was a state of solace for which he was striving. By March 19, 1960, he was so captivated by its beauty that he was already in the midst of composing what would eventually turn out to be over 4,000 separate haiku. In response to his friend and Dutch translator Margrit de Sablonière, Wright said that he had returned to poetry and added, "During my illness I experimented with the Japanese form of poetry called haiku; I wrote some 4,000 of them and am now sifting them out to see if they are any good" (qtd. in Hakutani and Tener 270). In his discussion of this monumental enterprise, Michel Fabre notes that Wright's interest in haiku also led him to research the works of the great Japanese masters, Buson, Bashō, and Issa. He ignored the European and American forms that were also becoming popular in the 1950s. Fabre further observes that Wright made "an effort to respect the exact form of the poem," but adds that it was curious for Wright to become so interested in haiku at a time when he was fighting a deleterious illness. As Fabre reasons, "Logically he should have been tempted to turn away from 'pure' literature and to use his pen instead as a weapon" (1973 *UQ* 505–6). In other words, Wright had diverted his attention away from his usual sociopolitical mantle that appears in his fictions, nonfictions, speeches, lectures, and early poetry in order to pursue aesthetic spirituality.

Just as curiously, Constance Webb refers to none of this haiku material as bearing great significance. She merely says that Wright had lost his physical energy and that "while lying against the pillows one afternoon he picked up the small book of Japanese poetry and began to read it again." It had been given to him earlier and he read and reread with enthusiasm about its style. She notes that Wright "had to study it and study to find out why it struck his ear with such a modern note," and adds that Wright "would try to bring the life and consciousness of a black American" to its form. According to her, the haiku "seemed to answer the rawness he felt, which had, in turn, created a sensitivity that ached. Never had he been so sensitive, as if his nervous system had been exposed to rough air." In a letter to Paul Reynolds, his friend and literary agent, Wright explained that he had sent to William Targ of the World Publishing Company an eighty-two-page manuscript of haiku titled "This Other World: Projections in the Haiku Manner." He remarks that "these poems are the result of my being in bed a great deal and it is likely that they are bad. I don't know" (Webb *Biography* 43–46).

That manuscript[2] was not published in its entirety until 1998, and was less than one-fourth of the total sum of 4,000 haiku.[3] Until we read all of his 1998 published poems and his remaining unpublished haiku, we will probably never know fully the reasons that Wright turned to haiku during the last years of his life. But that knowledge is unnecessary for us to read, appreciate, and enjoy the newly published haiku. A reading of the haiku in *This Other World* indicates that Wright, turning away from the moral, intellectual, social, and political problems that he had dealt with in his prose work, found in nature his latent poetic sensibility. Gwendolyn Brooks has called Wright's haiku in *This Other World* "a clutch of strong flowers."[4] "[These] haiku," Julia Wright, Wright's daughter, remarks in her introduction, "not only helped him place the volcanic experience of mourning under the self-control of closely counted syllables, but also enabled him to come to terms with the difficult beauty of the earth" ("Introduction," *OW* xi). And Wright's discovery of haiku, as Michel Fabre has noted, "brings to light an often neglected aspect of the writer's personality: his intimate sense of the universal harmony, his wonder before life, his thirst for a natural existence, all these tendencies which nourished his courageous and incessant battle against all that prevents an individual from fully belonging to the world" ("Poetry" 271).

As previously stated, Constance Webb noted that Wright, in studying the haiku form, "would try to bring the life and consciousness of a black American to its form" (Webb, *Biography* 43–46). In other words, Wright never forgot his racial or native heritage while writing prose or poetry. The genesis of his African American perspective, directions for cultural preservation, and poetic sensibility is clearly stated in "Blueprint for Negro Writing," even though his theory is Marxist and, hence, political rather than literary. An African American writer's point of view, says Wright, "is that part of a poem, novel, or play which a writer never puts directly upon paper. It is that fixed point in intellectual space where a writer stands to view the struggles, hopes, and sufferings of his people" ("Blueprint," *RWR* 45). Wright demonstrates how this vantage point in "intellectual space" operates in *Black Boy*, his nonfictional autobiography. At the same time, he consciously creates a poetic vision out of nature through which and against which he reports the acts of racial conflict continuously occurring in his environment. Indeed, the poetic passages in *Black Boy* signify Wright's incipient interest in the exaltation of nature and the usefulness of natural images for demonstrating his poetic sensibility.

The Eastern poetics influencing Wright's artistic sensibility come from a number of external sources. One of the salient characteristics of haiku is the utmost attention that poets give to natural objects. Unlike Western Romantic poetry and even the earlier Japanese poetry called *waka*, haiku, as R. H. Blythe has observed, "is as near to life and nature as possible, as far from literature and fine writing as may be, so that the asceticism is art and the art is asceticism" (*History* 1:1). Blythe's definition of haiku as an ascetic art means that classic haiku by such masters as Bashō, Buson, and Issa are strictly concerned with objects in nature. A haiku is not a haiku if it is an expression or representation of human subjectivity. In a haiku, the poet as subject is absent. As Roland Barthes has demonstrated in *Empire of Signs*, haiku is a form of decentered writing during which the poet is dethroned. Jacques Lacan would have said that the Zen master is "kicked out," let alone his ego.[5]

In some respects, the focus on nature rather than on the master in Eastern forms of haiku explains why Wright would see its connection to the African philosophy of life. Just on the basis of Wright having read Dr. J. B. Danquah's *The Akan Doctrine of God*[6] while in Ghana, he was persuaded by the beliefs of Africans that spirits reside in inanimate objects like trees, stones, and rivers—things of nature that are far removed from the poet. He also witnessed how and why Africans believe in ghosts and in the spirits of the dead. Not only was Wright fascinated with the African concept of death, he must have been contemplating death in general and his own death in particular while writing haiku in late 1959. To Wright the regenerated, intuitive, African American haiku poet, death was a most striking, mysterious *signifier* of nature. Although to him the concept of death seemed to be something abstract, to Africans, it is reified as a natural aspect of life. Moreover, for Africans, life and death are not diametrically opposed. "Life in the ghost world," remarked Wright, "is an exact duplicate of life in this world. A farmer in this world is a farmer there; a chief here is a chief there. It is, therefore, of decisive importance when one enters that world of ghostly shades to enter it in the right manner. For you can be snubbed there just as effectively and humiliatingly as you were snubbed here" (1954 *BP* 214).

African religion does not recognize the existence of hell and sin or distinguish between good and evil. "When the family is the chief idea," Wright quotes Danquah as saying, "things that are dishonorable and undignified, actions that in disgracing you disgrace the family, are held to be vices, and the highest virtue is found in honor and dignity. Tradition is the determinant of what is right and just, what is good and done" (1954 *BP* 215–16). Africans, thus, reject the notion of original sin espoused in Christian doctrine: "The notion that, because two remote ancestors had sexual relations and bore a child, there was imposed upon all mankind a threat of suffering, is, to the African mind, simply ridiculous" (216–17). Whereas the Akan and Christian religions share the concept of life after death, the Akan religion resembles more closely other religions such as Buddhism and Hinduism in its belief in reincarnation and in the existence of a soul in the nonhuman living. "Death," Wright observes, "does not round off life; it is not the end; it complements life." To him, African religion looks "terrifying" but not "primitive" (217), as any Eastern religion would seem to strike Westerners as being something terrifying rather than primitive.

Before commenting on Ashanti life, he quotes a passage from Edmund Husserl's *Ideas*:

> Not only might human development have never overstepped the pre-scientific stage and been doomed never to overstep it so that the physical world might indeed retain its truth whilst we should know nothing about it; the physical world might have been other than it is with systems of law other than those actually prevailing.

> It is also conceivable that our intuitable world should be the last, and "beyond" it no physical world at all. (1954 *BP* 239)

Husserl's passage suggests the preeminence of the physical world over the scientific vision of that world and the primacy of nature itself over human subjectivity in the search for truth. Wright thus applies Husserl's idea of human beings and their environment to his analysis on the concept of African existence. Wright interprets the primal outlook in African culture to mean the primacy of spirit over matter. The primacy of the spirit of nature over the strife of human beings is further pronounced in his later work, especially haiku. In "Blueprint for Negro Writing," one of the theoretical principles calls for an African American writer's exploration of universal humanism or what is common among all cultures. "Every iota of gain in human thought and sensibility," Wright argues, "should be ready grist for his mill, no matter how far-fetched they may seem in their immediate implications" ("Blueprint," *RWR* 45). After a journey into the Ashanti kingdom in West Africa in 1953, when he was forty-five, he wrote in *Black Power*:

> The truth is that the question of how much of Africa has survived in the New World is misnamed when termed "African survivals." The African attitude toward life springs from a natural and poetic grasp of existence and all the emotional implications that such an attitude carries; it is clear, then, that what the anthropologists have been trying to explain are not "African survivals" at all—they are but the retention of basic and primal attitudes toward life. (266)

Wright's exploration of the Ashanti and their "poetic grasp of existence" convinced him that their "retention of basic and primal attitudes toward life" meant for Africans a consistent renewal of faith in themselves. He realized for the first time in his life that African culture was buttressed by universal human values—such values as awe of nature, family kinship and love, faith in religion, and a sense of honor that had made "African survivals" possible. For the purpose of writing haiku, this African primal outlook upon life had a singular influence on his poetic vision.

Indeed, Wright's interpretation of the African philosophy of life recalls a teaching in Zen Buddhism. Unlike the other sects of Buddhism, Zen teaches that every individual possesses Buddhahood and all he or she must do is to realize it. One must purge one's mind and heart of any materialistic thoughts or feelings and appreciate the wonder of the world here and now. Its emphasis on self denial is derived from the prophetic admonishment Gautama Buddha is said to have given to his disciples: "Seek within, you are the Buddha." *Satori* in Zen is an enlightenment that transcends time and place and even the consciousness of self. The African primal outlook upon existence, in which a person's consciousness, as Wright explains, corresponds to the spirit of nature, has a closer resemblance to the concept of enlightenment in Zen than it does to Emersonian transcendentalism. Emerson defines *human enlightenment* as the subject's consciousness of the over-soul, itself "a light" that "shines through us upon things and makes us aware that we are nothing, but the light is all" (*Complete Essays* 263–64). This light is so powerful that one becomes "a transparent eyeball" (*Emerson* 4:7) that cannot see beyond one's state of mind. In Zen, one is taught to annihilate this eyeball before *satori* is attained: *satori* is the achievement of a state of *mu*, nothingness. The state of nothingness is free of human subjectivity and free of any thought or emotion that such a consciousness or "the unconscious" corresponds to the state of nature.

In Zen, if the enlightened person sees a tree, for instance, the person sees the tree through his or her enlightened eye. The tree is no longer an ordinary tree; it now exists with a different meaning. In other words, the tree contains *satori* only when the viewer is enlightened. From a perspective similar to *satori*, Wright saw in African life a closer relationship between human beings and nature than that between human beings and their social and political environments:

> Africa, with its high rain forest, with its stifling heat and lush vegetation, might well be mankind's queerest laboratory. Here instinct ruled and flowered without being concerned with the nature of the physical structure of the world; man lived without too much effort; there was nothing to distract him from concentrating upon the currents and countercurrents of his heart. He was thus free to project out of himself what he thought he was. Man has lived here in a waking dream, and, to some extent, he still lives here in that dream. (1954 *BP* 159)

Africa evokes in one "a total attitude toward life, calling into question the basic assumptions of existence," just as Zen teaches one a way of life completely independent of what one has been socially and politically conditioned to lead. As if echoing Zen enlightenment, Wright says: "Africa is the world of man; if you are wild, Africa's wild; if you are empty, so's Africa" (159).

Its discussion of the African concept of life is also suggestive of Zen's emphasis on transcending the dualism of life and death. Zen master Dogen (1200–1254), whose work *Shobogenzo* is known in Japan for his practical application rather than his theory of Zen doctrine, observed that because life and death are beyond human control, there is no need to avoid them. Dogen's teaching is a refutation of the assumption that life and death are entirely separate entities, as are seasons or day and night.[7] To Sigmund Freud, the unconscious includes a death instinct, an instinct in opposition to libido—an instinct to turn into elements in opposition to reproduction of organisms. To Lacan, the death instinct is not "an admission of impotence, it isn't a coming to a halt before an irreducible, an ineffable last thing, it is a concept" (70). Lacan takes issue with Freud because Freud defines death as the opposite of life: the pleasure principle underlying life is opposed to the death wish, which "tends to reduce all animate things to the inanimate" (80). Lacan, on the other hand, defines this change from life to death as "human experience, human interchanges, intersubjectivity" (80). Lacan's concept of death has a strong resemblance to Dogen's.

Dogen's doctrine of intersubjectivity versus separateness corresponds to the Ashanti's philosophy of life and death. The funeral service that Wright saw occurring in an Ashanti tribe showed him that "the 'dead' live side by side with the living; they eat, breathe, laugh, hate, love, and continue doing in the world of ghostly shadows exactly what they had been doing in the world of flesh and blood" (1954 *BP* 213). He was fascinated by the reverence of Africans for the nonhuman living, a primal African attitude that also corresponds to the Buddhist belief. He thus observed:

> The pre-Christian African was impressed with the littleness of himself and he walked the earth warily, lest he disturb the presence of invisible gods. When he wanted to disrupt the terrible majesty of the ocean in order to fish, he first made sacrifices to its crashing and rolling waves; he dared not cut down a tree without first propitiating its spirit so that it would not haunt him; he loved his fragile life and he was convinced that the tree loved its life also. (261–62)

The concept of unity, continuity, and infinity underlying that of life and death is what the Akan and Buddhist religions share. Wright's reading of the African mind conforms to both religions in their common beliefs that humankind is not at the center of the universe. The Akan religion and Buddhism both de-emphasize human subjectivity. It is this continuity of relationships emulating nature that holds true for human beings; it reveals how the African primal outlook upon life is akin to Zen Buddhism.

Achieving *Mu* (Nothingness)

De-emphasizing the self is the goal of *satori,* which calls for deflecting all social and political trappings as well. The self must *not* be identifiable as African American, African, or Japanese in order to achieve the highest state of *satori.* Several haiku in Wright's collection focus their poetic visions on humanity's union with nature. In some of these pieces, Wright offers simple, direct scenes where human beings and nature exist in harmony in contrast to those complex, intriguing scenes in society where people's live are strife-ridden:

42. Seen from a hilltop,
Shadowy in winter rain,
A man and his mule. (*OW* 11)

377. In the winter dusk,
A thin girl leads a black cow
By a dragging rope. (*OW* 95)

541. After the sermon,
The preacher's voice is still heard
In the caws of crows. (*OW* 136)

"Seen from a Hilltop" (42) finds unity in humankind and nature: a man, a mule, a rain, a meadow, and a hill. "In the Winter Dusk" (377), like "Seen from a Hilltop" (42), is a direct description of the scene where a girl lives in harmony with nature. It is not clear whether a girl leads a cow or a cow leads her: creating such an ambiguous image intensifies the unity and harmony between them. In "After the Sermon" (541), the seasonal reference is ambiguous but Wright finds unity and an analogy between humanity and nature, "the preacher's voice" and "the caws of crows."

Whether perceiving nature for its own sake or in its relation to humankind, Wright's haiku thrive on the subtle interactions of the senses captured in seventeen syllables. For instance, in

47. The spring lingers on
In the scent of a damp log
Rotting in the sun. (*OW* 12)

the poet seems to detach himself from a natural scene. The feeling of the warm sun, the scent of a damp log, and the sight and silence of an outdoor scene all coalesce into an image of spring. In the process, the overall image has evolved from the separate visual images of the sun, of the log, and of the atmosphere. The three images of sight, moreover, are intertwined with the images of warmth from the sun and the rotting log as well as with the image of smell from the log, thereby causing all five senses to interact with one another. Because the poet is away from his own life and is concerned with natural objects, these images are symbolic rather than imaginary: they constitute representations of nature, the other, instead of the self. Because the poet perceives the natural phenomena, however, these images also reflect subjectivity. The reader, too, is likely to have similar sensations, given a similar situation. Such a well-written haiku thrives on intersubjectivity. Wright's best haiku strictly follow the well-established tradition and principle that a haiku is not an expression of human subjectivity.

In attempting haiku, Wright initially modeled his after classic Japanese poets such as Moritake (1472–1549), Bashō (1644–94), Kikaku (1661–1707), Buson (1715–83), and Issa (1762–1826). Two haiku have a thematic resemblance to Moritake's famous *hokku*:

626. Off the cherry tree,
One twig and its red blossom
Flies into the sun. (*OW* 157)

669. A leaf chases wind
Across an autumn river
And shakes a pine tree. (*OW* 168)

Moritake's poem is in Japanese and in Blythe's translation:

Rakka eda ni Fallen petals
Kaeru to mireba Seemed to return to the branch,—
Kocho kana A butterfly![8]

—Moritake

Both of Wright's haiku, "Off the Cherry Tree" (626) and "A Leaf Chases Wind" (669) create an illusion similar to Moritake's haiku. In "Off the Cherry Tree" a twig with its red blossom flies into the sun as if a bird flew off the cherry tree. Likewise, "A Leaf Chases Wind" captures a scene as though a leaf were chasing the wind and shaking a pine tree rather than the other way around.[9]

It is this haiku by Moritake that influenced Ezra Pound's composition of the famous metro poem, "In a Station of the Metro." Pound acknowledged for the first time in his career his indebtedness to Japanese poetry in general and the art of haiku in particular. In his essay "Vorticism," he quoted Moritake's haiku, "The fallen blossom flies back to its branch: A butterfly" (Pound, "Vorticism" 462), just before discussing his "In a Station of the Metro," often regarded as the first published haiku written in English.[10] What impressed Gwendolyn Brooks in calling Wright's haiku "a clutch of strong flowers" as mentioned earlier, suggests that the imagery in Wright's haiku is charged with energy. According to Margaret Walker, Wright was fascinated by the American modernist poets, including Pound.[11] As Pound explained in his essay, the image is not a static, rational idea: "It is a radiant node or cluster; it is what I . . . call a VORTEX, from which, through which, and into which ideas are constantly rushing. One can only call it a VORTEX. From this necessity came the name 'vorticism'" ("Vorticism," 469–70). A year later, Pound stated that the image "may be a sketch, a vignette, a criticism, an epigram or anything else. . . . It may be impressionism, it may even be very good prose." As a vortex, the image must be "endowed with energy" ("Imagisme" 349). To Pound, the haiku image conveys objective, impersonal truth rather than a subjective, personal point of view ("Vorticism" 464).[12]

Whether Wright was directly influenced by Pound's imagism is difficult to determine. But many of Wright's haiku bear a close resemblance to classic Japanese haiku, thereby showing that he, an African American, had mastered Eastern poetics. A pair of his haiku in *This Other World*, in style and content, are reminiscent of two of Bashō's most celebrated haiku. Wright's "In the Silent Forest" echoes Bashō's "It's Deadly Quiet":

316. In the silent forest
A woodpecker hammers at
The sound of silence. (*OW* 79)

It's deadly quiet:
Piercing into the rocks
Is the shrill of cicada.

—Bashō

As Bashō expresses awe of quietude, Wright juxtaposes silence in the forest to the sound of a woodpecker. Similarly, Wright's "A Thin Waterfall" is akin to Bashō's "A Crow":

569. A thin waterfall
Dribbles the whole autumn night,—
How lonely it is.

A crow
Perched on a withered tree
In the autumn evening.

—Bashō[13]

Bashō focuses on a single crow perching on a branch of an old tree, as does Wright upon a thin waterfall. In both haiku, the scene is drawn with little detail and the mood is provided by a simple, reserved description of fact, a phenomenon in nature that has nothing to do with the poet except for his attempt to describe the scene for its own sake. As parts of the scene are painted in dark colors, so is the background. Both haiku create the kind of beauty associated with the aesthetic sensibility of *sabi* that suggests loneliness and quietude as opposed to overexcitement and loudness. Whether Wright and Bashō felt themselves lonely when writing the haiku is moot.

It is legend that Bashō inspired more disciples than did any other haiku poet and that Kikaku is regarded as Bashō's most innovative disciple. Two of Wright's haiku bear some resemblance to Kikaku's "The Harvest Moon"[14] because both poets emphasize an interaction between humanity and nature in the creation of beauty:

106. Beads of quicksilver
On a black umbrella:
Moonlit April rain. (*OW* 27)

670. A pale winter moon,
Pitying a lonely doll,
Lent it a shadow. (*OW* 168)

The harvest moon:

Lo, on the tatami mats
The shape of a pine.

—Kikaku

In Kikaku's haiku, the beauty of the moonlight is not only humanized by the light shining on the human-made object but also intensified by the shadows of a pine tree that fall upon the mats. The beauty of the shadow reflected on the intricate pattern of an ageless pine tree as it stamps the dustless mats intensifies the beauty of the moonlight. Not only does such a scene unify an image of humanity and an image of nature, but it also shows that humanity and nature do interact. In Wright's first haiku, an element of nature, "Beads of Quicksilver," is reinforced by a human-made object, "a black umbrella." In "A Pale Winter Moon," while the second line portrays the loneliness of a doll, a pale winter moon, a beauty of nature, is intensified by the presence of a human-made object. In contrast to Wright's and Bashō's haiku ("A Thin Waterfall"; "A Crow"), these three haiku by Wright and Kikaku lightly include human subjectivity in appreciating natural beauty, but the focus of their visions is on nature. In Wright's "Beads of Quicksilver" and "A Pale Winter Moon," the images of "a black umbrella" and "a lonely doll," and, from Kikaku's "The Harvest Moon," "the tatami mats" slightly reflect human sentiment and subjectivity because these objects are human-made. But the central image in each haiku represents a natural object: "Moonlit April rain," "A pale winter moon," "The harvest moon," respectively.

This Other World includes a number of haiku that depict seasonal, climatic changes in nature like those by classic Japanese haiku poets. Wright's "I Would Like a Bell" is comparable to Buson's well-known "On the Hanging Bell" in their simple depiction of a spring scene:

13. I would like a bell
Tolling in this soft twilight
Over willow trees. (*OW* 4)

On the hanging bell
Has perched and is fast asleep,
It's a butterfly.

—Buson

Buson was well known in his time as an accomplished painter, and many of his haiku reflect his singular attention to color and its intensification. Wright's "A Butterfly Makes" is reminiscent of Buson's "Also Stepping On":

82. A butterfly makes
The sunshine even brighter
With fluttering wings. (*OW* 21)

Also stepping on
The mountain pheasant's tail is
The spring setting sun.

—Buson

For a seasonal reference to spring, Buson links an image of a bird with the spring sunset because both are highly colored. As a painter, he is also interested in an ambiguous impression that the scene he has drawn gives him; it is not clear whether the setting sun is treading on the pheasant's tail or the tail on the setting sun. In any event, Buson has made both pictures beautiful to look at, just as Wright has drawn the pictures of a butterfly and the sunshine, themselves highly colorful and bright, which, in turn, intensify each other.

In another fine haiku, Wright portrays humanity's relationship with nature in terms of art:

571. From across the lake,
Past the black winter trees,
Faint sounds of a flute. (*OW* 143)

Unlike "The Spring Lingers On" (47), discussed earlier, this haiku admits a human involvement in the scene: someone is playing the flute as the poet is listening from the other side of the lake. Through a transference of the senses between the faint sounds of a flute and the black winter trees, an interaction of humanity and nature takes place. As the sound of a man and the sight of nature affect each other, Wright has created delightful images of humankind as well as of nature. Wright's "From across the Lake" has an affinity to Kikaku's "The Harvest Moon," noted earlier, for both haiku are expressions of beauty as reified in objects, not in subjects or the poets themselves. As the image of beauty in Kikaku's haiku is intensified through the interaction of the moon and "the tatami mats," natural and human objects, so is Wright's image of beauty, the "sounds of a flute," appreciated through natural objects, "the lake" and "the black winter trees."

The haiku in its portrayal of humankind's association with nature often conveys a kind of enlightenment, a new way of looking at human beings and nature. In some of the haiku, as the following examples indicate, Wright follows this tradition.

720. A wilting jonquil
Journeys to its destiny
In a shut bedroom. (*OW* 180)

722. Lines of winter rain
Gleam only as they flash past
My lighted window. (*OW* 181)

"A Wilting Jonquil" (720) teaches the poet a lesson that nature out of its environment cannot exhibit its beauty. In "Lines of Winter Rain" (722), the poet learns that only when an interaction between human beings and nature occurs can natural beauty be savored.

This revelatory tradition, derived from Zen philosophy, often informs many of Wright's haiku. Several of Wright's conscious efforts to emulate Eastern philosophy occur in pieces that Wright included toward the end of *This Other World*. For example, in

721. As my anger ebbs,
The spring stars grow bright again
And the wind returns. (*OW* 181)

Wright tries to attain a state of *mu*—nothingness in Zen—by controlling his emotions. This state of nothingness is not synonymous with a state of void, but is functional, and its function is perceived by the senses. For the enlightened viewer, natural objects such as "the spring stars" and "the wind" are no longer mere facts: they exist with different meanings. They exhibit *satori* only when the viewer is enlightened. This enlightened state of nothingness leads one to achieve what Wright calls in *Black Power* "a total attitude toward life" that calls into question "the basic assumptions of existence" (1954 *BP* 159). "So violent and fickle," he writes, "was nature that [the African] could not delude himself into feeling that he, a mere man, was at the center of the universe" (262). In "As My Anger Ebbs," as the poet relieves himself of anger and achieves solace, he begins to see the stars "grow bright again" and "the wind" return. Only when he, the tricultural poet, reaches the heightened Zen "state of nothingness" or *mu* inclusive of the Ashanti stage of " a total attitude toward life" does Wright perceive nature by means of his enlightened senses. How closely this perception of nature is related to Wright's latent interest in Zen can also be seen in such a haiku as

809. Why did this spring wood
Grow so silent when I came?
What was happening? (*OW* 203)

This haiku suggests the kind of questions asked by a Zen master who teaches ways of attaining the state of *mu*. Wright here tries to give an admonition—as he does in many of his other haiku—that only with the utmost attention can human beings achieve, through nature, "the African primal outlook upon life," and truly see themselves. Overall, Ashanti culture and philosophy convinced Wright that the world of nature is preeminent over the human subjective vision of that world. Nature is omnipotent. Thus, in writing and syncretizing African American and African outlooks upon life and emulating Eastern forms of classic haiku, Wright the ill poet not only achieved solace by acknowledging the supremacy of the natural world, but also conveyed in many of his haiku that he had created a poetic Wrightean form of haiku. His haiku teach us that human subjectivity, egotism, and desire stand in the way of seeking truth and of attaining the ultimate state of *mu*.

Notes

1. Before trying his hand at composing haiku, Wright consulted the four volumes of haiku by R. H. Blythe, *Haiku.*

2. This manuscript consists of a title page and eighty-two pages. Page 1 has the first seven haiku and each of the other pages have ten. The manuscript, dated 1960, is deposited among the Richard Wright Papers, Beinecke Rare Book and Manuscript Collection, Yale University.

3. See Wright, *Haiku: This Other World.* Each of the haiku is numbered consecutively 1–817. Subsequent references appear parenthetically in the text as *OW,* using these numbers.

4. See Gwendolyn Brooks's quote featured on the cover of the Random House edition (2000) of *Haiku: This Other World.*

5. Barthes found an empty center in signs of traditional Japanese culture, such as its food, its landscape, and its quintessential poetic form, haiku (*Empire* 3–37). Lacan's first published seminar opens with a reference to a Zen master whom he wanted to emulate: "The master breaks the silence with anything—with a sarcastic remark, with a kick-start. That is how a Buddhist master conducts his search for meaning, according to the technique of Zen. It behooves the students to find out for themselves the answer to their own questions" (1).

6. See J. B. Danquah, *The Akan Doctrine of God: A Fragment of Gold Coast Ethics and Religion* (London: Frank Cass, 1944), a work by an anthropologist and philosopher from which Wright quoted many passages in *Black Power.*

7. For Dogen's teaching on death, see Kodo Jurebayashi, *Introduction to Dogen Zen* (Tokyo: Taiho Rinkaku, 1984).

8. The original and the translation are from Blythe, *History,* 2:56.

9. A literal translation of the first two lines, "Rakka eda ni / Kaeru to mireba," is "A fallen flower appears to come back to its branch."

10. Pound, "Vorticism" 463. For the influence of haiku on Pound's imagism, see Hakutani, "Ezra Pound."

11. In *Richard Wright: Daemonic Genius,* a biographical and critical study, Margaret Walker remarks: "He felt a close affinity to all modern poets and their poetry and read poetry with a passion—Shakespeare, Hart Crane, T. S. Eliot, Yeats, Ezra Pound, Dylan Thomas, and Walt Whitman. . . . In the last years of his life, Wright discovered the Japanese form of poetry known as Haiku and became more than a little interested in . . . an exercise in conciseness—getting so much meaning or philosophy in so few words" (1988 Amistad ed. *DG* 313–14).

12. Pound thought of an image not as a decorative emblem or symbol but as a seed capable of germinating and developing into another organism. Imagism is further contrasted to symbolism: "The symbolist's *symbols* have a fixed value, like numbers in arithmetic, like 1, 2, and 7. The imagiste's images have a variable significance, like the signs *a, b,* and *x* in algebra" ("Vorticism" 463).

13. The English translation is from Blythe, *History,* 2:xxix.

14. The original of this haiku is found in Harold G. Henderson, *An Introduction to Haiku* (New York: Doubleday, 1958), 58.

Works Cited

Adell, Sandra. "Richard Wright's *The Outsider* and the Kierkegaardian Concept of Dread." *Comparative Literature Studies* 28, no. 4 (1991): 379–94. Print.

Algren, Nelson. "Interview." *Paris Review* 11 (Winter 1955): 37–58. Print.

Alkebulan, Adisa A. "The Spiritual Essence of African American Rhetoric." *Understanding African American Rhetoric*. Ed. Ronald L. Jackson, et al. New York: Routledge, 2003. 23–39. Print.

Anderson, Carol. *Eyes Off the Prize: The United Nations and the African American Struggle for Human Rights, 1944–1955*. Cambridge: Cambridge University Press, 2003. Print.

Anon. "Murder Is Admitted by Negro Musician." *New York Times*. 3 December 1941. n.p. Print.

———. "People." *Time* (20 October 1941): n.p. Print.

———. "Tract in Black and White." *Time* (27 October 1958): 95–96. Print.

Appiah, Kwame Anthony. "Rooted Cosmopolitanism." *The Ethics of Identity*. Princeton, NJ: Princeton University Press, 2005. 213–72. Print.

Baldwin, James. "Alas, Poor Richard." *Nobody Knows My Name: More Notes of a Native Son*. 1961. Rpt. New York: Vintage, 1993. Print. 181–216.

———. *Nobody Knows My Name: More Notes of a Native Son*. 1961. Rpt. New York: Vintage, 1993. Print.

Balibar, Etienne. "Ambiguous Universalism." *Differences: A Journal of Feminist Cultural Studies* 7, no. 1 (Spring 1995): 48–57. Print.

Baraka, Amiri. *Daggers and Javelins*. New York: Quill, 1984. Print.

Barthes, Roland. *Empire of Signs*. Trans. Richard Howard. New York: Hill and Wang, 1982. Print.

———. "Interview." Transcript of a Radio Broadcast on ORTF, Paris, France. 1956. *Conversations with Richard Wright*. Eds. Keneth Kinnamon and Michel Fabre. Jackson: University Press of Mississippi, 1993. 166–68. Print.

Bashō, Matsuo. *On Love and Barley: Haiku of Bashō*. Trans. and introduction by Lucien Stryk. New York: Penguin, 1985. Print.

Beaty, Bart. *Frederick Wertham and the Critique of Mass Culture*. Jackson: University Press of Mississippi, 2005. Print.

Bell, Derrick. *Race, Racism, and American Law*. Boston: Little, Brown, 1980. Print.

Bergler, Edmund. *Neurotic Counterfeit-Sex: Impotence, Frigidity, "Mechanical," and Pseudosexuality: Homosexuality*. London: Grune and Stratton, 1951. Print.

———. *The Writer and Psychoanalysis*. 1951. Rpt. New York: International Universities Press, 1992. Print.

Birt, Robert E. "The Bad Faith of Whiteness." *What White Looks Like: African-American Philosophers on the Whiteness Question*. Ed. George Yancy. New York: Routledge, 2004. 55–64. Print.

Blythe, R. H. "Buddhism and Haiku." *Monumenta Nipponica* 7, no. 1–2 (1951): 311–18.

———. *Haiku*. 4 vols. Tokyo: Hokuseido, 1949. Print.

———. *A History of Haiku*. 2 vols. 1963. Rpt. Tokyo: Hokuseido, 1964. Print.

Bogues, Anthony. *Black Heretic, Black Prophets: Radical Political Intellectuals*. New York: Routledge, 2003. Print.

Bontemps, Arna. "Review of *The Outsider*." *Saturday Review* 36 (28 March 1953): 16–17. Print.

Borstelmann, Thomas. *The Cold War and the Color Line: American Race Relations in the Global Arena*. Cambridge, MA: Harvard University Press, 2001. Print.

Branch, Taylor. *Parting the Waters: America in the King Years, 1954–1963*. New York: Simon and Schuster, 1988. Print.

Brenner, Charles, MD. *An Elementary Textbook of Psychoanalysis*. Rev. ed. New York: Anchor, 1974. Print.

Brigano, Carl. *Richard Wright: An Introduction to the Man and His Works*. Pittsburgh: University of Pittsburgh Press, 1970. Print.

Brooks, Gwendolyn. Cover blurb. *Haiku: This Other World*. Eds. Yoshinobu Hakutani and Robert L. Tener. New York: Random House, 2000. Print.

Bryant, Earle. "Sexual Initiation and Survival in *The Long Dream*." *Southern Quarterly* 21, no. 3 (1982): 57–67. Print.

Butler, Robert J. *The Critical Response to Richard Wright*. Westport, CT: Greenwood Press, 1995. Print.

Capra, Fritjof. *The Tao of Physics: An Exploration of the Parallels between Modern Physics and Eastern Mysticism*. 4th ed. Boston: Shambhala, 2000. Print.

Carpenter, Frederic Ives. *Emerson and Asia*. Cambridge, MA: Harvard University Press, 1930. Print.

Chiwengo, Ngwarsungu. "Gazing through the Screen: Richard Wright's Africa." *New Reflections: Richard Wright's Travel Books*. Ed. Virginia Whatley Smith. Jackson: University Press of Mississippi, 2001. 20–44. Print.

Clark, Edward D. "Richard Wright." *Dictionary of Literary Biography: Afro-American Writers, 1940–1953*. Ed. Trudier Harris. n.p.: Gale, 1988. 449–451. Print.

Cohen, Jean L., and Andrew Arato. *Civil Society and Political Theory*. Cambridge, MA: MIT Press, 1992. Print.

Confucius. *The Analects*. Trans. Raymond Dawson. Oxford: Oxford University Press, 1993. Print.

Cuvier, Georges Leopold. "Varieties of Human Species." *Walkin' the Talk: An Anthology of African American Studies*. Ed. Vernon D. Johnson and Bill Lyne. Upper Saddle River, NJ: Prentice Hall, 2003. 54–57. Print.

Davies, Peter. Ed. *American Heritage Dictionary of the English Language*. New York: Dell, 1976. Print.

Davis, Charles T. *Black Is the Color of the Cosmos*. New York and London: Garland, 1982. Print.

Davis, Jane. "More Force Than Human: Richard Wright's Female Characters." *OBSIDIAN II* (Winter 1986): 68–83. Print.

De Genova, Nick. "Gangster Rap and Nihilism in Black America: Some Questions of Life and Death." *Social Text* 13, no. 2 (1995): 89–132. Print.

Demirtürk, Lâle. "Mapping the Terrain of Whiteness: Richard Wright's *Savage Holiday*." *MELUS* 24, no. 1 (Spring 1999): 625–34. Print.

Derrida, Jacques. "Cosmopolitanism and Forgiveness." *Cosmopolitanism and Forgiveness: Thinking in Action*. New York: Routledge, 2006. 27–30, 306. Print.

———, and Maurizio Ferraris. *A Taste for the Secret*. Cambridge, MA: Polity Press, 2001. Print.

Dienstag, Joshua F. *Pessimism: Philosophy, Ethics, Spirit*. Princeton, NJ: Princeton University Press, 2006. Print.

Domanick, Joe. *To Protect and to Serve: The LAPD's Century of War in the City of Dreams*. New York: Pocket Prints, 1994. Print.

Dostoevsky, Fyodor. *Demons*. Trans. Richard Pevear and Larissa Volokhonsky. New York: Alfred A. Knopf, 1994. Print.

Douglas, Ann. "Periodizing the American Century: Modernism, Postmodernism, and Postcolonialism in the Cold War Context." *Modernism/Modernity* 5, no. 3 (1998): 17–36. Print.

Douglass, Frederick. *The Life and Times of Frederick Douglass in His Own Words: The Complete History of an American Freedom Fighter*. 1855. A Facsimile Edition. Kensington, UK: Citadel Press, 1983. Print.

———. *Narrative of the Life of Frederick Douglass, an American Slave, Written by Himself*. 1845. New York: W. W. Norton, 1997. Print.

Du Bois, W. E. B. 1903. *The Souls of Black Folk*. New York: Dodd, Mead, 1961. Print.

Dudziak, Mary I. *Cold War Civil Rights: Race and the Image of American Democracy*. Princeton, NJ: Princeton University Press, 2000. Print.

Eagleton, Terry. *Marxism and Literary Criticism*. 1976. London: Routledge, 1989. Print.

Early, Gerald. "Afterword." *Savage Holiday*. By Richard Wright. 1954. Rpt. Jackson: University Press of Mississippi, 1994. Print.

Edwards, Brent. *The Practice of Diaspora: Literature, Translation, and the Rise of Internationalism*. Cambridge, MA: Harvard University Press, 2003. Print.

Ellison, Ralph. "Richard Wright's Blues." *Antioch Review* 5 (1945): 198–211. Print.

Emerson, Ralph Waldo. *The Complete Essays and Other Writings of Ralph Waldo Emerson*. Ed. Brooks Atkinson. New York: Modern Library, 1940. Print.

———. *Emerson*. 4 vols. New York: Tudor, 1900. Print.

———. *Journals of Ralph Waldo Emerson, 1820–1872*. Ed. E. W. Emerson and W. E. Forbes. Boston: Houghton Mifflin, 1911. Print.

"Entretien avec Richard Wright." *L'Express*. 18 August 1960. Trans. Michel Fabre. *Dictionary of Literary Biography: Afro-American Writers, 1940–1953*. Ed. Trudier Harris. n.p.: Gale, 1988. 449. Print.

Evans, Roger. *How to Read Music*. New York: Crown, 1978. Print.

Fabre, Michel. "The Poetry of Richard Wright." *Critical Essays on Richard Wright*. Ed. Yoshinobu Hakutani. New York: G. K. Hall, 1982. 252–72. Print.

———. *Richard Wright: Books and Writers*. Jackson: University Press of Mississippi, 1990. Print.

———. "Richard Wright, French Existentialism, and *The Outsider*." *Critical Essays on Richard Wright*. Ed. Yoshinobu Hakutani. Boston: G. K. Hall, 1982. 182–98. Print.

———. "Richard Wright: The Man Who Lived Underground." *Richard Wright: A Collection of Critical Essays*. Eds. Richard Macksey and Frank E. Moorer. Englewood Cliffs, NJ: Prentice Hall, 1984. 207–20. Print.

———. *The Unfinished Quest of Richard Wright*. 1973. New York: William Morrow. Rpt. Urbana: University of Illinois Press, 1993. Print. [*UQ*]

———. *The World of Richard Wright*. Jackson: University Press of Mississippi, 1985. Print.

———, and Robert E. Skinner. *Conversations with Chester Himes*. Jackson: University Press of Mississippi, 1995. Print.

Fanon, Frantz. *Black Skin, White Masks*. New York: Grove Press, 1967. Print.

———. "On National Culture." *Wretched of the Earth*. Trans. Constance Farrington. New York: Penguin, 1967. 206–48. Print.

Farnsworth, R. M., and C. T. Davis. Eds. *Richard Wright: Impressions and Perspectives*. Ann Arbor: University of Michigan Press, 1974. Print.

Feagin, Joe R. *Racist America: Roots, Current Realities, and Future Reparations*. New York: Routledge, 2000. Print.

Ferguson, Roderick. "The Nightmares of Heteronormative." *Cultural Values* 4 (October 2000): 423–40. Print.

Forni, P. M. *Choosing Civility*. New York: St. Martin's Press, 2002. Print.

Foucault, Michel. *Discipline and Punish: The Birth of the Prison*. Trans. Alan Sheridan. New York: Vintage, 1979. Print.

Frye, Northrup. *The Great Code: The Bible and Literature*. New York: Harcourt Brace, 1982. Print.

Garland, David. *The Culture of Control: Crime and Social Order in Contemporary Society*. Chicago: University of Chicago Press, 2001. Print.

Gates, Henry Louis, Jr. *Figures in Black: Words, Signs, and the Racial Self*. New York: Oxford University Press, 1987. Print.

———. *The Signifying Monkey: A Theory of African-American Literary Criticism*. New York: Oxford University Press, 1986. Print.

———, and Kwame Anthony Appiah. Eds. *Richard Wright: Critical Perspective Past and Present*. New York: Amistad, 1993. Print.

Gayle, Addison. *Richard Wright: Ordeal of a Native Son*. Garden City, NJ: Anchor Press/Doubleday, 1980. Print.

Geiger, Jeffrey. "Unmaking the Male Body: The Politics of Masculinity in *The Long Dream*." *African American Review* 33, no. 2 (1999): 197–207. Print.

Gibson, Donald. "Richard Wright: Aspects of His Afro-American Literary Relation." *Critical Essays on Richard Wright*. Ed. Yoshinobu Hakutani. Boston: G. K. Hall, 1982. 82–90. Print.

Gilroy, Paul. *The Black Atlantic: Modernity and Double Consciousness*. Cambridge, MA: Harvard University Press, 1993. Print.

Giroux, Joan. *The Haiku Forum*. Rutland, VT: Turtle, 1974. Print.

Glave, Dianne D. *Rooted in the Earth: Reclaiming the African American Environmental Heritage*. Chicago: Lawrence Hill, 2010. Print.

Glover, Jonathan. *Humanity: A Moral History of the Twentieth Century*. New Haven, CT: Yale University Press, 1999. Print.

Goldfarb, Jeffrey C. *Civility and Subversion: The Intellectual in Democratic Society*. New York: Cambridge University Press, 1998. Print.

Gooding-Williams, Robert. *Zarathustra's Dionysian Modernism*. Stanford, CA: Stanford University Press, 2001. Print.

Gordon, Lewis R. *Existential Africana: Understanding Existential Thought*. New York: Routledge, 2000. Print.

———. "Through the Zone of Nonbeing: A Reading of *Black Skin, White Masks* in Celebration of Fanon's Eightieth Birthday." *C. L. R. James Journal* 11, no. 1 (Summer 2005): 1–43. Print.

Gounard, J. F., and Beverly Gounard. "Richard Wright's *Savage Holiday*: Use of Abuse of Psychoanalysis." *CLA Journal* 11 (1979): 334–49. Print.

Green, Tara. "The Virgin Mary, Eve, and Mary Magdalene in Richard Wright's Novels." *CLA Journal* 46, no. 2 (December 2002): 168–93. *Bloom's Modern Critical Views: Richard Wright.* Ed. Harold Bloom. New York: Infobase, 2009. 35–53. Print.

———. "Women in Richard Wright's Fiction." *The Richard Wright Encyclopedia.* Eds. Jerry W. Ward Jr. and Robert J. Butler. Westport, CT: Greenwood Press, 2008. Print.

Gurga, Lee. "Richard Wright's Place in American Haiku." *Valley Voices* 8, no. 2 (2008): 34–43. Print.

Gussow, Adam. *Seems Like Murder Here: Southern Violence and the Blues.* 2nd ed. Chicago: University of Chicago Press, 2002. Print.

Hahn, Harlan, and Judson L. Jeffries. *Urban America and Its Police: From the Postcolonial Era through the Turbulent 1960s.* Boulder: University Press of Colorado, 2003. Print.

Hakutani, Yoshinobu. *Cross-Cultural Visions in African American Modernism: From Spatial Narrative to Jazz Haiku.* Columbus: Ohio State University Press, 2006. Print.

———. "Ezra Pound, Yone Noguchi, and Imagism." *Modern Philology* 90 (August 1992): 46–69. Print.

———. "Richard Wright's Haiku, Zen, and the African 'Primal Outlook upon Life.'" *Cross-Cultural Visions in African American Literature: West Meets East.* Ed. Yoshinobu Hakutani. New York: Palgrave Macmillan, 2011. 3–21. Print.

———. "Richard Wright's *The Long Dream* as Racial and Sexual Discourse." *African American Review* 30, no. 2 (1996): 267–80. Print.

———. "Richard Wright's *The Outsider* and Albert Camus's *The Stranger.*" *Mississippi Quarterly* (Fall 1989): 364–78. Print.

———. *Richard Wright and Racial Discourse.* Columbus: University of Missouri Press, 1996. Print.

———, and Robert L. Tener. "Afterword." *Haiku: This Other World.* By Richard Wright. New York: Arcade, 1998. 245–300. Print.

Hansberry, Lorraine. "The Outsider." *Freedom* (April 1953): 55. Print.

Harrington, Ollie W. *Why I Left America and Other Essays.* Jackson: University Press of Mississippi, 1993. Print.

Harris, Trudier. "Native Sons and Foreign Daughters." *New Essays on 'Native Son.'* Ed. Keneth Kinnamon. New York: Cambridge University Press, 1990. 63–84. Print.

Hawthorne, Nathaniel. *The Marble Faun; or, The Romance of Monte Beni. The Centenary Edition of the Works of Nathaniel Hawthorne.* Ed. William Charvat, et al. Vol. 4. Columbus: Ohio State University Press, 1967–1997. Print.

Hayes, Floyd W., III. "The Concept of Double Vision in Richard Wright's *The Outsider*: Fragmented Blackness in the Age of Nihilism." *Existence in Black: An Anthology of Black Existential Philosophy.* Ed. Lewis R. Gordon. New York: Routledge, 1997. 173–93. Print.

Henderson, Harold Gould. *The Bamboo Broom: An Introduction to Japanese Haiku.* New York: Houghton Mifflin, 1934. Print.

———. *An Introduction to Haiku: An Anthology of Poems and Poets from Basho to Shiki.* New York: Doubleday, 1958. Print.

Hernton, Calvin. "The Sexual Mountain and Black Women Writers." *Black American Literature Forum* 18 (Winter 1984): 139–45. Print.

Higashida, Cheryl. "Aunt Sue's Children: Reviewing the Gender(ed) Politics of Richard Wright's Radicalism." *American Literature*. 75. (June 2003): 395–425. *Bloom's Modern Critical Views: Richard Wright—New Edition*. Ed. Harold Bloom. New York: Infobase, 2009. Print. 73-98.

Higginbotham, A. Leon. *In the Matter of Color: Race and the American Legal Process—The Colonial Period*. New York: Oxford University Press, 1978. Print.

Howard, William. "Richard Wright's Flood Stories and the Great Mississippi Flood of 1927: Social and Historical Backgrounds." *Southern Literary Journal* 16, no. 2 (Spring 1984): 44–62. Print.

Hughes, Langston. "The Negro Speaks of Rivers." *The Collected Poems of Langston Hughes*. Ed. Arnold Rampersad. New York: Knopf, 1995. Print.

Hume, David. "Of National Characteristics." *Walkin' the Talk: An Anthology of African American Studies*. Ed. Vernon D. Johnson and Bill Lyne. Upper Saddle River, NJ: Prentice Hall, 2003. 49–51. Print.

Hunsaker, Stephen. "Introduction." *Autobiography and National Identity in the Americas*. Charlottesville: University of Virginia Press, 1999. 1–12. Print.

Hurston, Zora Neale. *Mules and Men*. 1935. Rpt. Bloomington: Indiana University Press, 1978. Print.

———. "Stories of Conflict." *Saturday Review of Literature* (2 April 1938): 3. Print.

James, C. L. R. *American Civilization*. Cambridge: Blackwell, 1993. Print.

———. "Black Studies and the Contemporary Student." *At the Rendezvous of Victory*. London: Allison and Busby, 1984. 186–201. Print.

Jameson, Fredric. *The Cultural Turn, Selected Writings on the Postmodern, 1983–1998*. London: Verso, 1998. Print.

JanMohamed, Abdul R. *The Death-Bound Subject: Richard Wright's Archaeology of Death*. Durham, NC: Duke University Press, 2005. Print.

———. "Negating the Negation as a Form of Affirmation in Minority Discourse: The Construction of Richard Wright as a Subject." *Cultural Critique* (Fall 1987): 245–66. Rpt. *Richard Wright: A Collection of Critical Essays*. Ed. Arnold Rampersad. Englewood Cliffs, NJ: Prentice Hall, 1995. 107–23. Print.

Jefferson, Thomas. "From *Notes on the State of Virginia*." *Walkin' the Talk: An Anthology of African American Studies*. Ed. Vernon D. Johnson and Bill Lyne. Upper Saddle River, NJ: Prentice Hall, 2003. 43–48. Print.

Johnson, Barbara. "The Re(a) and the Black in Richard Wright's *Native Son*." *Richard Wright's Native Son*. Ed. Harold Bloom. New York: Chelsea House, 1988. 120–31. Print.

Julien, Eileen. "Terrains de Recontre: Césaire, Fanon, and Wright on Culture and Decolonization." *Yale French Studies: The French Fifties* 98 (2009): 149–66. Print.

Jung, Hwa Yol. Ed. *Existential Phenomenology and Political Theory: A Reader*. Chicago: Henry Regnery, 1972. Print.

———. "An Introductory Essay: The Political Relevance of Existential Phenomenology." *Existential Phenomenology and Political Theory: A Reader*. Ed. Hwa Yol Jung. Chicago: Henry Regnery, 1972. xvii–lv. Print.

Kant, Immanuel. "On National Characteristics." *Walkin' the Talk: An Anthology of African American Studies*. Ed. Vernon D. Johnson and Bill Lyne. Upper Saddle River, NJ: Prentice Hall, 2003. 52–53. Print.

Keady, Sylvia Neale. "Richard Wright's Women Characters and Inequality." *Black American Literature Forum* 18 (Fall 1976): 100–105. Print.

Keene, Donald. "Japanese Aesthetics." *Philosophy East and West* 19, no. 3 (1969): 293–306. Print.

Keiji, Nishitani. *The Self-Overcoming Nihilism*. Trans. Graham Parkes. Albany: State University of New York Press, 1990. Print.

Kent, George E. "Richard Wright: Blackness and the Adventure of Western Culture." *Richard Wright: A Collection of Critical Essays*. Eds. Richard Macksey and Frank E. Moorer. Englewood Cliffs, NJ: Prentice Hall, 1984. 37–54. Print.

Kierkegaard, Soren. *The Concept of Dread*. Trans. Walter Lowrie. Princeton, NJ: Princeton University Press, 1957. Print.

Kinnamon, Keneth. *The Emergence of Richard Wright: A Study of Literature and Society*. Urbana: University of Illinois Press, 1972. Print.

———. *New Essays on 'Native Son.'* New York: Cambridge University Press, 1990. Print.

———. *A Richard Wright Bibliography: Fifty Years of Criticism and Commentary: 1933–1982*. With the Help of Joseph Benson, Michel Fabre, and Craig Werner. Westport, CT: Greenwood Press, 1988. Print.

———, and Michel Fabre. Eds. *Conversations with Richard Wright*. Jackson: University Press of Mississippi, 1993. Print.

Kiuchi, Toru. "Zen Buddhism in Richard Wright's Haiku." *Valley Voices* 8, no. 2 (Fall 2008): 18–33. Print.

Kodama, Sanehide. "Japanese Influence on Richard Wright in His Last Years: English Haiku as a New Genre." *Tamkang Review* 15, nos. 1–4 (1984–85): 63–74. Print.

Kristeva, Julia. *Power of Horror: An Essay on Abjection*. Trans. Leon S. Roudiez. New York: Columbia University Press, 1993. Print.

Kurebayashi, Kodo. *An Introduction to Dogen Zen*. Tokyo: Taiho Rinkaku, 1984. Print.

Lacan, Jacques. *The Seminar of Jacques Lacan, Book II: The Ego in Freud's Theory and the Theory and Technique of Psychoanalysis*. Ed. Jacques-Alain Miller. Trans. Sylvana Tomaselli. New York: W. W. Norton, 1988. Print.

Locke, Alain. Ed. *The New Negro*. 1925. Rpt., New York: Simon and Schuster, 1997. Print.

Locke, John. "Essay Concerning Human Understanding." *The Heath Anthology of American Literature*. Vol. A. 5th ed. Ed. Paul Lauter. Boston: Houghton Mifflin, 2006. 635–36. Print.

Lynch, Michael F. *Creative Revolt: A Study of Wright, Ellison, and Dostoevsky*. New York: Peter Lang, 1990. Print.

———. "Haunted by Innocence: The Debate with Dostoevsky in Wright's 'Other Novel' *The Outsider*." *African American Review* 30, no. 2 (Summer 1996): 255–56. Print.

Macksey, Richard, and Frank E. Moorer. Eds. *Richard Wright: A Collection of Critical Essays*. Englewood Cliffs, NJ: Prentice Hall, 1984. Print.

Marable, Manning. *How Capitalism Underdeveloped Black America: Problems on Race, Political Economy, and Society*. Boston: South End Press, 1983. Print.

Margolies, Edward. *The Art of Richard Wright*. Carbondale: Southern Illinois University Press, 1969. Print.

———. "Wright's Craft: The Short Stories." *Richard Wright: A Critical Perspective Past and Present*. Eds. Henry Louis Gates Jr. and Kwame Anthony Appiah. New York: Amistad, 1993. 75–97. Print.

Massey, Douglas, and Nancy Denton. *American Apartheid*. Cambridge, MA: Harvard University Press, 1993. Print.

Mbiti, John. *African Religions and Philosophy*. 2nd ed. New York: Heinemann, 1999. Print.

McLean, Helen V. "Racial Prejudice." *American Journal of Orthopsychiatry* 24 (October 1944): 706–13. Print.

McMahan, David L. *The Making of Buddhist Modernism*. New York: Oxford University Press, 1971. Print.

McMahon, Frank. "Rereading *The Outsider*: Double-Consciousness and the Divided Self." *Mississippi Quarterly* 50 (Fall 1997): 289–305. Print.

Melamed, Jodi. "The Spirit of Neoliberalism: From Racial Liberalism to Neoliberal Multiculturalism." *Social Text* 89, no. 4 (Winter 2006): 1–24. Print.

Mills, Charles. *The Racial Contract*. Ithaca, NY: Cornell University Press, 1997. Print.

Monkkonen, Eric. *Police in Urban America*. New York: Cambridge University Press, 1983. Print.

Moore, Brooke Noel, and Kenneth Bruder. *Philosophy: The Power of Ideas*. 7th ed. New York: McGraw-Hill, 2008. Print.

Mootry, Maria K. "Bitches, Whores, and Woman Haters: Archetypes and Typologies in the Art of Richard Wright." *Richard Wright: A Collection of Critical Essays*. Eds. Richard Macksey and Frank E. Moorer. Englewood Cliffs, NJ: Prentice Hall, 1984. 117–27. Print.

Morrison, Toni. "Rootedness: The Ancestor as Foundation." *Black Women Writers (1950–1980)*. Ed. Mari Evans. New York: Anchor, 1984. 339–445. Print.

Natanson, Maurice. *The Erotic Bird: Phenomenology in Literature*. Princeton, NJ: Princeton University Press, 1998. Print.

———. "Phenomenology and the Social Sciences." *Phenomenology and the Social Sciences*. Vol. 1. Ed. Maurice Natanson. Evanston, IL: Northwestern University Press, 1973. 3–44. Print.

Nelson, Jill. Ed. *Police Brutality: An Anthology*. New York: W. W. Norton, 2000. Print.

Nietzsche, Friedrich. *Beyond Good and Evil*. Trans. Walter Kaufman. New York: Vintage, 1966. Print.

———. *Thus Spoke Zarathustra*. Trans. R. J. Hollingdale. New York: Penguin, 1969. Print.

———. *The Will to Power*. Ed. Walter Kaufmann. New York: Vintage, 1967. Print.

Nott, Josiah, and George R. Gliddon. *Types of Mankind*. 1854. *Clotel; or, The President's Daughter*. Ed. Robert S. Levine. Boston: Bedford/St. Martin's, 2000. 386–90. Print.

Novak, Philip. *The World's Wisdom: Sacred Texts of the World's Religion*. New York: HarperCollins, 1994. Print.

O'Brien, Gail W. *The Color of Law: Race, Violence, and Justice in the Post–World War II South*. Chapel Hill: University of North Carolina Press, 1999. Print.

Olson, Joel. *The Abolition of White Democracy*. Minneapolis: University of Minnesota Press, 2004. Print.

Omi, Michael, and Howard Winant. *Racial Formation in the United States: From the 1960s to the 1990s*. Rev. ed. New York: Routledge, 1994. Print.

Patterson, Orlando. *Rituals of Blood: Consequences of Slavery in Two American Centuries*. New York: Basic Books, 1998. Print.

Piccinato, Stefania. *Testo e contesto nella poesia di Langston Hughes*. Roma: Bulzoni Editore, 1979. Print.

Poe, Edgar Allan. "The Narrative of Arthur Gordon Pym." *Poetry and Tales*. New York: Library of America, 1984. 1003–1182. Print.

———. *Selected Writings of Edgar Allen Poe*. Ed. Edward Davidson. Boston: Houghton, 1956. Print.

Pound, Ezra. "As for Imagisme." *New Age* 14 (1915): 349. Print.

———. "Vorticism." *Fortnightly Review* 573, n.s. (September 1914): 461–71.

Rampersad, Arnold. Ed. *Richard Wright: A Collection of Critical Essays*. Englewood Cliffs, NJ: Prentice Hall, 1995. Print.

Reddick, L. D. "A New Richard Wright." *Phylon* 14 (Second Quarter 1953): 213–14.

Redding, J. Saunders. *Baltimore Afro-American*. 19 May 1953. 15–16. Print.

Reilly, John M. "Richard Wright and the Art of Non-Fiction: Stepping Out on the State of the World." *Callaloo* 9, no. 3 (Summer 1986): 507–20. Print.

———. "Richard Wright's Curious Thriller *Savage Holiday*." *CLA Journal* 23 (1977): 218–23. Print.

Robinson, Cedric J. *Black Marxism: The Making of the Black Radical Tradition*. London: Zed Press, 1983. Print.

Rosenberg, Joel. "Jeremiah and Ezekiel." *The Literary Guide to the Bible*. Ed. Robert Alter and Frank Kermode. Cambridge, MA: Harvard University Press, 1985. Print.

Ross, George. "So This Is Broadway." *New York Telegram*. 2 April 1944. 19. Print.

Rowley, Hazel. *Richard Wright: The Life and Times*. New York: Henry Holt, 2001. Print.

Rubeo, Ugo. *Agghiaccianti simmetrie. Dinamche testuali in the Narrative of A. Gordon Pym di Edgar Allen Poe*. Roma: Lozzi e Rossi Editori, 2000. Print.

———. "Fragments of an Agon": Metafictional Aspects of *As I Lay Dying*." *The Artist and His Masks: William Faulkner's Metafiction*. Ed. Agostino Lombardo: Roma: Bulzoni Editore, 1991. 201–12. Print.

Rugoff, Milton. *New York Herald Tribune Book Review*. 22 March 1953. 4. Print.

Rushdie, Salman. *Imaginary Homelands: Essays and Criticism 1981–1991*. New York: Penguin, 1992. Print.

Said, Edward. *Out of Place: A Memoir*. New York: Alfred Knopf, 1999. Print.

———. *The World, the Text, and the Critic*. Cambridge, MA: Harvard University Press, 1983. Print.

Sartre, Jean Paul. *Being and Nothingness: An Essay on Phenomenological Ontology*. New York: Philosophical Library, 1956. Print.

Sharf, Robert H. "Buddhist Modernism and the Rhetoric of Meditative Experience." *Numen* 42 (1995): 228–83. Print.

———. "The Zen of Japanese Nationalism." *History of Religion* 33 (1993): 1–43. Print.

Shirane, Haruo. *Traces of Dreams: Landscape, Cultural Memory, and the Poetry of Bashō*. Stanford, CA: Stanford University Press, 1998. Print.

Shoket, Eric. "Modernism and the Aesthetics of Management, or T. S. Eliot's Labor Literature." *Left of the Color Line. Race, Radicalism, and Twentieth-Century Literature of the United States*. Ed. Bill V. Mullen and James Smethurst. Chapel Hill: University of North Carolina Press, 2003. 13–35. Print.

Singh, Amritjit. "Afterword." *The Color Curtain. Three Books from Exile: Black Power; The Color Curtain; and White Man, Listen!* 1957. Rpt. New York: HarperPerennial, 2008. 611–29. Print.

———. "Richard Wright's *The Outsider*: Existentialist Exemplar or Critique?" *CLA Journal* (June 1984): 357–70. Print.

Singh, Nikhil Pal. *Black Is a Country: Race and the Unfinished Struggle for Democracy*. Cambridge, MA: Harvard University Press, 2004. Print.

———. "Culture/Wars: Recoding Empire in the Age of Democracy." *American Quarterly* 5, no. 3 (September 1998): 471–522. Print.

Skerett, Joseph. "Composing Bigger: Wright and the Making of *Native Son*." *Richard Wright's Native Son*. Ed. Harold Bloom. New York: Chelsea House, 1988. Print.

Smith, Kimberly K. *African American Environmental Thought*. Lawrence: University of Kansas Press, 2007. Print.

Snead, James. "Repetition as a Figure of Black Culture." *Black Literature and Literary Theory*. Ed. Henry Louis Gates Jr. New York: Methuen, 1984. 59–79. Print.

Tate, Claudia. "Christian Existentialism in Richard Wright's *The Outsider*." *CLA Journal* (June 1982): 371–95. Print.

———. "Rage, Race, and Desire: *Savage Holiday* by Richard Wright." *Psychoanalysis and Black Novels: Desire and the Protocols of Race*. New York: Oxford University Press, 1998. 86–118. Print.

Tener, Robert L. "The Where, the When, the What: A Study of Richard Wright's Haiku." *The Critical Essays of Richard Wright*. Ed. Yoshinobu Hakutani. New York: G. K. Hall, 1982. 273–98. Print.

Thiele, Leslie P. *Friedrich Nietzsche and the Politics of the Soul: A Study of Heroic Individualism*. Princeton, NJ: Princeton University Press, 1990. Print.

Thoreau, Henry David. *Walden; or, Life in the Woods*. New York: Holt, Rinehart and Winston, 1948. Print.

Todorov, Tzvetan. *The Fantastic: A Structural Approach to Literary Genre*. Trans. Richard Howard. Ithaca, NY: Cornell University Press, 1973. Print.

Ueda, Makoto. "Bashō and the Poetics of 'Haiku.'" *Journal of Aesthetics and Art Criticism* 21, no. 4 (1963): 423–31. Print.

Vassilowitch, John, Jr. "'Erskine Fowler': A Key Freudian Pun in *Savage Holiday*." *English Language Notes* 43, no. 3 (March 1981): 206–8. Print.

Venui, Lawrence M. Ed. *The Translation Studies Reader*. New York: Routledge, 2000. Print.

"Virginia Slave Laws of 1662 and 1669." *The Heath Anthology to American Literature*. 4th ed. Ed. Paul Lauter. New York: Houghton Mifflin, 2002. 14. Print.

Von Eschen, Penny. *Race against Empire: Black Americans and Anticolonialism, 1937–1957*. Ithaca, NY: Cornell University Press, 1997. Print.

Walker, Margaret. "Richard Wright." *Richard Wright: Impressions and Perspectives*. Ed. David Ray and Robert Farnsworth. Ann Arbor: University of Michigan Press, 1971. Print.

———. *Richard Wright: Daemonic Genius*. New York: Amistad/HarperCollins, 1988. Rpt. *Richard Wright, Daemonic Genius*. New York: Warner Books, 1988. [*DG*].

Ward, Jerry W., and Robert J. Butler. *The Richard Wright Encyclopedia*. Westport, CT: Greenwood Press, 2008. Print.

Warren, Mark. *Nietzsche and Political Thought*. Cambridge: MIT Press, 1988. Print.

Warren, Nagueyalti. "Black Girls and Native Sons: Female Images in Selected Works by Richard Wright." *Richard Wright: Myths and Realities.* Ed. James C. Trotman. New York: Garland, 1988. 69–71. Print.

Wasserstein, Bernard. *Barbarism and Civilization: A History of Europe in Our Time.* New York: Oxford University Press, 2007. Print.

Watkins, Patricia D. "The Paradoxical Structure of Richard Wright's 'The Man Who Lived Underground.'" *Richard Wright: A Collection of Critical Essays.* Ed. Arnold Rampersad. Englewood Cliffs, NJ: Prentice Hall, 1995. 148–61. Print.

Webb, Constance. *Richard Wright: A Biography.* New York: O. Putnam's Sons, 1968. Print.

Webb, Tracy. "Role of Water Imagery in *Uncle Tom's Children.*" *Modern Fiction Studies* 34, no. 1 (Spring 1988): 5–16. Print.

Webster, Harvey C. "Richard Wright's Profound New Novel." *New Leader* 36 (6 April 1953): 17–18. Print.

Weimer, David. *The City as Metaphor.* New York: Random, 1966. Print.

Weinstein, Michael. *Culture Flesh: Explorations of Postcivilized Modernity.* Lanham, MD: Rowman and Littlefield, 1995. Print.

Wertham, Frederick. "An Unconscious Determinant in *Native Son.*" *Journal of Clinical Psychology and Psychotherapy* 6 (July 1944): 111–15. Print.

West, Cornell. "Introduction." *Three Books from Exile: Black Power; The Color Curtain; and White Man, Listen!* 1957. Rpt. New York: HarperPerennial, 2008. vii–xiii. Print.

Whitted, Qiana J. "Using My Grandmother's Life as a Model: Richard Wright and the Gendered Politics of Religious Representation." *Southern Literary Journal* 36, no. 2 (2004): 13–30. *Bloom's Modern Critical Views: Richard Wright—New Edition.* Ed. Harold Bloom. New York: Infobase, 2009. Print. 131–36.

Widmer, Kingsley. "The Existential Darkness: Richard Wright's *The Outsider.*" *Wisconsin Studies in Contemporary Literature* (Fall 1960): 13–21. Print.

Williams, Raymond. *Keywords: A Vocabulary of Culture and Society.* New York: Oxford University Press, 1983. Print.

———. *The Long Revolution.* New York: Broadview, 2001. Rpt. New York: Parthiam Books, 2012.

Williams, Sherley Anne. "Papa Dick and Sister Woman: Reflections on Women in the Fiction of Richard Wright." Rpt. *Richard Wright: A Collection of Critical Essays.* Ed. Arnold Rampersad. Englewood Cliffs, NJ: Prentice Hall, 1995. 63–82. Print.

Wright, Ellen, and Michel Fabre. Eds. *Richard Wright Reader.* New York: Harper and Row, 1978. Print. [*RWR*].

Wright, Julia "Introduction." *A Father's Law.* New York: HarperPerennial, 2008. v–xiii.

———. "Introduction." *Haiku: This Other World.* By Richard Wright. New York: Arcade, 1998. vii–xii. Print.

Wright, Richard."Almos' a Man." *Harper's Bazaar* (January 1940): 40+. Print.

———. "Between the World and Me." *Richard Wright Reader.* Eds. Ellen Wright and Michel Fabre. New York: Harper and Row, 1978. 246–47. Print.

———. *Black Boy.* 1945. New York: HarperPerennial, 1987. [*BB*]. Rpt. *Black Boy/American Hunger.* The Restored Edition of the Library of America. New York: HarperPerennial, 1993. Print. [*BB/AH*].

———. *Black Power: A Record of Reactions in a Land of Pathos*. 1954. New York: HarperPerennial, 2008. 1–427. Print. [*BP*].

———. "Blueprint for Negro Writing." *Richard Wright Reader*. Eds. Ellen Wright and Michel Fabre. New York: Harper and Row, 1978. 36–49. Rpt. *Within the Circle*. Ed. Angelyn Mitchell, 1938. Durham, NC: Duke University Press, 1994. 97–106. Print.

———. "Down by the Riverside." *Uncle Tom's Children*. 1938. New York: HarperPerennial, 1991. 62–124. Print.

———. *Eight Men*. 1961. New York: HarperPerennial, 1996. Print.

———. *A Father's Law*. New York: Harper, 2008. Print. [*FL*].

———. "Foreword." *Blues Fell This Morning*. By Paul Oliver. New York: Cambridge University Press, 1990. xii–xvi. Print.

———. *Haiku: This Other World*. By Richard Wright. Eds. Yoshinobu Hakutani and Robert L. Tener. New York: Anchor, 1998. Rpt. Anchor 1998. Rpt. Random House, 2000. Print. [*OW*].

———. "How 'Bigger' Was Born." *Native Son*. The Restored Text Established by the Library of America. 1945. New York: Perennial Classics, 1993. Rpt. 1998. 433–62.

———. "I Choose Exile." Richard Wright Papers. Beinecke Rare Book and Manuscript Collection. Yale University. Manuscript. n.p. [RWP].

———. "Interview with Richard Wright," *L'Express* (1960). *Conversations with Richard Wright*. Eds. Keneth Kinnamon and Michel Fabre. Jackson: University of Mississippi Press, 1993. 201–7.

———. *Lawd Today!* New York: Walker, 1963. Rpt. Boston: Northeastern University Press, 1993. Print.

———. *The Long Dream*. 1958. New York: Harper and Row, 1986. Print. [*LD*].

———. *The Man Who Lived Underground*. 1941. *Eight Men*. New York: HarperPerennial, 1989. 3–84. Print.

———. "Memories of My Grandmother." Richard Wright Papers. Beinecke Rare Book and Manuscript Collection. Yale University. Typescript. [RWP].

———. *Native Son*. 1940. New York: HarperPerennial, 1987. The Restored Text Established by the Library of America. New York: Perennial Classics, 1993. Rpt. 1998. [*NS*].

———. "This Other World: Projections in the Haiku Manner." Richard Wright Papers. Beinecke Rare Book and Manuscript Collection. Yale University. [RWP]

———. *The Outsider*. 1953. New York: HarperPerennial, 1965. The Restored Text by the Library of America. New York: HarperPerennial, 1991. Rpt. 1993. Print.

———. "Psychiatry Comes to Harlem." *Free World* (September 1940): 49–51. Print.

———. "Richard Wright: I Curse the Day When for the First Time I Heard the Word 'Politics.'" *L'Express* (18 October 1955), 8. *Conversations with Richard Wright*. Eds. Keneth Kinnamon and Michel Fabre. Jackson: University of Mississippi Press, 1993. 163–65. Print.

———. *Rite of Passage*. New York: HarperCollins, 1994. Print. [*RP*].

———. *Savage Holiday*. 1954. Jackson: University Press of Mississippi, 1994. Print. [*SH*].

———. "Tarbaby's Dawn." Richard Wright Papers. Beinecke Rare Book and Manuscript Collection. Yale University. Typescript. [RWP].

———. *Three Books from Exile: Black Power The Color Curtain; and White Man Listen!* New York: HarperPerennial, 2008. 659–812. Print.

———. *12 Million Black Voices: A Folk History of the Negro in the United States.* New York: Viking, 1941. Rpt. New York: Thunder's Mouth Press, 1985. Rpt. 2002. [*12MBV*].

———. *Uncle Tom's Children.* 1938. New York: Harper and Brothers, 1940. Rpt. New York: HarperPerennial, 1965. *Richard Wright: Early Works.* 1938. New York: Library of America Restored Edition, 1991. 221–44. Print.

———. *White Man, Listen!* New York: HarperCollins, 1957. Rpt. New York: Anchor, 1957. [*WML!*].

Yancy, George. *Black Bodies, White Gazes: The Continuing Significance of Race.* Lanham, MD: Rowman and Littlefield, 2008. Print.

———. "Introduction." *What White Looks Like: African-American Philosophers on the Whiteness Question.* Ed. George Yancy. New York: Routledge, 2004. 1–23. Print.

Yarborough, Richard. "Introduction." *Uncle Tom's Children.* By Richard Wright. 1938. New York: HarperPerennial, 1991. ix–xxix. Print.

Contributors

Robert J. Butler is a professor of English at Canisius College in Buffalo, New York. He is the author of *Native Son: The Emergence of a New Black Hero* (1995), *The Critical Response to Richard Wright* (1995), *Contemporary African American Literature: The Open Journey* (1998), and *The Critical Response to Ralph Ellison* (2001). He is the coauthor of *The City in African American Literature* (1995) and *The Critical Response in Japan to African American Writers* (2003). His articles have appeared in *African American Review, CLA Journal, American Studies, MELUS*, and the *Southern Quarterly*.

Ginevra Geraci earned her PhD from Università di Roma 3 and wrote her dissertation on "Imagining the Other: Representations of the Jew in Zora Neale Hurston, Chester Himes, and Alice Walker." She has contributed to the Italian translations of early African American authors appearing in *Libri Parlanti* (Paravia, Torino, 1999) edited by Alessandro Portelli. Geraci has also published on James Baldwin, Venture Smith, Jonathan Safran Foer, Ann Petry, and Bernard Malamud.

A professor of English at Kent State University, Ohio, **Yoshinobu Hakutani** is also a University Distinguished Scholar at this institution. Among his numerous books and editions are *Haiku: This Other World* by Richard Wright (coedited with Robert L. Tener; Random House, 2000); *Haiku and Modernist Poetics* (Palgrave Macmillan, 2009); *Art, Music, and Literature 1897–1902* by Theodore Dreiser (University of Illinois Press, 2007); *Cross-Cultural Visions in African American Modernism: From Spatial Narrative to Jazz Haiku* (Ohio State University Press, 2006); and editor of *Cross-Cultural Visions in African American Literature: West Meets East* (Palgrave Macmillan, 2011).

Floyd W. Hayes III received his PhD from the University of Michigan and is a senior lecturer, Department of Political Science, and coordinator of programs and undergraduate studies, Center for Africana Studies, at Johns Hopkins University. The author of numerous articles and book chapters, Hayes focuses on Africana political philosophy, politics, and policy. He is the editor of *A Turbulent*

Voyage: Readings in African American Studies. Hayes is working on a book titled "Domination and Resentiment: The Desperate Vision of Richard Wright."

An associate professor of English at Binghamton University, SUNY, **Joseph Keith** specializes in twentieth-century literatures of the United States, comparative race and ethnic studies, and postcolonial theory. Keith has published in *Interventions: International Journal of Postcolonial Studies*, *Postmodern Culture*, and the *Black Scholar*. His current book is titled "Unbecoming Americans: Race, Alienage, and the Shadow Narratives of the Transnational, 1945–1960."

Toru Kiuchi is a professor of English at Nihon University, Japan. He is coauthor of *The Critical Response in Japan to African American Writers* (Peter Lang, 2003). He is also the Japanese translator of many works inclusive of Richard Wright's *Haiku: This Other World* (Sairyusha Press, 2000), and *A Langston Hughes Reader* by Hans Ostrom (Yushodo Press, 2006). Kiuchi's article "Zen Buddhism in Richard Wright's Haiku" appeared in *Valley Voices* in fall 2008.

John Lowe is the Barbara Methvin Professor of Southern Literature at the University of Georgia, Athens. He is the author or editor of seven books, including *Jump at the Sun: Zora Neale Hurston's Cosmic Comedy*; his most recent book, *Calypso Magnolia: The Caribbean Side of the South,* will be published in 2016 by the University of North Carolina Press.

A professor of American literature and gender studies at Tsuru University, Yamanashi, Japan, **Sachi Nakachi** served as a visiting fellow at the University of Cambridge, United Kingdom, and as a Fulbright scholar at New York University and University of California, Berkeley, during 2009 and 2010. She has published on African American literature and art/cinema, and on American *Japonisme* literature in the Japanese *Journal of Black Studies*, the *Journal of Japonisme Studies*, and other venues.

Virginia Whatley Smith is retired as an associate professor of English at the University of Alabama at Birmingham. Smith is editor of *Richard Wright's Travel Writings: New Reflections* (University Press of Mississippi, 2001). Her essay on "African American Travel Literature" appeared in *The Cambridge Companion to American Travel Writing* in 2009, and her essay on "Jean Toomer Revisited in James Emanuel's Postmodernist Jazz Haiku" appeared in *Cross-Cultural Visions in African American Literature* edited by Yoshinobu Hakutani (Palgrave Macmillan, 2011).

John Zheng is a professor of English and chair of the Department of English and Foreign Languages, Mississippi Valley State University. He has received scholarships, fellowships, and grants from the Fulbright programs, the National Council for the Humanities, and the Mississippi Arts Commission. He serves as editor of the *Journal of Ethnic American Literature* and *The Other World of Richard Wright: Perspectives on His Haiku* (University Press of Mississippi, 2011).

Index

CPSIA information can be obtained at www.ICGtesting.com
Printed in the USA
BVOW05*1134260516

448450BV00007B/3/P

9 781496 803801